**THE ROBERT GORDON UNIVERSITY
LIBRARY**

THE
**ROBERT GORDON
UNIVERSITY**
ABERDEEN

This book is due for return on or before the last date shown below.

WYTHENSHAWE
The Story of a Garden City

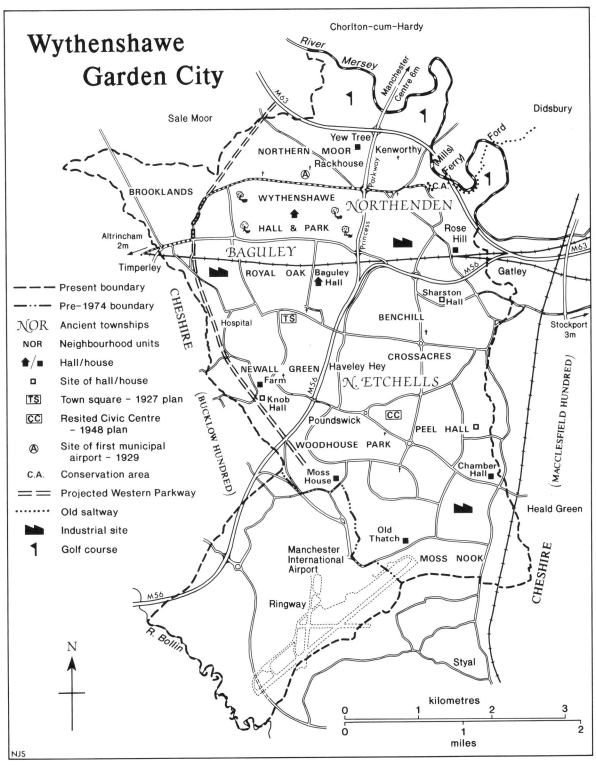

Wythenshawe Garden City

Chorlton-cum-Hardy

River
Mersey
Manchester
Centre 6m

Didsbury

Sale Moor

Yew Tree
NORTHERN MOOR
Kenworthy
Rackhouse

Ford

(Mills)
(Ferry)

BROOKLANDS

Parkway

C.A.

WYTHENSHAWE
NORTHENDEN

HALL & PARK

Rose
Hill

Altrincham
2m

Princess

BAGULEY

M56

Gatley

M63

Timperley

CHESHIRE

ROYAL OAK

Baguley
Hall

Sharston
Hall

Stockport
3m

Hospital

TS

BENCHILL

CROSSACRES

NEWALL GREEN
Farm

Haveley Hey

N. ETCHELLS

(MACCLESFIELD HUNDRED)

(BUCKLOW HUNDRED)

Knob
Hall

Poundswick

CC

PEEL HALL

WOODHOUSE PARK

Chamber
Hall

Moss
House

Heald Green

Old
Thatch

Manchester
International
Airport

MOSS NOOK

CHESHIRE

Ringway

R. Bollin

Styal

Legend

- — — — Present boundary
- — · — · Pre-1974 boundary
- *NOR* Ancient townships
- NOR Neighbourhood units
- ♠/■ Hall/house
- ▫ Site of hall/house
- TS Town square – 1927 plan
- CC Resited Civic Centre – 1948 plan
- Ⓐ Site of first municipal airport – 1929
- C.A. Conservation area
- ══ Projected Western Parkway
- ····· Old saltway
- ◤ Industrial site
- 1 Golf course

N

kilometres
0   1   2   3
0   1   2
miles

NJS

Wythenshawe.

WYTHENSHAWE
The Story of a Garden City

Baguley and Royal Oak, Benchill and Sharston, Brooklands,
Brownley Green and Haveley Hey, Crossacres, Northern Moor
and Rackhouse, Newall Green, Peel Hall and Poundswick,
Northenden, Woodhouse Park — and Ringway.

Edited by
Derick Deakin

Phillimore

1989

Published by
PHILLIMORE & CO. LTD.
Shopwyke Hall, Chichester

ISBN 0 85033 699 6

Printed and bound in Great Britain by
STAPLES PRINTERS ROCHESTER

Contents

Editorial Team

Derick Deakin	Convener, Editor, Chapters 1, 2, 3, 4, 8 and 10.
Jean Greatorex	Social Life, Chapters 5, 9 and 11 — and advice.
Michael Redhead	The War, Chapters 6 and 7 — and advice.
Jill Groves	Road, Rail and Air Transport throughout the book, new research, especially concerning the Civil War period in Chapter 1.
Jim Pugh	Early reminiscences and Medical Services throughout the book.

Acknowledgements

We wish to acknowledge the generous help and wealth of information that has been so freely given. These ranged from long written reports and taped interviews to snippets of information passed on in the street. A few contributors are listed here and a list of witnesses appears below.

Jack Close — British Legion; Dr Winifred Hall — Northwerthen Guild; Eileen and Alex Merchant — Jackson and Simon; Deryck Moore — Adult Education; Cleone Simons — 1930s; Elfrida and Harry Warner — Baguley Hall; officials of the Police, Fire and Ambulance Services; many Wythenshawe head teachers; Rod Blayden, Stephen Ruffley and all who helped at Wythenshawe, Northenden and Central Libraries; officials at the Town Hall and of countless other organisations.

John Boyle — publication of the first restricted edition of Chapters Two to Eleven; Carol Hyne — initial typing of Chapters Five and Six; Rita Oughton and John Rhodes — initial impetus; William Shercliffe — advice; Bill Williams — interviewing techniques; Ray Harris — additional research, especially on illustrations; Elaine Mercer — final typing of complete manuscript; Northern Writers Advisory Services — copy-editing and keyboarding of typescript onto computer disc for photo-typesetting.

Eye witnesses, listed after the chapter in which they first appear: Chapter Two, Mrs. T. Carol, George Brown, Syd Heslop, Florence Weatherby. Chapter Three, Graham Pearson, Jim Pugh, Annie Chandley, Ray Harris, Winifred Garner, Frank Glover, Jack Riley, John Organ. Chapter Four, Dr. Winifred Hall, Helen McGraph, F. Ray, Chris Heap. Chapter Five, Wilf Halligan, Les Davies, Roy Whittaker. Chapter Six, Douglas Howard, Ethel Price, Les Jones, Carrie Griffiths. Chapter Seven, Joan Lawrence.

Unattributed quotations, except where the source is obviously otherwise, are from local papers, including the *Manchester Evening News*, *Wythenshawe Express* and *Wythenshawe World*. Occasionally an unattributed quotation may simply reflect a prevailing sentiment; in all cases it must be remembered that quotations 'may illustrate an issue — but never prove a point'.

Illustrations

Acknowledgements

The authors thank the following for permission to reproduce illustrations in this book: jacket and other photographs — John Hill-Wilson; Lilywhite Postcards; Manchester Cultural Services — David Owen, John Davies, Rod Blayden, George Turnbull — and Arthur Royle Collection; Manchester City Council; Manchester Education Committee; Ruth Jones and Mike Edkins, Arden College; Manchester International Airport Archives — Brian Robertson; *Wythenshawe Express*; *Wythenshawe World* — Susan Eades, John Oatway; Rev. and Mrs. Albert Atherton, Pete Brennan, Charlotte Brunt per Noreen Eckersley, Les Davies, Mrs. Leslie Dukinfield, Rev. Greg Forster, Frank Freeman, Pat, Helen and Paul Gaunlett, Russell Hancock, Ray Harris, .Douglas Howard, Charles Millward, Frank Mitchell, Jim Pugh, Michael Saul per David Mycock, Denis Thorpe and *The Guardian*, Nic Scarle, Alan Smyllie, Alan Sutton, Keith Warrender and Willow Publishing, Stephen Weeks, Edwin Woodall.

President's Message

*by Sir William Downward, formerly Lord Lieutenant of Greater Manchester,
President, Northenden Civic Society*

This book has been assembled by a team of local writers, each with their own style, expertise and outlook. While covering the complete history of Wythenshawe, the emphasis is on more recent times, especially the period from 1926 to the present. The last sixty years have seen rapid and fundamental changes in the area, not least of which has been the tremendous increase in the population, with its consequent social and domestic problems.

I trust that those of us who are striving to improve our environment and living conditions will be inspired by the vision and enthusiasm of the pioneers of the Wythenshawe estate, and will try to learn and profit from this account of their failures and successes.

William Downward

Foreword

by The Rt. Hon. Alfred Morris, M.A. (Oxon.), Member of Parliament for Wythenshawe and Vice-President of the Northenden Civic Society

This book is not only for specialists in local history. Nor is it just for the people of Wythenshawe or, indeed, for Mancunians as a whole. It is a book that will interest everyone who cares about civic leadership and the making of social policy. At the same time, it is a book of special importance to the young people of our community, for, if tomorrow's citizens are not to be left unaware of their heritage, books like this should have an honoured place in all our schools. My hope is that this work will give more and more of our young people a pride in their heritage and that deeper sense of belonging that flows from learning about the origins of one's own community.

Many who are not so young will recall the pledge given to provide 'homes for heroes to live in' for Britain's fightingmen who lived through the carnage of the First World War. Instead, they mainly returned (most of the surviving 'Manchester Pals' among them) to homes that were as dilapidated as they were insanitary. Yet, fortunately, among Manchester's civic leaders there were some with the will to try to make good the default. Informed by the vision of a garden city, and undaunted by the problems recounted in this book, they built new and better homes for all the ex-servicemen's and other families they rescued from Manchester's decaying slums. The story, indeed drama, of their efforts is one of fellowship and man's humanity to man.

It was to visit one of the newly-rehoused 'heroes' that I first came to Wythenshawe in the years covered by some of the earlier chapters in this book. My father, one of Manchester's war disabled, had recently died. It was 1936 and I stayed briefly with my father's brother and his wife in Benchill. Even now I can still vividly recall the striking contrast between the old Manchester and the new. After what seemed a marathon journey, I was amazed by what I saw. It was summer and sunlit. This new Manchester was green and pleasant, spacious and memorable.

My own memories, of course, are subjective. What the authors of this book have sought to achieve is an objective account of the events they describe. That is never easy to do, and especially not when it is recent events that are being described. Yet the task of sifting and assessing the mass of documentary evidence available to them has been undertaken with both admirable fairness and skill. Happily their book will much increase public respect for the men and women who conceived and then created modern Wythenshawe.

Northenden Civic Society has achieved much since its inception. This book adds notably to its achievements. In warmly congratulating the authors, I very much hope that their book will reach the very wide readership it deserves.

A Y Morris.

Preface

This book covers the history of Wythenshawe from earliest times to the present, with the focus on the prodigious, record-breaking development of the area that had been, up to the 1920s, entirely rural in character into the garden city of Wythenshawe.

The history of the earlier period is covered in Chapter One, and particularly in this sphere the present authors must acknowledge their debt to the writers of *Wythenshawe: A History of the Townships of Northenden, Northen Etchells and Baguley to 1926*; we owe much to L. Wharfe, Winifred Garner, Mary Morrow, E. Hunt, Anne Lowcock and especially the editor, Bill Shercliffe, who pointed us in the right direction for this present book.

In almost any history the chapters covering recent and contemporary years are possibly the most difficult to write because they seem less like 'history'; happenings of one, two or more centuries ago seem intrinsically interesting because, however trivial the detail, time will have given it a patina of importance. In the instance of Wythenshawe, the area has an impressive past, but at the start of the 20th century its greatest moment of triumph — a few cynics have said disaster — was yet to come.

The machinery to create the first large garden city, with a population more than double any previous attempt, had yet to be assembled in 1926, though the first hesitant moves had been made. The primacy of Wythenshawe — its eventual population greater than that of Cambridge, twice that of the Isle of Man and almost twice that of its former county town, Chester — has yet to be recognised.

A problem that confronted the writers on the earlier part of Wythenshawe's history was of shortage of evidence. The opposite problem, a surfeit of material, confronts writers on its recent history. The minutes of the Wythenshawe Estates Special Committee, the body created by Manchester City Council to oversee the new garden city, alone run to 13 very large volumes. The problem of what to include was paramount and compounded by the fact that the dust of controversy, hearsay and familiarity tended to cloud important elements of recent occurrences. To include every event or mention every society would have produced a dry catalogue or unwieldy treatise. We have, therefore, tried to outline the main course of events, occasionally giving a more detailed account to illustrate the main themes rather than to suggest that a topic has particular significance.

We hope this book will be of interest and help to the present and future generations.

Derick Deakin

Chronicle of Notable Events

The Mersey, ford and land to the south used by settlers and travellers from Bronze Age or earlier.

Settlement — and church dedicated to St Wilfrid who died A.D.709.

Tata left Rostherne — set up Tata's tun — start of Tatton dynasty.

1086	Domesday book includes Norwordine and Bagelei.
1119	Massey family grants Northenden to the abbey at Chester: half leased back 1270.
1286	Tatton manors pass to the Masseys. Etchells manor known to be with De Stokeport family.
1297	Tattons first mentioned at Kenworthy, Northenden.
1311	William the miller granted land at Northenden. 'Northen Boat' ferry nearby.
1316	Witenscaw (Wythenshawe) first mentioned — in a charter.
1348	Masseys acquire land at Northenden.
1349	Etchells passes to Ardernes, who build the Peele as manorhouse. (*See* 1408.)
1370	Tattons acquire Wythenshawe — it is presumed by marriage of Robert to Alicia de Massey.
14th C.	Leigh family at Baguley Hall — until 17th century.
1408	Etchells passes to Stanleys.
1515	Ringway — Chapel of Ease of Bowdon — annexed by Dissenters *c.*1642, regained by Anglicans 1721, redundant 1970. *c.*1535 Wythenshawe Hall — centre part rebuilt after fire.
1540	Monasteries dissolved — Chester looses control of Northenden; church to Macclesfield Deanery — 1933 to Manchester Diocese.
1557	Tattons acquire Etchells — after litigation become Lords of Manors of Northenden and Etchells — use Peel Hall as dower house.
1594	Newall Green Farm — one of earliest in brick.
1641	Map of Lordshippe of Northenden by Richard Martinscroft.
1641-1646	Civil War. Wythenshawe Hall, held by royalists, besieged and surrenders February 1644. *Boathouse Inn*, Northenden used as parliamentary barracks. Rector Mallory replaced by Henry Dunster, puritan clergyman, 1645. After siege Robert Tatton flees to Chester, then Oxford, returning to Wythenshawe in 1647.
1659	Robert Tatton's son in Cheshire Rising.
1661	Restoration of Charles II. Mallory returns. *c.*1691 William Boardman has school in Northenden. Knob Hall rebuilt and enlarged — demolished 1959.
*c.*1701	Sharston Manor and Hall. Demolished 1984.
1703	Chamber Hall rebuilt in brick.
*c.*1720	Joseph Collier making clocks at Moss Nook, followed by son David — family trade 16th-19th centuries.
1727	Death of Henry Hough of Shadow Moss, watchmaker and renowned engraver.
*c.*1740	Northenden Rectory rebuilt in brick.
1745	'Bonnie Prince Charlie' Stuart and his Scots army cross the Mersey.
1777	Gatley Congregational Church — replaced 1937.
1780	Tattons at Tatton Hall — until 1806, as 'Tatton- Egertons'.
1784	Quarry Bank Mill and garden village built at Styal by Samuel Gregg.
*c.*1790	Sharston School — rebuilt 1842, 1864 (*and see* 1901).
1801	First Census: Northenden, 538, Northen Etchells, approx. 620, Baguley, 423; Total, approx. 1,581. (*See* 1851.)
1816	Methodists at James Renshaw's cottage, Northenden. (*See* 1828.)
1819	Peterloo Massacre, Joseph Johnson imprisoned. At his Northenden home with Absolem Watkin plans moves towards the Reform Bill. Edward Watkin born — 'Railway Doctor', Channel tunnel planner.
1821	Stockport-Altrincham Road turnpiked — toll bars at Cheadle and Timperley.

1828	First Methodist chapel; larger building 1877. Floods.
1832	Absolem Watkin settles at Rose Hill, Longley Lane.
1835	Shadow Moss school/mission church. Demolished 1961.
1839	Maps by Tithe Commissioners. Ordnance Survey 1842-43.
1851	Census: Northenden, 679, Northen Etchells, 659, Baguley, 570; Total, 1,898. (*See* 1901.)
1859	Brooklands Station on Manchester South Junction & Altrincham Railway (1849).
1861	Girder footbridge over Mersey at Northenden — incites 'New Road', now Palatine Road. Toll at Barlow Moor Road.
1862	Heyhead Congregational church.
1866	Working Men's Club, Church Road — in time library, evening school, dance school and nursery.
1867	Horse-drawn omnibus, Northenden to West Didsbury. Piped water.
1868	St John's church, Brooklands.
1869	Baguley Congregational church.
*c.*1870	Footbridge with toll replaces ferry at *Tatton Arms*. Schooling compulsory.
1872	Gas into Northenden church.
1873	Northenden church demolished except the tower. Rebuilt by 1876.
1874	Bridge with carriageway replaces footbridge of 1861 over Mersey.
1879	St John's School, Baguley.
1881	St James's church, Gatley. Tolls abolished on Palatine and Wilmslow Roads.
1888	Cheshire County Council formed. (*See* 1894.)
1892	Mercantile Bank, Palatine Road. 1919 District Bank.
1894	Bucklow Rural District Council formed — administers Northenden, Northen Etchells and Baguley, which have parish councils.
1895	Sewage works, Longley Lane.
1898	First local car owner — Mr. Towell, Longley Lane.
1901	Census: Northenden, 2,127, Northen Etchells, 758, Baguley, 834; Total, 3,719. Footbridge by Henry Simon over ford to Didsbury. Methodist Day School, Victoria Road. National School, Palatine Road, Kenworthy Lane. Sharston School sold as tea rooms — demolished 1934. Forty hexagonal gas street lights installed.
1902	Cheshire C.C., by Education Act, runs local schools. Murder at Bradley Gate Farm, Longley Lane. Manchester establishes Baguley Sanatorium fever hospital in Wythenshawe.
1904	Catholics buy Ziba Ward's church of 1901, Kenworthy Lane.
1905	Old Café Pavilion, Palatine Road, destroyed by fire.
1906	County takes over the Methodists' school — new buildings in Bazley Road, 1910. Manchester's first trial of motor buses — to Northenden — adopted 1910.
1910	Coronation of George V — hall built on Longley Lane becomes Coronation Cinema, 1911 — last years as bingo hall — demolished 1987.
1913	Church Rooms, Kenworthy Lane, built. Volunteer Corps of 300 formed, probably first in country.
1914	Beech House, Yew Tree Lane, in use as Red Cross Hospital.
1915	Rose Hill in use as Ophthalmic Children's Hospital.
1920	Manchester notes the Abercrombie Report — Wythenshawe 'eminently suitable for housing'. Locally resisted. Northenden Comrades of Great War founded. New premises 1926.
1921	Census: Northenden, 3,236, Northen Etchells, 906, Baguley, 1,325. Total, 5,487. (*See* 1939 and 1964.) Northenden Amateur Dramatic Society formed. Parochial Church Council established.
1923	Murder at Carrs Wood, Longley Lane.
1926	Manchester City Council buys Tatton Estates; Ernest Simon gives Wythenshawe Hall to City Council as a park; Grand Fête.
1927	Parliament backs Bucklow R.D.C. and Cheshire — they retain control. Wythenshawe Committee set up. Parker to plan a true garden city.
1929	City's plans mangled by Bucklow — only 142 houses approved; slum clearance delayed. First municipal airport at Northenden.
1930	Parliament agrees to incorporation into city. Parkway commenced.
1931	Wythenshawe joins Manchester. First issue, *Wythenshawe Gazette*.

1932	Princess Parkway opened. Mersey floods. First 400 houses complete.
1933-1934	Schools, shops, churches, Northenden cinema built. Chamber of Trade, community associations and clubs formed. Eastern (Sharston) Industrial Estate began.
1935	Population reaches 32,000.
1938	Ringway Airport in operation. Benchill, Rackhouse, Royal Oak in use.
1939	War; population 40,000. Wythenshawe Hospital conceived. Cinema, baths and town square plans aborted. Temporary shops built.
1941	Sharston Hall used by Police, Fire, Ambulance, Home Guard, A.R.P. Avro planes assembled in bus depot. Paratroopers at Ringway.
1945	Nicholas Plan reshapes Wythenshawe. Building resumes erratically. Government insists on housing priority.
1948	First Civic Week; shoal of post-war schools going up.
1950	Eveline Hill M.P.; airport extended.
1951	Wythenshawe Hospital established; Northenden Festival.
1953	*Plan and Reality* publicises Wythenshawe. Police and fire stations being built.
1957	B.E.A. Viscount crashes on Woodhouse Park.
1961	Sharston Baths and some Civic Centre shops open.
1962	Northenden Stadium gutted by fire.
1964	Population passes 100,000; 'Wythenshawe complete'. Alf Morris M.P.
1965	Maternity Hospital open. Rail passenger stations closed.
1967	Airport runways extended. Government saves Baguley Hall; Peel Hall lost.
1970	Impact '70, first Wythenshawe Arts Festival. Motorways sprouting.
1971	Civic Centre Forum open — sports, theatre, library.
1974	Northenden A.B.C. Forum closes. Wythenshawe Hospital open. Ringway part of Manchester.
1979	Last issue of *Wythenshawe Express*.
1980	*Iceberg* painting from Rose Hill sells for record £2m.
1981	Northenden Conservation Area designated.
1982	Northenden Library opened.
1983	Wythenshawe Law Centre established.
1984	Northenden Health Centre and Police Station built.
1985	Sharston Hall replaced by offices retaining name and building style.
1989	Wythenshawe Health Care Centre at Benchill.

Chapter One

1086 and All That

The Story of the Townships of Northenden, Baguley and Northen Etchells

1. The entry in Domesday Book for Northenden and Baguley.

Thus in the Domesday Book of 1086 we have the first record of Northenden and Baguley. It was made for William the Conqueror after the redistribution of land from the English to the Normans following his invasion in 1066. In spite of the Latin and the abbreviations, it is not hard to follow, in the text above, that

> ... IN Bucklow Hundred
> ['*In Bochelau hd*' — the area of north Cheshire centred on Bucklow which is just north of Knutsford] Ranulf and Bigot held Northenden which was previously the manor of Wulfgeat, a freeman [*lib. ho.*], that there were about two hundred cultivated acres [1 *hida*] liable to tax [*geld*], land for two ploughs, a church [*eccla*] and woodlands [*siluae*]. Its value was three shillings. In the time of King Edward the Confessor [*T.R.E.*] it had been worth ten shillings. Baguley and nearby Sunderland were now held by Gilbert, Ranulf and Hamon — four manors, now also worth three shillings.

The 'total waste' (*wasta. e tota*) reflects the devastation in the north following a rebellion in 1069-70 and William's savage 'harrying of the North' afterwards.

The story of Wythenshawe is the story of the three ancient townships of Northenden, Baguley and Northen Etchells. Northenden in the north of Wythenshawe and Baguley in the west appeared in the Domesday entry above. The trinity was completed with Northern Etchells, the eastern part of Wythenshawe. Down the centuries the fortunes of the three rural townships, Northenden, Baguley and Northern Etchells were interwoven: the forces that bound them together were partly the waters of the River Mersey and the Fairywell, Baguley and Gatley Brooks and partly the matrimonial webs spun by the Tattons, the archetypal country squires of Wythenshawe Hall.

1

The trio of townships, by the 20th century called civil parishes, were formally welded together as the suburban Garden City of Wythenshawe when they became part of Manchester in 1931. The Tattons have now gone but, in spite of the bricks and mortar and the glass and aluminium, the rural atmosphere and clean air are still present.

The name *Northenden* (Northen to many locals) tells us that the place existed as a *northern-den* in the Saxon kingdom of Mercia (whose northern boundary was the Mersey). At this point in its course the Mersey is likely to have been forded and used by Man from the earliest times, and axe-hammers of the Bronze Age have been found in and around Northenden. Early farmers would have found the sandy soil of the Mersey terrace, which formed a shelf about a mile wide south of the river, easier to cultivate than the boulder clay just a little further south. The nearest Roman roads were at Sale (Watling Street) and Stockport, but again the Mersey and its banks would have been used as a link.

Topping the small hill that rises from the Mersey at Northenden is the church dedicated to St Wilfrid, the seventh-century Bishop of Ripon who established the Roman form of Christianity in Britain. During the rebuilding of the church in the 1870s, rubble walls, possibly of Saxon origin, were found. The dedication to Wilfrid may be a pointer to the date of the founding of the church but it would be wishful speculation to assert that the saint visited Northenden.

Friend and foe, the Mersey has always been a key feature of Northenden. The river would have shifted its course in the flood plain many times before being set into the present channel following drainage work, possibly in the 14th century. The change accounts for the old county boundaries differing from the present river course. For centuries its water-powered corn mills and the ford, near the Didsbury end of Ford Lane, helped determine the route of one ancient saltway through Northenden from the Cheshire saltfield to northern England. Because the ford made a bridge less necessary, it slowed down the general development of the area, and when a bridge was at last built in the 19th century Northenden became a rural haven for Mancunians, with boats, teahouses and fairs. The Mersey and its flood plain was also a barrier to expanding Manchester that was not breached until 1931. One victim of its steady toll of floods and drownings was William, son and heir to Robert Tatton, the lord of the manor, in 1616.

South of the river much of the land was wooded. Wythenshawe means a *willow-shaw*, *shaw* being a word still in use for a wood. Sharston might have been a boundary cornerstone by a wood, a *shaw-stone*, Baguley is a *badger lea* (*lea* — a clearing) and similarly we have Kenwor*thy*, Long*ley* and Have*ley*. Other woody local names are Cringlewood, Hazelhurst (hillock), Poundswick (*wick* — an oak), Royal Thorn (Royle or Ryle Thorn originally) and Yew Tree. It was this fertile but wooded land that at the Conquest the Normans discovered and reallocated to their own advantage. The Anglo-Saxons already had a system of shires and hundreds (a hundred families) with sheriffs (shire-reeves) and onto this the Normans grafted their feudal system. At the top was the king, the local chief was the lord of the manor and at the bottom were the freemen, villeins, bondsmen and cottagers, the latter two classes effectively slaves: each had to serve the rank above him in return for the security of the system — fine if you were a king but security you could well manage without if you were a cottager.

Hamon de Massey (the Hamo in the Domesday entry and the 'Massey' in Dunham Massey) gave Northenden church in 1119 to the Abbey of St Werburgh, the abbot becoming lord of the manor of Northenden. The Masseys were rewarded in 1270 with the lease back of half the manor of Northenden. This was possibly the area around Wythenshawe Hall as there has been a Massie's field recorded nearby from the time of the earliest maps.

Meanwhile the Tatton family, who were destined to oversee most of Wythenshawe down to the present century, were established in the manor of Tatton. In Anglo-Saxon times, an adventurous villager named Tata left his home in Rostherne to set up Tata's tun, hence Tatton, on the site of the present Old Hall at Tatton Park. After Domesday the manor was left partly under the control of Order of St John of Jerusalem. As the knights of this order had links with both the Tattons and the Crusades, this might explain the presence of the Middle-Eastern variety of autumn crocus whose display in Ford Lane is one of the finest in the country. The twin manors of Tatton were passed through an heiress to Sir Richard Massey in 1286; by what course we do not know, but very soon afterwards, in 1297, we have the first record of the Tattons at Kenworthy in Northenden.

The first mention of the name Wythenshawe is in a charter of 1316 when Thomas de Mascy of Wythenschawe granted land to his son and to his neighbour Sir William Baggelegh. The land passed to the Tattons by the presumed marriage of heiress Alice Massey to Robert Tatton in 1370. Beginning with Nicholas as Baron of the Exchequer of Chester in 1451, through a well placed in-law, the Tattons began to be the regular holders of the office of sheriff of Chester. Later they acquired, usually by marriage, much of the manors of Baguley and Etchells and, for a quarter of a century after 1780, their old homestead, Tatton Hall.

We know nothing of the first Wythenshawe Hall, but we do know from a footnote to a deed that Robert Tatton rebuilt most of it after a fire in the 1530s (hence the moat discovered in the 1953 renovations). The new hall, of timber frame, consisted of the square hall with a passage on the north side. On the opposite end was the kitchen with a solar above to which the lord and his wife would retire. Originally the front was on the west where a studded oak door remains. Outside were other kitchens, dairies, a brewhouse, gatehouse and moat. A chapel was added to the north and in Elizabeth's time the west was rebuilt in brick. A Bacchus-like figure and a workman's graffiti dating from these early alterations remained hidden till the 1980s. Over the next three hundred years a library, billiards room, smoking room and a tenants' hall spread to the north; guests and servants' quarters were built to the south and over existing rooms. A coating of stucco helped to give it a unified appearance — and dry rot.

Baguley also changed hands by marriage, initially in this case in the 13th century, passing from the Masseys to the Baguleys, whose money came from salt mines. Sir William Baguley was granted Ryle Thorn and Alveley Hey by the de Stokeport family and around 1320 built Baguley Hall. Probably the finest medieval hall in the area, it is built in the Viking style of an upturned boat of heavy planks. To the original central hall, with a passage to the north, a later medieval wing was added, later refaced in brick, and a wing to the south in Georgian times. The manor passed through the marriage of Isabel Baguley to the Leghs of Booths, near Knutsford, in 1355. At the end of the 17th century, after the death of the last of the Leghs in 1691, it passed through the hands of Allens, Jacksons and Masseys before becoming part of the Tattons' estates in the mid-18th century and being leased out as a farmhouse until 1931.

It was a tennis ball that helped shape the story of Etchells. The name *Et-chells* means 'extra cleared land' — the part of Wythenshawe that is today east of Baguley Brook, the line of the M56. After 1086 it was split along the old hundred boundary marked by Gatley Brook (later moved west to the boundary between Baguley and Northenden). The halves were held at times by the Stokeports and the Ardernes, who built Peel Hall. Later it was held by the Stanleys until in 1508 John Stanley, the sole heir, was killed by a tennis ball. Because there were no rightful claimants the land was acquired by the crown, under feudal law, in an early version of '. . . in the interests of national security'. The Tattons were a suitably righteous and loyal family and in 1556 Etchells was sold to William Tatton who already had bought Ryle Thorn. So by the 1560s the Tattons owned Northenden and Northen Etchells and, being sufficiently landed, they became, after some dispute, full lords of the manor. Their stewards held manorial courts from 1580. Peel Hall (a peele being a small castle) was used as the Tatton dower house, although in 1578 Dorothy Tatton, widow of Robert Tatton, was installed at Northenden Rectory because Peel Hall . . . 'is not sufficiently buylded for her to dwell'. The stone bridge that crossed the moat alone remains and Peel Hall Farm, which replaced the hall in the 18th century, has itself now been demolished.

The authority of each of the lords of the manors was enforced by court leets and court barons. (The original manuscript records of these for Northenden are in the John Rylands Library, Manchester, and those for Etchells in Manchester's Central Library. Many libraries, including Wythenshawe, have transcripts of the court leet records, which make fascinating reading.) Rents and charges such as heriots (the best beast, chattel or a sum of money paid to the lord of the manor on the death of each tenant) were checked by the courts, and to this end the paid steward was backed up by burleymen (bylawmen), bailiffs, ale founders, assessors and appraisors of the lays or local taxes.

In the records offenders were 'pained' (fined) for unrepaired property, Mary for not 'scouring her brucke' (cleaning her brook of debris), John for 'putting a scabbed mare on the common', William for failing 'to dick his dyke' (dig and clean his hedge-side ditches) and there were lesser fines for 'tale-telling' or 'setting up of dissension'. Encroachment on the moors (often with the lord's consent) also appears in the records. Piecemeal enclosure of the two moors in Northenden and Etchells, Northern Moor and Shadow Moss, was taking place throughout the 17th century. Subtenancies were also dealt with by the manor courts and show a pattern of elder sons taking up subtenancies when they married and before they inherited their fathers' tenements. Subtenanting was also a good way of ensuring the future of younger sons so that they did not have to move too far away.

The original courthouse for Etchells was Chamber Hall (which shows signs of having medieval foundations — and probably a medieval roof beam — in its central section), less than half a mile south of Peel Hall, the original manor house. In the late 16th century the court leets and court barons moved to Gatley, which was nearer Wythenshawe Hall, to a building later known as the Old Court House. The courts for Northenden were held in the *Boat Inn* (now the *Tatton Arms*) in the 18th century.

More income for the lord came from his right to ensure all tenants ground their corn at his mill, for which the fee was one twenty-fourth part of the corn ground. William the miller was granted a strip of land in Northenden in 1311. The Tattons had two mills at one time and they also controlled the ferry at this point. In the early 17th century, the Tattons had a legal battle with a Lancashire landowner, Rowland Moseley, over the weir and ferry, known as Northenden Boat. The last mill was demolished in 1966, by which time it was being used simply for the retailing of animal feed stocks. Only the weir remains.

The Black Death made labour scarce and helped the demand for higher wages. Gradually, the power of the lords of the manor declined and parliamentary acts were increasingly enforced through parish and township officials. In Elizabeth's time, churchwardens and householders were nominated as Overseers of the Poor who could raise local taxes, set adults to work and bind children as apprentices, although the task of discovering strangers who might be a charge on the parish and making sure that they were sent on their way still fell to the court leet. The overseers were, in time, given other duties and by the end of the 18th century there were paid officials, parish clerks and highway surveyors. From the 16th century onwards enforcement was by local magistrates at quarter sessions, of which records for Cheshire survive from 1559. One persistent local rowdy was a certain James Anderton, who was arrested in Marple in 1577 as a wandering rogue.

The Civil War of the 1640s brought into question not only the divine right of kings but the powers persisting in the manorial system. Since the Cheshire gentry were equally divided between royalists and parliamentarians, the war divided families and brought distress (the brothers-in-law of the then lord of the manor, Robert Tatton, were parliamentarians, whilst he was a staunch royalist), but it also brought excitement if one believes the highly dubious account of the rector of Northenden, Thomas Mallory (a descendant of Sir Thomas Mallory of *Morte d'Arthur* fame). The cleric is supposed to have described how, on 25 November 1643, they found parliamentarian soldiers at the church, where the east windows with the figures which included 'the form of the blessed Saint Wilfrid [were] . . . smashed', the font 'ground to pieces . . . and our fair and goodly temple laid to waste'. (The truth is probably that the 'account' was written much later, perhaps even in the late 19th century.)

The account then says that the rector, a royalist, went to stay at the ferry house (which was being used as a parliamentarian outpost — Mallory actually went to Wythenshawe Hall) 'with a godly family, the Swindells' (the ferryman was called James Dean and he too was a member of the royalist garrison).

In the Puritan purge of High Church 'idolatry', Mallory and the rector of Cheadle, Dr. William Nicholls (who was Robert Tatton's stepfather), were ejected in September 1643. Nicholls and his wife fled to Chester (where he was later appointed Dean of Chester as successor to Mallory's father). Mallory stayed and helped to garrison Wythenshawe Hall.

With the latter and Robert Tatton, there were also Edward Legh of Baguley, a number of yeomen from the surrounding areas of Didsbury, Altrincham and Hale, and some tenants from Northenden, Etchells and Baguley. The local parliamentarian regimental commander, Colonel Duckenfield of Stockport, sent 30 soldiers under Captain Adams to besiege the hall. The siege lasted from 21 November 1643 to 25 February 1644: they finally took the hall by storm with two cannons brought from Manchester (the weather and the roads had been too bad for them to have been brought before). On the same day someone shot Captain Adams. The dubious so-called Mallory account has it as an act of revenge by a maidservant named as Mary Webb for the death of her fiancé. There are depositions (i.e. statements) amongst the Tatton family papers taken by the parliamentarians at Stockport from members of the garrison and none of them mention the incident. Captain Adams was shot, but by someone unknown. He was buried at Stockport on 27 February, according to Stockport parish register.

Robert Tatton fled to Chester, where he was appointed High Sheriff of Cheshire a few months before its surrender. He then went to support the king at Oxford, which finally surrendered to the New Model Army on 24 June 1646.

Robert was not the only heroic member of the family. In true 'secrets in her curlers' fashion, Mistress Anne Tatton smuggled letters out of Chester. She had travelled to Chester in March 1645 with rent moneys for her husband and stepfather, who were in desperate need of money. On 10 March Sir George Booth the elder of Dunham, a prominent Cheshire parliamentarian and neighbour, gave her a safe conduct pass out of the city for herself, her servant, William Tomlinson, and two other ladies. They were stopped at Tarvin by an enemy patrol and their baggage searched. Mistress Tatton was found to be carrying letters from royalist ladies in Chester to royalist ladies in Manchester, which were of great interest to the enemy for they mentioned the movements of a royalist army marching north to relieve Chester. Mistress Tatton and her friends were sent back to Chester but were later allowed to return to their homes.

The most eminent of the local parliamentarians was Henry Cockson, Robert Tatton's cousin and steward of his courts. Cockson was also Solicitor for Sequestrations for Cheshire, and in this capacity helped Edward Legh briefly regain control of his estates and later, in the 1650s, helped Robert mortgage the two manors. But for the help and influence of Henry Cockson, the Tattons would have been forced to sell their estates. Another notable parliamentarian from this area was William Barrett, sequestrator for the Macclesfield Hundred Sequestration Committee, and lay (i.e. unordained) minister for the Independent congregation which used the chapel at Ringway, and which probably included many from Northenden, Etchells and Baguley.

Robert Tatton 'compounded for his delinquency' (i.e. agreed to pay a fine for taking up arms against parliament) between July 1646 and April 1649. The original fine was set by the Macclesfield Sequestration Committee at £806 10s., but this was finally reduced to £707 13s. 4d. after a pleading letter by Robert's wife, Anne, and the intervention of Sir Thomas Fairfax, the Commander-in-Chief of the New Model Army.

Charles I was beheaded in Whitehall in 1649, but two years later, in 1651, his son, the future Charles II, brought down an army from Scotland. It was routed by Cromwell at Worcester and the remnants straggled back to Scotland, some crossing the Mersey at the Northenden ford. A story still heard in golfing circles tells how 11 Scottish soldiers are buried on the second fairway south-east of Simon's bridge: it is said that the site, formerly marked by a stone, can still be traced by a cross-shaped mound, 'so low that it is almost invisible'.

An early attempt at the restoration of the monarchy, the Cheshire Rising of 1659, was led by Sir George Booth of Dunham Massey. The then constable of Northenden, William Whitelegg, raised four soldiers but had problems in also raising the leys or taxes to pay them. At the Restoration in 1660 Robert Tatton was rewarded by Charles II with a silver snuff box. Two odd legacies are the Cromwell Room in the hall, at the top of the original staircase, and a Cromwell Cottage by the church, which dates only from the 18th century.

Edmund Shelmerdine, a local roundhead captain, did not accept the Restoration. He was arrested in 1662 for saying in a Northenden alehouse that

> there never was such great taxes laid upon the country as now there were, and that there would never be peace and quietness till they did as in Germany and that is to rise and cut the throats of all the gentry in England, wherein he said he will be as ready as any man . . .

Shelmerdine had fought hard to overturn the manorial system, but now he saw it re-established nearly as vigorously as before.

Francis Shelmerdine, once Puritan curate of Cheadle, also suffered in the Restoration. He was ejected from his living at Mottram-in-Longdendale, came back to live at Chamber Hall in Etchells, and, as well as farming, was forced to learn linen weaving, the main industry of the area, to enable himself and his family to eat. (By doing so he founded a clothier family.) At the end of his life he was granted a licence to have Presbyterian meetings in his house.

When the hall was surrendered an inventory was taken for Colonel Duckenfield and to help the sequestrators administer the estate. It lists hundreds of items, including these examples picked at random:

	£	s.	d.
Six longe fine flaxen Table Cloths	12	0	0
Braceletts of color Amber and Cristoll	1	13	0
One gilt Booke of the heavenly Meditations	1	2	0
In the Chamber over the Kitchen			
One Truckle bed and curtains	4	0	0
In the Buttery			
Six pewter flagons	1	10	0
In the Kitchen			
Nine brasse potts	1	0	0
Quicke Goods [livestock]			
One graye Stone Horse	20	0	0
One old Chesnutt Mare	1	0	0

Corn growing on the ground came to £207 and the overall total was £1,649 2s. 8d., with another £232 6s. 8d. for bricks and timber ready for building a new kitchen and brewhouse.

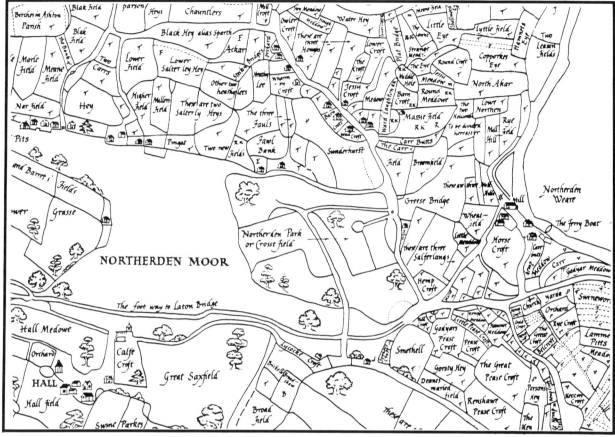

2. A detail of Martinscroft's map of the Lordship of Wythenshawe, surveyed in 1641, from the transcript made by Frank and Teretta Mitchell. Wythenshawe Hall is on the left, the Mersey, Northenden weir and ferry are on the right. The original map had north at the bottom, but in this copy north is at the top.

In the Porter's Ward was 'The Mappe of the Whole Lordshippe of Northern £1 0s 0d'. It was made a year before the Civil War broke out by Richard Martinscroft, an enterprising son of a physician. He taught mathematics, mended clocks, helped convert the collegiate church (now the Cathedral) buildings in Manchester (on the site of the manor house) into Chetham's Hospital and Library for the philanthropic clothier, Humphrey Chetham, and his nephew George, and clasped and chained the books for the Library. The refurbishment had been delayed until after the death of Humphrey Chetham because the original sum laid out for this purpose was given as a mortgage on the manors of Northenden and Etchells to a very desperate Robert Tatton.

The map, with south at the top, is a real work of art and tells us a great deal about the extent of the lord's demesne land (his domain), the crops planted, the pasture and meadow lands. It reveals that one field, the Swineworth, was still divided into strips, or 'lounts' and 'doles' as they were called in this area, and shows as well as the lanes and rights of way, which were often mentioned in the court leet records. It was rediscovered in the Flat Iron Market by F.W. Clark in 1925.

It shows clearly that Northenden had a four-field Cheshire system of open field husbandry into the mid-17th century (in fact, some copyhold leases dating from the late 17th century were still referring to lands in the 'Townfield'). The Cheshire system differed from the Midland three-field system in that it was more flexible, with only small areas of an open field devoted to a single crop. Crops such as peas and beans could be introduced more readily and such mixtures as wheat and rye (called munk corn or maslin) could be sown together. When potatoes arrived in this area in the late 17th century, they were easily introduced into this system, which helped them to become an important crop in this area by the end of the 18th century.

Immediately following the ejection of Thomas Mallory as rector, Northenden had as part-time minister a young curate, Henry Roote, who went on to be minister of Sowerby in Yorkshire, and several visiting ministers, including Francis Shelmerdine. In 1645 the living was given to Henry Dunster. A survey of 1649 tells us that he was 'an honest, able minister' and that the Great Tithes and the Lesser Tithes were worth £100. His first wife, Alice, and his daughter Felicia were buried in Northenden churchyard. When Dunster died in 1662, only a few months before he would have been ejected under the Act of Uniformity, his cousin Henry Newcombe, minister at Gawsworth and who helped found the Dissenters' Meeting House on Cross Street in Manchester, pronounced, 'Poor family. Poor people'. He was buried under the east window, his gravestone being recently re-discovered.

At Ringway in the manor of Hale, only a short step away from the southern boundaries of Northenden, Etchells and Baguley, the chapel of ease, which dated from 1515 and came within the parish of Bowdon, was taken over by a Nonconformist congregation headed by William Barrett and later by the Presbyterian minister John Brereton. The Cheshire historian and royalist, Sir Peter Leycester, described Ringway Chapel as 'a receptacle for nonconformists; in which dissolute times [the Civil War] every pragmatical illiterate person, as the humour served, stepped into the pulpit, without any lawful calling thereunto, or licence of authority'.

After the Restoration, Ringway Chapel continued as a place of Nonconformist worship, despite the Act of Uniformity, under the patronage and protection, firstly, of the ex-parliamentarian general, Sir William Brereton of Handforth, and later under John Crewe of Crewe and his widow. Not until 1721 was the chapel returned to the Anglicans. The minister, Mr. Waterhouse, was 'seized by the collar and turned, with the congregation, out of the church'. The Dissenting congregation continued at Hale in a new building built on a field called the Butts. In the hands of the Anglicans, Ringway Chapel was twice rebuilt, being finally re-established as All Saints, Hale Barns.

As a postscript to the Civil Wars, in 1745 Charles Edward Stuart, the Young Pretender and great-grandson of Charles I, marched south from Scotland and caused great excitement in this area. A High Church party in Manchester, led by Colonel Townley and the family of Dr. Thomas Deacon, fêted the Prince. In opposition, the Earl of Derby brought out the militia and bridges to the south of Manchester were demolished. Trees were felled for makeshift crossings and it has been assumed that the ford at Northenden was also used, possibly by the Prince. The temporary bridges are mentioned in the diaries of Elizabeth (Beppy) Byrom, daughter of John Byrom, the composer of *Christians Awake!* She often travelled to her uncle, John Houghton, a noted literary scholar who lived at Baguley. She also recorded that 'the Manchester pack of fox-hounds met . . . at Northenden Ferry', how Bonnie Prince Charlie had seized the Whitworth's *Manchester Magazine* press, and how they went to watch the Prince and his stragglers, after turning tail at Derby, returning to Scotland

and defeat at the battle of Culloden. One Northenden hostage was freed at Wilmslow but had to walk home without his boots.

A gentleman who would have missed all this local excitement was The Revd. Dr. Samuel Peploe. We learn from the diocesan visitations that he was one of the absentee rectors and pluralists common in the 18th century; by using a curate to serve Northenden he was able to reside in Chester whilst holding the posts — and the salaries — as Rector of Tatton Hall, Chancellor of Chester, Archdeacon of Richmond and Warden of Manchester. We learn too that the parish, which included part of Etchells and Baguley, had 160 houses and was growing slowly. The curate's salary was £50 a year and he lived at the Rectory, which in 1735 consisted 'of five Bays of Timber-building Cover'd with Slate. One barn of four bays and another of three bays With a swine Coat annex'd to ye nearer side of it and a stable Containing two little bays of Buildings with a Garner over it . . .' (a bay was approximately 15 feet). The Rectory was rebuilt in classical Georgian style sometime between 1735 and 1754 in brick and slate.

Macabre tales of the churchyard include the undertaker, Bailey, who decapitated tall bodies to fit his coffins, the rector who exorcised a ghost known as the Gatley Shouter and the body snatchers, who were finally foiled by battens of straw and twigs being mixed with the covering soil.

Although the church and its festivals remained a focus of the social life at this time, the inns, alehouses and farming customs played their part. In addition to the services, Christmas had its feasting and yule log, its mummers acting out the St George story, the Lord of Misrule, waits and carol singers. Easter had its Easter Monday peace-egging (a custom of rolling eggs down a slope, which later degenerated into begging), Whitsun its female finery and All Souls its soul cakes. Births and marriages were times for pranks and celebrations. After the last respects at the burial, funerals too could be times for feasting. On May Day the May Queen paraded, maypoles sprouted and, until Victoria ruled, Guy Fawkes Day was a holiday.

Stemming from the farming year were the harvest festival and harvest home, ploughing days to help new tenants, and ploughing matches. Cheese was an important local product and there were rites with stones at the cheese weighing sales. Bull and badger baiting, and cock fighting were illegal by 1830 but still took place at the inns. Prison Bars was a favourite form of line tag for boisterous drinkers at pubs and there was hunting for the rich and poaching for the poor. A rite dating back to the laws of Alfred was that of walking the boundaries of the parish on Rogation Sunday. Officials took with them boys carrying willow wands to 'beat the bounds' — or the beater — to ensure the next generation knew the extent of their parish. As beer flowed freely at the finish the custom was popular, and in Northenden there were detailed records kept until the 18th century when the practice was dropped as maps and the population, slowly creeping past the 1,000 mark, became more plentiful.

New or rebuilt houses for all classes were a feature of the 17th and 18th centuries. This is known to architectural historians as the 'Great Rebuilding'. As has been mentioned, Northenden Rectory, in the 17th century a half-timber house of 16 rooms, was rebuilt in brick in the mid-18th century, using the same sandstone plinth and cellars.

The earliest known brick-built house is Newall Green Farm in Baguley, dated 1594. Built in the symmetrical 'E', fashionable in the late 16th and early 17th centuries, Newall Green, with its stone quoining and porch, is also one of the earliest examples in this area of a building other than a manor house not built in the local vernacular style.

Cottages acquired brick chimneys in the 17th century and brick replaced the wattle-and-daub infill in timber-framed houses. Thomas Barlowe's kitchen chimney in Northenden was built in brick before 1671. Building in brick by the local gentry was taking place from at least the early 17th century onwards. John Vawdrey of Bank Hall in Bowdon had a brick

3. Northenden old church. The church was the setting for many
dramatic incidents in the 17th century. The body of the church shown
in this photograph of about 1850 was rebuilt in 1874 but the 15th-
century tower has been retained.

4. Newall Green farm. One of the earliest brick-built houses in the area, it is also one of a very few working farms
within modern Wythenshawe.

kiln listed in his inventory dated 1626. Bricks also appear in the inventories of the ordinary folk of Northenden, Etchells and Baguley from the 1660s onwards. The bricks used were largely locally made, as fines by the Etchells court leet in the early 18th century for making bricks on Shadow Moss show.

Chamber Hall, the original medieval courthouse of Etchells, had two wings of differing proportions added at different times before 1674 and was encased in brick in 1703 by its owner, Matthew Shelmerdine. It still has its original medieval roof beam and 16th-century front door, and wooden latches on some of the doors. From the inventories of successive generations of Shelmerdines, we know it had 15 rooms, including a cellar and two lofts, in 1674, in 1711 and in 1732, and it still has nearly the same number of rooms today, in spite of slight changes since the mid-18th century.

Kenworthy Hall, Knob Hall, Floats Hall and Benchill were farmhouses, mainly from the 18th century built in brick, but these were lost as the new estates advanced. Sharston Hall had three storeys, an opulent staircase and ornate Victorian additions. The Worthingtons had been a local family from 1511 but the Hall only dates from 1701. In the early 19th century Thomas Worthington made his money as an early umbrella tycoon. In 1827 the Earl of Chester's Yeoman Cavalry, when resting near the Hall, were entertained by Thomas. His son was posted as a Cornet two months later and in 1848 helped to put down the Chartist (demanding a people's charter) riots in Stockport. The Hall stood until 1986 but it was eventually defeated by neglect and dry rot and replaced by offices built in an 18th-century style evocative of the old hall, and houses.

At Quarry Bank in Styal, just south of Wythenshawe, a new house, a new factory and a model village were founded in 1784: the cotton mill (now a working National Trust museum) and the houses of Samuel Gregg and his employees. The enterprise was significant in two ways. Firstly, it was the true beginning of the Industrial Revolution in this area. Secondly, Gregg created a village for the workers, complete with school, church and shops; the first industrial garden village and a prologue to the garden city movement in which Wythenshawe would ultimately figure so prominently. Gregg's apprentices came from the Poor Law Commissioners and had no wages, but were fed, clothed and boarded in the Apprentices' House, which may still be inspected.

The cloth trade, the leather trades, clockmaking and, in the early 19th century, market gardening, were other local industries. Fustian, a coarse cotton/wool or linen/wool cloth, was woven in Northenden. Linen weaving (using locally grown hemp and flax until the 18th century, then higher quality flax from Ireland or around Manchester) took place everywhere and was the principal type of weaving until the advent of Gregg's mill. In 1750 William Roscoe from Bradshawe near Bolton established a 'factory' for hand spinning cotton and linen, using the big Yorkshire wheel, near Gatley Hall. Later the Alcock family, John and Samuel, established a smallware weaving shed in the same building. There were a great number of handloom smallware weavers around Gatley Green and their cottages had cellars for storage and well-lit upper rooms for the looms.

Tanning and the rest of the leather industries in the area were as important as the cloth industry in the 17th century, but they declined rapidly in the 18th century. Meanwhile a small watch/clock industry established itself for a short time in Shadow Moss towards the end of the 17th century, beginning with Henry Hough, who first appears in the copyhold leases of the Tatton estates in 1699 (he was a tenant for some years before that). As houses became more comfortable and their occupants wanted to appear more affluent, there was a demand for clocks and watches. But Henry Hough was more than a watchmaker, he appears to have enjoyed a considerable local, and possibly even national, reputation as an engraver. At his death in 1727 a memorial was set up to him in Northenden Church which read

Here lieth the Body of Henry Hough of Etchells in Northerden Parish Famous throughout the

Kingdom for his Skill in the Art of Engraving in which he has not left his Equal. He lived admired and died lamented upon ye 30 of December Anno. Dom. 1727.

He was followed by the Collier family. Joseph Collier made clocks first at Moss Nook (Etchells on the clocks) from 1720 onwards and his son David continued the craft after him.

Amongst the more unusual trades to be found in the area, there were two gunsmiths in Northenden towards the end of the 17th century, Richard Goulden of Northern Moor and his son James. Richard Goulden began life as a whitesmith (i.e. a smith who finished off the work of others), but with the increase in demand for sporting guns in the latter half of the 17th century he easily turned to finishing guns. The lock would have been made elsewhere but he would have put lock, barrel and stock together.

Alehousekeepers, both licensed and unlicensed, seem to have done a good trade in the area through the 17th and 18th centuries. In the late 17th century, the court leet records show that there were up to ten unlicensed alehouses in Northenden and Etchells, and probably only two or three licensed ones. In 1742 Edward Dean, grocer and innkeeper, sold sugar and 'Spanish juice' to his customers as well as beer made in his brewhouse.

Market gardening began in the early 19th century, with the emphasis on soft fruits, onions, lettuce and rhubarb (locally called 'Baguley beef'). With the coming of the railways and the rapid expansion of the populations of Manchester and Stockport, market-garden produce from this area travelled to London and Chester, as well as the local markets. The industry continued to expand well into the 20th century.

The railway and population growth also changed another agricultural product from this area by the mid-19th century. Instead of turning all their milk into cheese, local farmers found it easier and more lucrative to supply liquid milk to the populations of Stockport and Manchester. William Palin in his *Cheshire Agriculture: Report for the Royal Agricultural Society*, published in 1848, noted that: 'The vast increase of population in manufacturing localities has occasioned a considerable demand for milk'.

Compared with the Worthingtons of Sharston and the Tattons, Samuel Gregg was a liberal, but there were two Northenden men of property, Joseph Johnson and Absolem Watkin, who were hard fighters for reform. The issues in the early 19th century were the price of bread, unemployment and votes for the poor.

Joseph Johnson, a brushmaker of Shudehill, was secretary to the Manchester Patriotic Society. It was he who proposed that Henry 'Orator' Hunt be invited to St Peter's Fields in Manchester in 1819, and he was with Hunt on the platform when the magistrates (one was Thomas William Tatton) ordered the yeomanry to charge. The slaughter that followed became known as Peterloo. Johnson, with Hunt and others, was imprisoned. His wife visited him at Lincoln Castle but she died within a year, as did his small son, and he was not allowed to attend their funerals. Their home was briefly Myrtle Grove on Sale Road, but when free again Johnson moved to Ravenswood House on the east side of Church Road, where he continued his campaign for reform. He was host there to William Cobbett (author of *Rural Rides* and editor of *The Political Register* in the 1830s and 1840s), and through his friend, Absolem Watkin, he knew Richard Cobden, Bright and others. A window in Northenden Church was dedicated to him after his death in 1872. Johnson's house, Ravenswood, was converted into shops at the turn of the century and demolished in the 1970s.

Absolem Watkin worked with Johnson on the Remonstrance concerning Peterloo and it was while visiting him in 1826 that he fell for 'the natural beauty of Northenden'. When he was again working with Joseph Johnson in 1830 on the famous Manchester Petition for the Reform Bill, he decided to buy Rose Hill, at the southern end of Longley Lane, with its 'commanding view of the river . . . the land is some of the best in Northen'. His family came from Shrewsbury. Aged 20, he became proprietor of his uncle's cotton mill. Besides his work for the Free Trade movement, in opposition to the Corn Laws which protected

5. Peterloo, 1819. This contemporary engraving shows Orator Hunt being arrested by the Military at A, and centre stage at B Joseph Johnson of Northenden, the instigator of the meeting, being arrested by the tipstaff.

farmers by excluding imports and keeping prices high, he was a J.P. and in 1873 Mayor of Manchester. He enlarged Rose Hill and collected a fine library that covered both science and the arts. In his *Extracts from His Journals 1814-1856*, he wrote 'Discursive reading has been the great enduring and uncloying pleasure of my life'.

His son, Edward Watkin, born in the year of Peterloo, left his father's business to become the Railway King or Doctor. The lines he remodelled included the Trent Valley, the Stafford to Rugby, the Manchester-Sheffield, Lincoln and Marylebone, Snowdon and the Canadian Pacific. Locally, he promoted the Cheshire Lines Committee, the joint railway that in serving Northenden and Baguley also ran through his estate, so giving him a personal service that he sometimes extended to Sunday School parties. To promote north London and its railway, the area later called 'Metroland', he began a copy of the Eiffel Tower, but at 60 feet the structure was abandoned, as were his Channel Tunnel (until recently) and Scottish-Irish Tunnel schemes.

As J.P., Manchester councillor, Liberal M.P., High Sheriff of Cheshire, Knight and Baron, Sir Edward campaigned on behalf of working people for better hours, half-day holidays and public parks. As Sir Edward Watkin, he was visited by Gladstone, Dickens and Disraeli. The enlarged Rose Hill included a chapel and the huge painting by Edwin Church of *Icebergs* (*see* Chapter Ten), and in the grounds he had a large glacial boulder or meteorite mounted on a tree stump.

After his death in 1901 Rose Hill became in turn a hospital for soldiers and then children, an orphanage and a remand home. His monument in Northenden church is next to the memorial window to Joseph Johnson.

The number of successful businessmen bringing their gains from the city of Manchester back to Wythenshawe much increased in the 19th century. We have seen how Thomas Worthington built Sharston Hall on umbrellas, Joseph Johnson's Ravenswood was supported on brushes and Absolem Watkin's Rose Hill reposed on cotton and later railway sleepers.

Samuel Brooks made a fortune from the useful combination of calico printing and running a bank that issued its own notes. In 1856 he bought much of Baguley, Timperley and Sale and built on it Brooklands Road, with a toll bar and its three mile extension to Prospect House at Hale Barns. St John's church in Brooklands Road was designed for him by Alfred Waterhouse, who later planned the new Manchester Town Hall. A fire in 1945 ruined the organ and reredos, but the church, of simple design, has since regained its aura of dignity. Nicholas Kilvert of Kilvert's Lard later lived on Brooklands Road at Woodcourt, a large house now widely known as a hotel and restaurant.

Another church was built with the money made by magnate James Watts, of S. & J. Watts, the proprietors of the famous warehouse for fancy goods on Portland Street. The church, Heyhead Congregational, was opened in 1862. Mr. Watts was twice Mayor of Manchester, a J.P., High Sheriff of Cheshire and host to the Prince of Wales. Early on in his career he took over The Bazaar in Deansgate from Samuel Brooks.

St Wilfrid's church, when it was rebuilt in 1877, obtained its new organ as a gift from Robert Percival, a wealthy property owner, who for a while lived at the top-end house on Ford Lane, Northenden. The new reredos, a carving after Leonardo da Vinci's *Last Supper*, was given in memory of his father-in-law of Beech House. This house, on Yew Tree Lane, later became a military hospital and then a health clinic. An arch, taken from Manchester Cathedral when it was rebuilt, adorned the grounds of Beech House and a second arch went to the Hollies on Royle Green Road in Northenden.

It was perhaps no coincidence that two old arches from Manchester Cathedral should come to Northenden as it was the same architect, J. S. Crowther, who before the Manchester rebuilding had rebuilt Northenden church. The rector at the time was the second local worthy by the name of Johnson — The Revd. Edward Ralph Johnson, who later became Bishop of Calcutta.

As has been mentioned, in the rebuilding rubble walls were traced, indicating a narrow church with a square chancel of Saxon or Norman work, and in the 12th century the Masseys gave the church to St Werbergh's Abbey in Chester. When Henry dissolved the abbey in 1540 and the Diocese of Chester was created, Northenden Parish passed to the Macclesfield Deanery and then joined the Diocese of Manchester in 1933. In 1537, during one of the periodic plague epidemics of those days, 'the newe sickness', Baguley residents were told to go to Bowdon church, although the Legh family of Baguley Hall were excused. The six bells date from 1750 and lie in the tower of about 1500. The tower did not need to be rebuilt except for its top stonework, which was replaced in 1924.

Although mainly a 16th-century building, many alterations had weakened it. The church consulted the architect J. S. Crowther in 1873; his work included St Mary's, Hulme, St Albans, Cheetham, and the rebuilding of Bury parish church, 'the gem of the diocese', as well as Manchester Cathedral in 1893.

The old church was demolished that year and Messrs. Clay & Son began work in April 1874 when T. W. Tatton laid the foundation stone, probably in a chancel arch and since covered. The afternoon of the ceremony began with a procession from the Rectory and ended with luncheon in the new *Boathouse Hotel*. In spite of a strike, an unforeseen collapse and rows between architect and builder, the new church was ready three years later, having cost £13,000.

A fine carved wooden screen in the south chapel, given by Robert Honford of Etchells in 1527, and memorials to the Tattons who had built both chapels were transferred to the new church. Robert Honford had also willed 'my goblet of silver & my worst silver spoons' towards the making of a chalice. The box pews were replaced and the roof raised six feet. The new organ was given a home in the south chapel, being moved to the position of the original organ, in the west gallery, in 1961.

The period around the 1870s was a busy time for other local churches. St James' church, Gatley, began in 1875 in a schoolroom on the site of the Old Court House: the building, of handmade bricks and with oak pews, followed in 1881.

Northenden Methodists' Chapel was built in 1876, immediately behind a small square one of 1826 which itself had replaced services in a cottage run by James Renshaw, a joiner. The new chapel was enlarged in 1908. A few years earlier a new Wesleyan Chapel had been built in Dobinett's Lane. Gatley's old Congregational Chapel was improved in the 1870s, but the building, which dated from 1777, was not replaced until 1937. Baguley Congregational Church dated from 1866 and for 22 years from 1876 it was also used as a school.

Before the Reformation in the 16th century St Wilfrids was, of course, a Roman Catholic church, but the re-establishment of a Roman Catholic church in Northenden came by an odd twist of fate. Mrs. Ziba Ward of Cringlewood on Yew Tree Lane had a black and white church built for 'the poorer classes', who she felt were put off by the formalities at St Wilfrids. The 'poorer classes' were still not attracted, so Ziba advertised the church for sale and the Roman Catholics bought themselves a ready-made church in 1904. The congregation flourished and 80 years later they replaced it with a smart new church.

While houses and churches had been refurbished over the centuries, roads were neglected. Sale Road was new, but although the Stockport to Altrincham road was turnpiked in the 18th century, access from Northenden to Manchester meant a ferry, a ford or a long detour. At last, in 1861, under pressure, the Manchester and Wilmslow Trust built a footbridge, and widened it by a lattice and girder construction in 1874 to make the present Palatine Road Bridge. A horse-drawn omnibus was operating by 1867 with five journeys to and from Manchester daily. The first motor buses in Manchester were tried out on the route in 1906 and used regularly from 1909. To replace the ferry, Mr. Tatton erected a footbridge in the 1870s and at first a toll was charged for it use. Tolls for the road bridge ceased in 1881 when the Highways Board took over.

Because of improved links and the use of omnibuses and cycles, Northenden began to grow as commuters from the city came to live in the area. Houses sprang up along what would become Palatine Road. Northenden also became the weekend playground for city workers, with boating on the river, golf to one side, a fairground with a pub on the other, tea-houses everywhere and open countryside all around.

The *Parish Magazine* of 1879 warns of Good Friday crowds and asks that 'not only those who trade in intoxicating drinks but others who may have intercourse with the visitors will do their best . . . to defend the moral character of the village'. T. A. Coward in his *Picturesque Cheshire* (1902) commented of the weekend trippers 'it is not the fine old church they go to visit, but the swing boats and booths and the river, for here the Mersey is navigable for craft of a sort'.

Meanwhile, seemingly unruffled by the influx of new residents and trippers, the Tattons still graced Wythenshawe Hall and owned most of Wythenshawe — but the power-base was shifting. Their power as lords of the manor waned, but that coming from the wealth of their estate persisted, and each Tatton in turn played the part of squire with just the right veneer of dignity and charm. From 1780 onwards they inherited their earliest stamping ground and for two generations became the Tatton-Egertons of Tatton Park and Wythenshawe. Both halls continued to grow and the number of servants likewise. Perhaps the last openly ostentatious display of largesse was the coming-of-age party of R. H. G. Tatton in 1904.

The income the Church received from tithes continued into the 20th century and the Rectory and its staff also grew. The tithe maps of 1839 were made to determine the state of play where tithes were still levied, and together with the early Ordnance Survey maps tell us much about the topography of the area. The parson and squire image was still current but increasingly the power of the new-rich was growing and of the elected and paid officials was being formalised.

The highways boards of the 1850s had grown out of the body of local dignitaries, the Poor Law Guardians, which from the 1830s met fortnightly as the Bucklow Union at Knutsford. The Guardians came into being with the New Poor Law in 1834 and were an elected body. Previously for generations the Overseers of the Poor, working with the churchwardens, had overseen the poor (checking also that they kept to their parish of birth or 'settlement'), the workhouses, and the granting of 'outdoor' relief (i.e. to those not in the workhouses); they appointed surveyors and under guidance from the Commissioners in London, had collected rates for local use. There were four paid Relieving Officers for the area and gradually their duties widened and other departments mushroomed. A paid assistant overseer, John Richardson, a former Sharston teacher, worked for the three townships from 1864. Finally, from 1888 onwards, Rural District Councils were created to take over the various boards — sanitary, highways, police and, from 1902, education. Parish Councils were left with little power except to make complaints. Northenden made several efforts to become an Urban District Council at this time, but in vain.

Educational provision was limited to a single school at Sharston Green for most of the 19th century. Reflecting the national situation, education was the sphere most due for change. Apart from small, private schools, such as the one in Northenden licensed in 1692 to William Boardman, Sharston was the first school to serve the area generally, beginning in the early 1800s, with new buildings in 1842 and 1864. William Richardson ran the school until the 1840s, when he was said to be 'not capable of much exertion'. He was succeeded by his son Thomas and later by John Richardson who, after two years, became parish clerk. The 1870 Act made fees and attendance compulsory. Fines and imprisonment could be and were imposed, but the remoteness of the school and the use of children as labour on farms made attendance 'by far the most irregular in the district'. The use of older pupil monitors as teachers, a common practice at the time, did not help.

A 'National' Church of England school served Moss Nook from 1835, and the building doubled as a Mission church. In Northenden an infants' school was built in Ford Lane, doubling as a church room and as a church during the 1870s rebuilding. Baguley was served by a Congregational school in 1860s and a C. of E. school, managed by Brooklands Church, opened in 1876. School fees were abolished in the 1890s and under government pressure for higher standards a new National School was built in 1901 at the corner of Kenworthy Lane and Palatine Road in Northenden to replace the Sharston and Ford Lane schools.

Also in 1901 the Methodists opened a school in Victoria Road and this became a council school in 1904. As children over the age of 11 had to travel to distant schools at this time, the council school was given new buildings in Bazley Road with 400 places and cookery, laundry and craftwork rooms. The old Sharston School became a tea-house and continued as a general-purpose meeting room until 1937. The Ford Lane school remained as the Church Rooms until the new ones opened behind the Kenworthy Lane school in 1913.

Adult education made a tentative start when the Working Mens' Club-come-reading room opened in Church Road in 1866. Talks were given by Edward Watkin, William Tatton and Mr. Worthington on topics that included local history. A night school for children and adults was staffed by volunteers and functioned from 1872. A Literary Society flourished from 1899 onwards and did not shirk from topics such as Socialism, River Pollution and Cholera.

With the use of the Mersey for boating, swimming and fishing, its pollution was of increasing concern to the Sanitary Board and a joint committee of all local authorities was set up. Sewage works were built off Longley Lane in 1895 and enlarged in 1907 and 1926, but the fight against industrial pollution from the Stockport region was as ineffectual then as it is today. Piped water had, however, come to Northenden in 1867 and gradually cholera was subdued.

Two particular fires point to the lack of fire brigade cover in Wythenshawe in the early 1900s. The parish council approved a voluntary brigade in the 1860s and there is a photograph of a team of eight on a horse and cart with a knife board along the middle taking part in Queen Victoria's Jubilee celebrations at Rose Hill. Actual fire cover came from the Sale and Ashton Brigade or the Cheadle and Gatley U.D.C., but the £21 2s. needed for a telephone link could not be met.

The first significant fire was at the Northenden Café which stood on Palatine Road opposite Mill Lane. It was built and run by Monsieur and Madame Logios, who provided dancing, entertainment and films with their sumptuous but expensive meals. On 4 November 1904 the brick-and-plaster fronted café caught fire, and by the time the Sale Brigade arrived it was practically destroyed. The *Stockport Advertiser* observed, 'It will be remembered that the original café on the same site suffered a similar catastrophe some four or five years ago'. Monsieur Logios committed suicide by shooting himself. The second fire to underline Northenden's isolation was at a motor garage in 1922, when the Manchester Fire Brigade arrived before the one from Sale.

The police force, represented by a sergeant and two constables, came under orders from Chester and Stockport. They were involved in a tragic incident at Bradley Gate House on Longley Lane on 26 February 1902. A servant named Cotterill shot his master, Mr. Dyson, in his bed. Reports vary as to whether he had been dismissed or whether he had had a row with the butler. When approached by the police he fired, the police withdrew to the street and in a shoot-out Cotterill was shot dead. Because he had the reputation of being pro-Boer and was nicknamed Kruger by the villagers, his body was taken from a stable behind the *Church Inn* and kicked along the road. The *Daily Dispatch* report, headed 'Northenden Sensation', continued, '. . . the intention of the village group was to throw the body in the river. Rumour having got abroad the timely arrival of the village constable led to the body being abandoned under a hedge in the lane leading to the boathouse'. The body is buried behind the pillar postbox (a rare V.R. one) in the churchyard.

The problems of the one-cell police station at Moor End figured in a second murder in 1923. A 14-year-old Ardwick boy, Percy Sharpe, was stabbed in Carrs Wood, also off Longley Lane, where it crosses the railway. The identification parade had to be held outside the police station before a hostile crowd and a named suspect, David Calthorpe, was dutifully picked out. Fortunately, at his trial he was found 'not guilty' and a Francis Booker, who after arrest was found to have the knife, the boy's trousers, diary and unemployment card, was eventually traced and hung.

Between these two murders came the much greater tragedy of the First World War. Before then there were lighter moments, starting with the 40 hexagonal gas street lamps that the parish council obtained in 1901. The following year there was lamb roasting off Longley Lane to mark the coronation of Edward VII. A four-day bazaar was held in 1910 in the riverside Stadium to raise money for the proposed Kenworthy Lane Parish Rooms. The Stadium had been opened about ten years earlier by Mr. Livingstone as a skating rink and boxing stadium and was the largest structure of its kind in the area. At the north end of Longley Lane, opposite the last surviving Northenden smithy, Peter Legh built a public hall in 1911. To mark the crowning of George V it became the Coronation Cinema, one of the first 'picture-houses' in the district. Conveniently, the proprietor also owned the *Farmers' Arms* next door and the intervals were suitably long. The screen was a whitewashed wall, the prices were 3d., 6d. and 9d., and children 2d., and it had its own generator for its electric light.

But as the lights went out over the so-called civilised world the focus of attention became the casualty list, coupled with the campaign to extort yet more and more food from the land. With the return of peace Wythenshawe began to realise that it was itself the object of scrutiny by the Manchester citizens across the waters of the Mersey — and this time what was wanted was the land itself.

6. Wythenshawe Hall. Home of the Tatton family, the archetypal squires of Wythenshawe down the centuries, it has now been inherited by the people of Manchester.

Chapter Two

Towards a New Wythenshawe
Dreamers and Schemers, Plotters and Planners

With a story stretching from the Bronze Age to well into the 20th century, it might be thought that Chapter One had covered the major part of Wythenshawe's history. In terms of time this is true. In terms of events normally thought of as historically significant, such as Saxon settlements, St Wilfrid and an ancient church, a Domesday entry, an ancient saltway, a Civil War siege, imagined links with Cromwell and Bonnie Prince Charlie, ejected clergymen, Peterloo conspirators and an ever-present paternalistic surveillance from the lord of the manor at the Hall, Wythenshawe indeed has an early history considerably more fascinating and varied than many towns in Britain. If we consider, however, that with the creation of the Wythenshawe project, which involved over a hundred thousand people in a vast, traumatic social experiment on such a scale that the importance has been recognised throughout Europe and beyond, then it may be argued that the most interesting and significant period of history of the area was only beginning in 1926.

During the building of Wythenshawe the community of Northenden increasingly, often reluctantly, shared the spotlight. As the number of houses, industrial areas, schools and shops grew, and activity spread over the wider Wythenshawe canvas, the interaction of the locals (particularly the settled populace of Northenden) with the pioneers was itself an interesting phenomenon in the area's development. In spite of the peripheral activity and the way maps show the village completely engulfed by Wythenshawe, Northenden has managed to maintain much of its independent character, and for that reason, and because of its long history, it is treated here as a separate entity.

There were few outward signs in the Northenden of 1926 to suggest that over the next forty years the land south of the village would become the site of one of the most interesting, exciting and arguably one of the greatest housing enterprises of recent times. To understand the circumstances that led to these great changes we have to follow two threads.

The first thread was the swelling pressure from the city of Manchester for more living space. At that time, in the eyes of the residents of Northenden, Manchester was a quite separate, smoky but sometimes useful, big brother north of the River Mersey. Few spoke of the threat across the water but it was perhaps felt in the bones. 'We all knew that the time might come when Manchester would take over Northenden, but we didn't really believe it would be in our time', was how one resident of the period put it fifty years later.

Annexations of adjoining territory had been made by Manchester and other big cities many times in the past, but the contrast between the industrialism and poverty in Manchester and the rolling estates of the landowners of Cheshire was so great, and the River Mersey and its flood plain such a psychological barrier, that further encroachment seemed impossible. Civic awareness, too, was stirring in the 1920s. For Cheshire landowners to watch the amputation would be galling. Yet it was clear to many that it was going to happen, and the facts that it took place under a spotlight at national, as well as local, level and is fully documented make the acquisition a particularly interesting piece of 20th-century history.

The move over the Mersey was spearheaded from Manchester Town Hall by such people of vision as Alderman Jackson and Councillors Ernest and Sheena Simon. Whether they were villains or benefactors would seem largely to depend on whether the person making the judgment was born south or north of the Mersey. Jackson was a Socialist and the Simons were Liberals, who became Socialists later (when they became peers), but there were Conservatives too, such as Lt.-Col. Westcott, who had faith in Manchester's ability to build a great garden city.

The other thread was spun by the professional garden city reformers and planners. These, too, were mostly men of vision, whose work had grown out of many campaigns in the previous century for better, even ideal, living conditions for working people. That there ought to be such aims was by no means obvious or acceptable to many town-hall planners in the 19th and 20th centuries. Many examples of blindness about this were to be seen in Britain as well as in Manchester itself. The planners who could dream of garden cities for artisans included Ebenezer Howard, generally regarded as the leading pioneer of the movement, Raymond Unwin, a disciple of Howard, and Unwin's partner and friend, Barry Parker, the man who was to become most associated with Wythenshawe. The coming together of the schemers from the Town Hall, Jackson and the Simons, with the dreamers from the drawing boards, Raymond Unwin and Barry Parker, created Wythenshawe, the eventual home for over 100,000 souls, mainly from Manchester, and the focus of attention of town planners from all over the world.

Acquiring Wythenshawe for Manchester's overflowing population had been mooted for some years, but in 1926 it was still only a dream. How did Mancunians of the early 1920s view the mirage, to some perhaps the promised land, south of the Mersey? An early resident of Wythenshawe, who visited the area in the 1920s before being rehoused there, recalled:

> We would take a tram to Barlow Moor Road and then walk into Northenden. When you reached the fields by the river you felt you were in the country. Then there were the places selling teas by the river and the boats you could go on and there was often a fair there.

A wounded soldier in Withington Hospital recalled:

> I was in Nell Lane Hospital in 1918. We were told that when we got to Northenden we were out of Manchester so we used to try to reach there in an afternoon. We felt we were getting better if we managed that far and somehow getting over the river into a village that was so different from Manchester made us feel better. It wasn't often that we walked in the other direction, to Manchester.

A member of a Manchester cycling club remembered Northenden as 'a first base where hot water for tea, at a 1d. a jug, and minerals at ½d., could be bought at the houses by the river'.

The area was popular, too, for organised outings as one former Sunday school member recalled in 1980.

> I expect our teachers were really kind, but to us, it seemed they were only nice three times a year: Christmas, Whitsunday and the yearly outing. Everyone was gay on that day. Some parents came to help the teachers. My father always came.
>
> My earliest memory of an outing was about 1921 or 1922. There were several carts pulled by horses. Tied down on the carts were the forms used in Sunday-school. Dressed in our best clothes we had to sit very still on these forms or we would have fallen off.
>
> We were jolted along from near Platt Lane, along Wilmslow Road then onto Palatine Road. As we crossed the River Mersey we all cheered. We were really in the country then. Just the village shops and a few cottages, cattle grazing in the fields, then on past Wythenshawe Park, which then belonged to Lord and Lady Simon, on until we came to a tiny village church school. There we were greeted by the country people who belonged to the church. They had tables laid out for us in the playground. We had a lovely time after our picnic and we all went home with flowers . . .

Someone who saw the trippers coming into the area was Mrs. Florence Weatherby, and in the 1970s she wrote of those days. Her account is quoted extensively to give a flavour of the enchantment of rural Northenden for city people. (The steamer referred to below would in fact have been a motor boat.)

7. Fire, Northenden Café 1904. The scene the morning after the second (or third) fire at the *avant-garde* café.

8. The River Mersey and *Tatton Arms, c.*1890. At this time the area was a venue for day trippers. Before the bridge, the inn (then called the *Boat House*) controlled a ferry here. By the bridge are toll booths and behind a fair and boats for hire.

Northenden was quite a pretty village as I remember it sixty-odd years ago. Lots of folks used to come from the town for a day out. The river was a great attraction. There was the old steamer which would not be complete without its 'Master Bob', who in his younger days had been a seaman. Showmen used to come and there were stalls etc., and most of the folk in Mill Lane used to cater for meals, mostly teas. My father was a baker and supplied them with slab cake at 4d. a pound, and it was good.

The Fair was a great attraction too at Easter and Whitsun. This brought trade to the few shops as the Fair people used to live well and spend well. The 'Wakes' ground was at the end of the Brett Street and was quite a space.

A few of the Northenden men had jobs in town. We called them 'the business men'. There wasn't much else to do except farming and market gardening. It was a common sight to see a chap fast asleep on his cart going home from early market. The old horse knew his way home. There were very few cars then, mostly horses . . .

We had very little excitement as children. I remember when the Tattons' coach was on its way to St Wilfrid's Church with the Squire and his wife on Sunday mornings, we used to dash upstairs to watch them go by. The maids walked behind in pairs, about twenty-four of them, all dressed in navy blue bonnets and long navy blue dresses. The coach was small and glass. The footman and driver looked smart, with white waistcoats and tall silk hats. I believe the coach is still at Wythenshawe Hall, and I wonder why they don't put it on show.

Mrs. Weatherby goes on to describe how the Mill Lane Mission Hall — converted to Mews homes in 1987 — was run by an Irish couple, Mr. and Mrs. Daley, who also ran a Reading Room and Coffee Tavern to support it.

As time went on they got too old and retired. It was handed over to the Manchester City Mission who ran it for a few years, then the Brethren, I think, run it now. Lots of folk had some very happy days there. I feel I should not be what I am today if it had not been for the faith and patience of some of the Sunday School teachers.

Later on a gentleman named Mr. Bowcliffe lived also in Fielden Park. He used to give a Garden Party and invite all the teachers and workers from all the Churches around. Speeches were made — all to do with Sunday School work. Even in those days we all met — Church, Chapel, Mission and all.

Where the Town Houses are now, opposite Mill Lane, there used to be a stone-front Café. A Frenchman kept it. His name was Mr. Lougous. They had an orchestra. The place was burnt down three times, which made it look suspicious. The first time we saw moving pictures was there. A party came along in caravans with Charlie Chaplin's pictures. They were silent. We paid 3d. to go in. Quite a lot of excitement for us children. They stayed a week and then moved on.

Some of you will remember Bradley Gate House on Longley Lane, where the Corporation have now built. A gentleman named Mr. Dyson lived there. It was a well kept house and farm. He was a business man in town. The coachman and the butler had a row one night. The butler came in late and rather drunk, and shot the coachman dead on his bed as he thought, but discovered it was his master he had shot. He then shot himself. This caused such a stir folk talked of nothing else. They wheeled the butler's body on a handcart down the village. After that we kids always said that the house was haunted.

A man called Mr. Bothwick began to run a private bus to West Didsbury at the cost of 2d.; but many people still walked, as 2d. was 2d. in those days. Then they took the train or horse bus to Manchester. Later the Corporation ran horse buses, open on top — you had to weather it! Then later motor buses and electric trams ran down to town from West Didsbury.

Near the Ford Cottage Tea-rooms there used to be a clay pit and a brick kiln where they made bricks for a firm at Stockport. The bungalow was still there, and my father-in-law lived there as a boy, as his father was in charge of the place. It was very dark at night, not a light anywhere. His father always kept a gun for shooting rabbits. One night the parents went out to the village and left two boys in, but the third boy was out. They thought they heard someone around and picked up the gun and went to the door. The gun went off, the bullets going into the door lintel. Good job they did or they might have hit the other brother. I believe the marks are there to this day.

My father-in-law used to say how one night there was a loud knocking long after they had all

9. The ford, a mile up river from the *Tatton Arms*, 1903.

gone to bed. When they asked who was there, it was a coachman saying, 'Can you come and help and bring a rope. We have stuck in the middle of the river'. Where Simons Bridge is now used to be a crossing, very shallow, and you crossed over into Didsbury as there was no bridge then. I have walked over many times. Well, they tugged and tugged, and could not move the coach. So Grandad looked in and said, 'I'm afraid, Ladies, you will have to get out!'. All in their Fancy Ball dresses and shoes. It was the only way. They used to fish in the river. I don't know what sort of fish it was they caught, it must have been cleaner then.

Near Heath's shop on Church Road used to be a farm. Ellesmere (now Elverston) Street was a pond. It used to ice over in winter and we used to slide on it. On the site of the old shops nearer the garage there was a big house with a very high wall round. A Captain Marsland lived there.

Outside the Church Inn there used to be a man selling pots. He used to stand there and shout and every now and then he would break a plate or a cup just to draw a crowd. The Tea people used to buy his pots cheap.

Now and then one of the Pubs would make a Hot Pot or pie with a thick crust on and bring it to our Bakehouse to be baked. It used to smell good. The Dairy on Church Road and Royle Green Road used to send a very large can of milk to be used in the bread which was ordered for each Monday, two dozen 2lb loaves, and I believe it kept lovely and moist all week. You couldn't enjoy bread kept a week these days.

When gas was brought to Northenden we thought it was wonderful. The lamplighter used to go round with his pole and turn the lamps on, and just before 12.00 p.m. he went round to turn them

out. It's very different today. There was no traffic on the roads then, the new estates were all
farmland.

    The mail was brought from Didsbury by the Postman, Mr. Battey. He pushed the truck up
Palatine Road and back. He always carried his umbrella and his shoes were polished. He did it for
years and looked smart. Also at that time a Mr. Joe Palmer used to be a Postman and Cobbler. He
lived in Northenden.

With such attractive images of the land just over the Mersey prevailing, it was clear that,
with the demand for living space exacerbated by the 1914-1918 World War, the advance
south could not be held forever. Slum clearance in Manchester began in 1841. Houses in
Market Street, London Road and Deansgate were in turn demolished to make way for shops,
businesses and stations. As the population in the heart of Manchester declined from 1850,
so the suburbs spread outwards. Cheetham Hill and Broughton in the north were matched
with Withington and Fallowfield in the south. With the aid of the horse omnibus, trains
and trams, the new middle class, the 'business men', could build in the fields round
Didsbury, Withington and, to a lesser extent, at Northenden, while the prosperous could
reach Bowdon, Alderley Edge, Cheadle and Wilmslow. Early in the 20th century it was
realised that vast numbers of new houses were also needed for those who could not afford
to build their own. The Housing of the Working Class Act of 1890 had permitted local
authorities to build houses to let, but offered them no help to do so. Because of the shortage
of houses towards the end of the First World War, however, more positive help and
encouragement of the building of new houses for renting was given.

As soon as the first murmurings of the cry that was to become a tumult, 'Homes fit for
Heroes', had been heard, the government of 1917 set up a committee under Sir John Tudor
Walters — the Housing (Building Construction) Committee. It was asked to 'investigate
the questions of building constructions in connection with the provision of dwellings, for
the working classes in England, Wales and Scotland'. Its influential report, made in October
1918, stressed the importance of an open layout with no more than 12 houses per acre, 70
feet between rows of facing houses, and a still greater width on roads carrying through
traffic. The report recommended that most houses should have three bedrooms, a large
living room of 180 square feet (five x four metres) with a sunny aspect, a small parlour, a
reasonably-sized scullery, a bathroom and a water closet approached under cover.

The future Wythenshawe had an important link with the Tudor Walters Commission as
an influential member of it was Raymond Unwin, partner and brother-in-law of Barry
Parker, the man Manchester would approve to mastermind its new garden city. Raymond
Unwin's influence can be detected in that the Commission looked further than the houses,
and in the recommendation that the site should be considered as a future location of a
community. The report affirmed that it was not sufficient merely to cover the ground with
streets and houses, but that the social, educational and other requirements of a living
community should also be considered. Cost, it claimed optimistically, need not be greater
than normal if sites were carefully planned.

Tied to the Tudor Walters report was the Addison Act. This accepted that private
enterprise could not provide enough working-class houses to let, and therefore government
money, 'grant-in-aid', would be made available for municipal housing over and above the
money raised locally by a penny rate. The act required local authorities to prepare and
carry out adequate housing schemes. A completely new era in the supply of working-class
houses, 'council houses', was thereby ushered in. Financed by the ratepayers and tax-payers
but watched over by the Treasury and the Ministry of Health, the onus for working-class
houses was now on the committees and officials of local authorities.

In Manchester, as in towns and cities all over the country, the translation of the various
reports and Acts of Parliament into actual homes, especially rented accommodation for the

working class, was the task of those concerned with local government. In every town hall the creation of homes had to be a co-operative venture of councillors and officials, and the conversion of rural Wythenshawe into the huge satellite township, or garden city, of Wythenshawe by Manchester was no exception. Nevertheless such a mammoth task was not achieved, indeed could not be commenced, without the foresight and leadership of a few devoted campaigners for this new concept. Of all those concerned there were three men, all Mancunians-by-adoption, whose lives and careers became so integrated with the Wythenshawe project that we need to look at their stories and relationship more closely. One of these was the professional garden city planner, Barry Parker, and the other two were militants on Manchester City Council, where they had to wage long and often bitter battles before the new Wythenshawe became a reality. These men of action were Alderman William Jackson and Alderman, later Lord, Ernest Simon.

Born in 1864, William Turner Jackson's early childhood was spent in the pretty village of Langwith, Nottinghamshire. At that time 15,000 so-called cave-dwellers could be found using Manchester cellars. At 14 he became a junior railway clerk on the old Manchester, Sheffield and Lincolnshire Railway at Worksop Station. Two years later he was transferred to Manchester and, as he recorded later, 'I was horrified to see the slums of Gorton, Openshaw and Ardwick'.

William Jackson became business manager to a firm of plasterers, but he spent his spare time listening to County Forum debates in a cellar in Market Street and, with the other handful of Labour members, was branded a dangerous revolutionary. This impression was reinforced by the fact that he was also attending lectures by Charles Beard, who came from America to help found the socialist-orientated Ruskin Hall.

In 1903 he was voted on to the city council as Labour member for the Harpurhey Ward and was soon appointed to the Sanitary Committee, which was already making municipal history and which later became the Public Health Committee. In 1912 Jackson became its chairman and after the war he proposed the building of a tubercular sanatorium of 100 beds for children on a farm on a Welsh hillside in Abergele. Rejected contemptuously at first, Jackson took some of the opposition to see the children he had brought to the farm at Abergele. Amazed at their improvement all doubts faded. In 1931 a start was made, but not without trouble. A well was needed and it was not until they had drilled within three feet of their stated limit of 400 feet that water was found and the sanatorium, and William Jackson's precarious position, were saved.

But it is as Jackson of Wythenshawe, the 'father of Wythenshawe', that he will be chiefly remembered. An alderman in 1918, Lord Mayor from 1923 to 1924, freeman in 1927, he had considerable influence. It was William Jackson who upset the city's conscience about its slums, who discovered the potential of Wythenshawe when he visited Baguley Sanatorium as Health Committee member, who called for the Abercrombie Report on the area and was made first chairman of the Wythenshawe Committee in 1927. 'His task was the monumental one of obtaining support for his idea and convincing the Council of its benefits. Throughout the campaign for Wythenshawe, Jackson remained a prominent spokesman both inside and outside the Council Chamber.'

Working with Ernest Simon, William Jackson kept faith with the project after the failure of the city to wrest control from Cheshire after the purchase of the land, and during the struggle to build under the Councils of Cheshire and Bucklow, who did their utmost to frustrate and cripple the scheme. Again it was the year 1931 that saw success for Alderman Jackson when Manchester was able to take complete control over Wythenshawe and build its great satellite garden city.

William Jackson's reputation as an authority on the subject was recognised at a national level when he was made a member of the Departmental Committee on Garden Cities and

Satellite Towns. He was able to watch the outsize operation of building Wythenshawe get under way in the 1930s and also see the halting of the work at a most critical time by the war. He died in 1945 just as preparations were being made for the automaton to come to life again for the completion of Wythenshawe.

Born in Didsbury in 1879, Ernest Darwin Simon was the son of Henry Simon, who had come from Germany 20 years previously and established two businesses, one at Cheadle Heath constructing flour mills and the other, Simon Carves Ltd., creating iron mills. It has been said that within twenty-one years of arriving in Britain, Henry Simon had revolutionised both flour mills and the production of coke ovens. Ernest Simon, after Rugby School and Cambridge University, qualified as an engineer and at 20 took over the family firms and expanded them into the Simon Engineering Group. He married Sheena Potter in 1912 and together they became totally involved in social reform.

Ernest Simon, after serving as a councillor from 1911, became the city's youngest Lord Mayor in 1921. He served as the Liberal Member of Parliament for Withington from 1923 to 1924, and towards the end of his second term from 1929 to 1931 he became a Parliamentary Secretary to the Minister of Health. In 1932 he was knighted by George V.

After purchasing Wythenshawe Hall and 250 acres of its estate to form a park, the Simons presented them to the city and it was for this that their names first come to mind. But this gesture was only part of a long campaign undertaken by the Simons, working closely with William Jackson and Barry Parker, to accelerate slum clearance and create a garden city. His publications, *The Smokeless City*, *A City Council From Within*, *How to Abolish Slums*, *The Anti-slum Campaign*, *The Rebuilding of Manchester*, *The Smaller Democracies*, *Rebuilding Britain* and *A Twenty Year Plan* made him respected as an authority throughout much of the world. His campaign for smoke control was to help make Wythenshawe one of the first clean, smoke-free areas in the country. Education fellowships to promote the teaching of civic and social science were also created by Ernest Simon. Sheena, too, was a guiding figure on the city's Education Committee until within two years before her death in 1972. It is also very probable that she was an important influence on her husband and an inspiration behind his dynamism. Whether this is the case or not and although they were always in accord on general principles, on some issues they displayed complete independence of each other.

The abundance of energy that Ernest Simon possessed, and was able to throw into the long campaign for the creation of the new Wythenshawe, had much to do with the successful fulfilment of the dream. His obituary in *The Times* made particular note of his vigour.

> Simon, physically robust and vigorous in mind, threw himself whole-heartedly into every activity which attracted him, being completely tireless, whether walking in Cheshire or in the Lake District (where for many years he had a country cottage) or following up his most recent interest. He played a useful game of tennis, one of his few relaxations until long after most men have become spectators. The late Professor T.W. Manson, when presenting him for the honorary degree, described him as 'the embodiment of perpetual youth, inexhaustible vigour, and insatiable appetite for experiment and adventure; who combines the qualities of a volcano in active eruption and a cornucopia in full production'.
>
> He not uncommonly failed to realise that others found his pace a trifle exacting; but his enthusiasm and abounding energy were infectious. Sometimes his urge to get things done led to impatience and impetuousness and a manner which appeared strangely autocratic for one who believed so passionately in democracy.

The strange schizophrenic mix of the autocrat and the radical was a puzzling feature to some, yet is understandable in one who was born in one world but whose breadth of education and daily contact brought him into another. A glimmer of Socialism had emanated from Ernest Simon from his earliest days, and it has been said that he wanted to become a Socialist in the 1920s but was concerned about the suspicion others might have of his reconciliation between his party allegiance and his income from an industrial empire. It was no surprise, therefore, when he joined the Labour Party in 1946 and accepted a peerage the following year. His duality, industrialist and idealist, was expressed in his title, Lord Simon of Wythenshawe. He was then able to strengthen the Labour support in the House of Lords and to offer his expertise on housing to the Party. In the same year he became Chairman of the BBC. He retained his links with Manchester, however, chiefly through his continued work for the University and for Wythenshawe. He was made a Doctor of Law in 1944 and he left his home, Broomcroft, at the Didsbury end of Ford Lane, as a Hall of Residence to the University. The City of Manchester made him a Freeman in the year before his death in 1960.

The first moves by Manchester City Council towards building the new Wythenshawe were made in 1920 when Ernest Simon, as Chairman of the Housing Committee from December 1919, produced a housing report which showed that 17,000 houses were urgently needed in Manchester. As a result of this a four-year plan was put into effect. Bricklayers were in short supply and Simon urged their release from the army.

10. Wagonette, 1912. From Sunday-school outings to pub crawls, the wagonette gave access to the countryside. This outing has reached the *Tatton Inn* at Moss Nook. The small boy holding the hand-rail is Charles Millward, now 81 and formerly a lead in the West Wythenshawe Operatic Society and St Wilfrid's choir.

Jackson was Simon's deputy on the housing committee but he was forced to step down on a technicality in January 1920. In this short time, however, he had persuaded the committee to ask the Professor of Civic Design at Liverpool, Patrick Abercrombie, for a report on the suitability of Wythenshawe for Manchester housing, an area Jackson knew from his visits to the Baguley Sanatorium.

The Abercrombie report noted that south of Northenden: 'there is virgin land, capable of being moulded to take whatever shape may be decreed, with hardly a village or large group of houses to interfere with or direct the line of development'. Road and tram services, it stated, could be extended into the area. A railway ran across the north of the land but this was less useful. The Baguley Sanatorium, Abercrombie observed, was a testimony to the healthy, non-polluted air. In short his report suggested that Wythenshawe was a most suitable area for development, larger than Letchworth, even if much of the land was retained for agriculture and for other amenities.

Professor Abercrombie saw the development chiefly in residential terms, with 'little interest in promoting a self-contained industrial area like Letchworth'. At this time the development of plots for light industrial firms using electrical power was not common and the report saw Wythenshawe more as a garden dormitory for Manchester, than as a self-contained, largely-autonomous garden city. On the other hand, he noted artfully, that if Manchester bought the land at agricultural prices it could make a fat profit. His report therefore backed Alderman Jackson's scheme and it suggested that a comprehensive and imaginative overall plan should be prepared. It is interesting that it was not Abercrombie but Barry Parker who was asked, in time, to draw up the Wythenshawe plan.

In a covering letter, however, Professor Abercrombie pointed out, ominously as it turned out, that purchase of the land would not give Manchester planning control over the area. If it had a mind to do so, and if it was aware of its rights, Bucklow Council could obstruct and delay the development.

Other city departments were asked for their views. The City Engineer and the Electricity Department were happy with the scheme, while the Gas men positively bubbled over at the prospect of selling more gas on a smokeless estate. The Chief Constable more cautiously thought Manchester could take more houses without extending its boundaries, while the Chief Engineer of the Waterworks Department said he believed that there was still up to 20,000 acres of spare land nearer at hand, which would be less costly to develop and less expensive when it came to travel. A yet more important point, he argued, was that good agricultural land was being used.

At the Housing Committee meeting that followed on 19 July 1920, Councillor Cundiff, a Conservative, claimed that the deal would not be profitable — 'nothing eats its head off like land'. Labour Alderman J. Johnston argued that they were too busy to consider the matter and Alderman Cook agreed with the Waterworks Engineer's criticisms. Lt.-Col. Westcott welcomed the scheme, however, and became a staunch ally of Jackson and Simon.

The report made by the Housing Committee suggested that Manchester could not help but benefit by buying the land at £80 an acre. Simon the optimist felt sure the price would rocket to £450 an acre once the market started to move. The Parliamentary Sub-Committee and the Finance Committee received the report in November 1920, with the recommendation that purchase should be by private treaty where possible and compulsory purchase where not.

Major obstacles loomed, however. T. E. Tatton, owner of the Tatton Estate and related to the Chairman of Cheshire County Council, resolutely refused to sell. Another obstacle appeared in the middle of 1921 when the Government cut the money it was giving for council housing through the Addison Act. It was not until 1923 that Neville Chamberlain restored a little help for municipal house-building, but only if and when an authority could prove to the Ministry of Health that they could do it better 'than if they left it to private enterprise'.

Delight grew out of despair on both counts for the 'Purchase Wythenshawe' camp in the following year, 1924. On the death of T. E. Tatton the new owner, R. H. G. Tatton, 'Mr. Peter', contending with death duties, was ready and very willing to sell. The first Labour Government was in power. In its short time in office it produced the Wheatley Act, giving encouragement and help to councils to build houses for renting to working-class families and regarding the action as a necessary social service. The unions relaxed their apprenticeship rules and agreed to cooperate generally.

In the sharing out of resources for house building, on the assumption that over two million municipal houses were needed over the next 15 years, Manchester was allocated 47,500 houses on the basis of between eight and ten houses to the acre. The land required was 4,165 acres. Once again eyes turned to Wythenshawe. The Medical Officer supported its purchase and the Housing Officer reported, in July 1924, 'The opportunity given by such acquisition . . . is of almost priceless value to the citizens of the future'.

The next hurdle appeared within the city council itself. The opposition of the Conservative Party and Ratepayers' Association came into the open with the municipal election of 1925. The Labour Party made the purchase of Wythenshawe for council housing part of a comprehensive programme that included education, employment and municipal banking. To counter this the Conservatives produced a leaflet entitled, *Some Reasons Why the Manchester Corporation Should Not Purchase Wythenshawe Estate*. It claimed to show that at the present rate of corporation building there was space available for the next 60 years. The leaflet also pointed out that if the land remained in Cheshire it would be Cheshire that would benefit from the rates of the houses built by Manchester. Not all Conservatives opposed the purchase. Lt.-Col. Westcott still supported the idea strongly and the candidate for Didsbury, Dr. H. Levenstein, believed it to be a business-like proposition.

As a result of city council elections in the winter of 1925 the Conservatives remained effectively in control. In December of that year the Housing Committee turned down the purchase of Wythenshawe. The behind-the-scenes work of the past five years now seemed wasted and there was a natural reaction from Jackson, Simon and others. A letter from E. C. Galts to the *Manchester Guardian* pointed out that at the worst the rate rise would be one fifth of a penny, the price of ten matches.

The decision to purchase or not to purchase the Tatton Estates would be made early in 1926. Ernest Simon, in a letter to the *Guardian* on 29 December 1925, wrote that the vote on Wythenshawe would probably be the most important decision to be taken by the city council for the next twenty years, equal in importance to the commitment to build the Ship Canal.

The main stint of wheeling and dealing by the council men of Manchester and elsewhere was yet to take place in 1926. We must look now across to the other thread woven into the genesis of Wythenshawe, that of the professional garden-city planners, especially, Barry Parker.

It has been claimed that the first realistic idea of a garden city is to be found in the works of Leonardo da Vinci, notably his plans for Milan. Included in his design was a scheme for separating the traffic from the pedestrians. For a more certain beginning of the modern garden city, however, we need go back no further than the middle of the 19th century and the efforts that preceded Ebenezer Howard, though the 18th century had produced a number of garden villages. Most villages that have grown naturally in the country are, by their setting, garden villages, but the same could not said of those hastily and haphazardly thrown into being round factories in the Industrial Revolution.

There were, however, a few instances of careful attempts being made to create attractive industrial garden villages. One of the first of these villages, and one of the most lasting, was that built next to Wythenshawe by the Gregg family in 1784 to serve their mill at Styal. The village contained houses, a village shop, a school, an apprentice house and a chapel. In *Remains of a Revolution* Anthony Burton describes the site:

> The village that Samuel Gregg built is undeniably pleasant, and to the pauper families that came
> must have seemed positively luxurious. Visiting the mill and village in Styal, the overriding

impression is of neat cottages, set in a pleasant open countryside, and it is clearly not difficult to see how it came to be upheld as a model of benevolent development. That it still stands is itself a reflection that the village was built to a higher standard than the houses of the speculative builders of other cotton towns.

Nevertheless, views differ on whether Samuel Gregg's village was built out of consideration for the workers or out of the necessity of attracting labour to a country site where there was convenient water power.

An influential step in the movement was the garden village, perhaps more a garden small-town, to house 10,000, planned by James Buckingham in 1849. Then followed a number of notable small garden cities, Port Sunlight in 1880 and Bourneville in 1893, where the factory had already existed for 14 years. That it was not easy to create a happy community was demonstrated in America, where the garden village of Pullman, designed in 1880, was dubbed an industrial squirearchy and was plagued for years by bitter rows. Curiously, the community of Saltaire in England, planned on exactly the same lines, worked well. Most successful of all garden villages, however, was New Earswick, three miles north of York. This was designed and built for the Joseph Rowntree Trust by the rising young architect, Barry Parker. However successful the garden villages were, they were too small to make a serious contribution to the urgently needed supply of working-class houses. Lewis Mumford wrote in 1927 'The garden-village is only a drop in the ocean. The aim of the garden city must be to change the shape of the bucket'. The men who changed the shape of the bucket were Ebenezer Howard and his disciples Raymond Unwin and Barry Parker.

Howard, through his writings, did more than anyone to further the cult of the garden city and his is the name most often associated with them. He was born into the family of a hard-working baker in 1850, and his first work was as a city clerk in London. When he was 20 he went to America and became an expert shorthand writer in Chicago. The city was recovering from the great earthquake and fire at the time. The rebuilding inspired the young Howard to think deeply about the possibility of planning a city with the same love and care that is taken in planning a garden. The term garden city had already been coined and Long Island in New York was built with some of the principles in mind, but Howard gave the term reality and became the leading figure in the movement.

On his return to England he became the official stenographer to the Royal Commission on Labour. In this work he came to know Keir Hardy and others concerned with the conditions in which many industrial workers lived, and he was influenced by the Socialism and idealism of Frederick Engels, John Ruskin and William Morris, all men who knew Manchester.

With interests both in Socialism and in the better planning of cities, Howard produced his first book, *Tomorrow: a Peaceful Path to Real Reform*. This was the book that launched the garden city movement. Reissued four years later in 1902 as *Garden-cities of Tomorrow*, it pictured the town and country as two magnets each attracting 'The People': the town offering work, society and amusements, but also harbouring high rates, dirt and disease; the country offering clean air, beauty and space, but lacking a social life, employment and sanitation. Howard claimed that the solution was the garden city. He had romantic ideals but he knew that industry and social life were as important as fresh air and good houses. That all was not ideal in country sanitation is suggested in the *Punch* rhyme of the time:

> The cottage homes of England, Alas! How strong they smell,
> There's fever in the cesspool, and sewage in the well.

Locally, in the 1880s, the Rector of Northenden condemned in the parish magazine the insanitary conditions in the area that caused repeated epidemics of cholera.

Howard was able to put his ideas into practice in 1899 when the Garden Cities Association was formed. By 1904 the first garden city, Letchworth, was being built. For partners Ebenezer Howard chose two young planners, Raymond Unwin and Barry Parker. In 1905 he moved into a house designed by them at Letchworth. Keenly interested in designing a shorthand typewriter and in the hybrid language of Esperanto, he proclaimed the virtues of garden cities all over Europe. Howard remained the inspiration of more garden cities from Welwyn to Wythenshawe, though his disciples, Parker and Unwin, increasingly became the active designers.

Bernard Shaw wrote of Howard that he should have had a barony for his book, an earldom for Letchworth and a dukedom for Welwyn. He died in April 1927, but he had lived just long enough to know of the decision to buy the Tatton Estates that would make up three-fifths of Wythenshawe, and that his torch would be carried safely to the new venture by his apostles and successors, Barry Parker and, aiding him and abetting him in the Ministry, Raymond Unwin.

Until Wythenshawe was built, the garden cities of Britain (Letchworth and Welwyn) and America, were not cities at all in any real sense but only moderately-sized towns in terms of population, all having well under fifty thousand inhabitants. Wythenshawe was to have a population of over 100,000 and so be the first to approach the proportions of a city, though in fact it would have even less say in its own affairs than its predecessors. Its architect, Parker, was the third man, after Jackson and Simon, to be most associated with the new Wythenshawe. He was to have a comparatively free hand in its planning. He dreamt of it as the ultimate in garden cities and he regarded it as his masterpiece.

Richard Barry Parker was born at Chesterfield on 18 November 1867, an eldest son. After education at Buxton and Wesley College he was apprenticed to T. C. Simmonds at his Derby art college, but his artistic initiative was first triggered when he was concerned with the Manchester Royal Jubilee Exhibition of 1887. In the same year he became articled to G. Faulkner Armitage of Altrincham, where the design of wallpapers was one of his tasks. While he was there he attended the annual lectures given by William Morris in Ancoats and became involved in the Northern Art Workers' Guild, founded in 1896. In that same year Raymond Unwin, whose parents had known John Ruskin, married Barry Parker's sister and the brothers-in-law set up at Buxton a consultancy that soon turned to town planning. Parker was more concerned with the artistic aspect of their work and Unwin with the engineering.

To Parker the village was a microcosm of society and a living symbol of life itself. As a Quaker, he was impressed by the compassion of Christianity and the concern for the less well off as expressed in Guild Socialism. He saw the communal spirit in the village as an important stabilising factor upon those living there: 'the village did not just exist together but lived and worked together with the cohesion of a single entity'.

Parker's first commission was for three houses on a large plot of land purchased by his father, manager of Evan's Bank, in the fashionable Park suburb of Buxton. The largest, Moorlands, became the Parker family home.

Modest success came to the partners in 1903 when they contributed a town planning exhibit to the Northern Art Workers Guild in Manchester and it attracted wide attention. In the same year they undertook the planning of New Earswick, near York, and this too enhanced their reputation. Barry Parker had been a Member of the Society of Architects from 1895 and now, for his third accolade of 1903 he was chosen, with Unwin, to work on Letchworth, under Ebenezer Howard. He retained the post of Consultant Architect to First Garden City Ltd. until 1943. Parker became a Fellow of the Royal Institute of British Architects (R.I.B.A.) in 1913, but that year also saw Unwin leave the partnership to join the Ministry of Health as Chief Town Planning Inspector.

Letchworth was Howard's Utopian dream. In practice, it was a compromise with Parker and Unwin's down-to-earth ideas about the need for economic balance. There was enough industry in Letchworth, with more commuters coming in than going out. One of the few criticisms of Letchworth was the failure to provide civic centre shopping facilities which resulted in piecemeal development. Wythenshawe's civic centre plan by Parker was accordingly revised and much enlarged after the Second World War. Nevertheless, the socially-balanced population of Letchworth rose to around thirty thousand in 1970. It had already been agreed to be a success within its first few years.

The government did not take up the idea of garden cities in spite of Letchworth's success, so Howard, now 69, again went to the drawing-board. Welwyn, the second garden city, began in 1919 and followed the Tudor Walters Report of the previous year. Houses were kept to 12 per acre and, as with Letchworth, there were footpaths for pedestrians and more than enough local industry. The population reached 40,000 in the 1970s, but long before then Welwyn Garden City, home of Shredded Wheat, had made a world-wide impression. America borrowed many of the English ideas and as part of Roosevelt's New Deal garden cities were built under the watchful gaze of Unwin on his American visits.

Raymond Unwin was born at Rotherham in 1863, went to school in Oxford but returned north as an engineer, first in Manchester, then at Chesterfield. Already related to the Parkers, he married Ethel and partnered Barry at Buxton. A strong Socialist, he campaigned for better working-class houses in *Cottage Plans and Commonsense*. He worked on Letchworth from 1906, was elected Fellow of the R.I.B.A. in 1910 and became second president of the Royal Town Planning Institute. He was knighted in 1932 and from that time on he was a

11. Garden-city dreamers, back left, Unwin, right, Parker, with relatives at Buxton in 1898.

Visiting Professor of Town Planning at Columbia University in America until he died at his daughter's home there in 1940. Throughout all this time he exchanged ideas with Barry Parker and in practical terms the partnership was as strong as ever.

New Earswick, Hampstead Garden Suburb, Letchworth and Welwyn were test pieces compared to the proposed full-scale garden city of Wythenshawe that Barry Parker would soon be invited to design. Raymond Unwin was no longer his partner, overtly at least, but he was conveniently placed as an Inspector with the Ministry of Health and it was Unwin, with a Mr. W. G. Weeks, who came to hold the local inquiry into the proposal to purchase land in Wythenshawe. Negotiations for the buying of the Tatton Estate of 2,568 acres had begun, but the Minister of Health's sanction for the borrowing of £210,000 was needed. The Minister gave his approval and intimated that he saw no objection in principle to a city buying land outside its boundaries. The Inspectors went further by suggesting that the city should purchase more land adjoining the Tatton Estate.

> In order to enable the scheme of development to be carried out and to secure the improved values
> for business, industrial and other purposes which the self-contained development of such an area
> will create, the Corporation should consider the desirability of purchasing such further areas as may
> be required to round off the estate.

A Wythenshawe committee was set up by Manchester City Council early in 1927 (we shall be following the tensions and drama of Manchester's fight to wrench the control of the land away from Cheshire in the next chapter). The committee almost immediately asked for a scheme from Barry Parker and for the next two decades he supervised and ordered the building of the new Wythenshawe. Generally, the relationship was amicable, though on more than one occasion his contract came close to the point of not being renewed. He lived to see work commence again after the 1939-1945 war, but he died at Letchworth in 1947. Whilst working on Wythenshawe he, in 1929, was appointed President of the Town Planning Institute. In 1941, when he retired as consultant architect-planner of Wythenshawe, he was awarded the Howard Medal for his services to the Garden City Movement.

The succeeding chapters will follow the manifestation of Parker's plan for Wythenshawe. Even the work undertaken after the Second World War, although modified in 1945 by Manchester's own architect, Nicholas, was based on the principles and general schema of Parker.

With all the aggression of the next few years during the takeover from Cheshire, the depression and the war, the Parker principles could easily have been submerged. The common bond between Jackson, Simon and Parker might be thought to be on Socialist principles and a concern for the working class. This is essentially true, although in other hands such principles have sometimes had unfortunate outcomes, such as the high-rise flats so confidently erected in London, Leeds, Liverpool, Birmingham and, fortunately less so, in Manchester, on the assumption that working people would want to avoid the labour of gardening.

Jackson and Simon had both been impressed by the work of Councillor T. R. Marr on various Improvement, Building and Housing Committees, and it was his firm belief that high-rise flats were aesthetically and socially less desirable than semi-detached and short-terraced houses in an open-garden setting. Parker and Unwin were both keen members of professional associations such as the Institute of Town Planners, and both men regarded the furtherance of good architectural standards in house building as an essential part of their creed.

Parker was a vegetarian as well as a Quaker. A reflection of his strict upbringing is seen in his battles to prevent over-ostentatious design in the larger houses in Northenden and in his campaign to ensure that council houses should be well-equipped and architecturally respectable. The houses he designed for the New Earswick Estate at York and the earlier council houses in Wythenshawe, built before the economic cutback in the 1930s, are generally held to be particularly pleasing to look at and comfortable to live in.

But there was still some time before the first houses, municipal or private, would be built in Wythenshawe. In 'The Review of the Municipal Year' in its 29 December 1925 issue the *Manchester Guardian* reminded readers that a further seven thousand people had registered for working-class houses in the year. It concluded:

> As a parting gift 1925 has bequeathed to its successor the question of the Wythenshawe Estates. The Council has toyed with the Wythenshawe idea for five years, but now it appears to be confronted point blank with the offer either to take or to leave it. The decision, whatever it may be, is bound to affect profoundly the chronicles of Manchester's development, not only fifty years hence but immediately.

Chapter Three

The Five-year War: 1926-31
From Parkland to Parkerland

'In 1926 the purchase [of the Tatton Estates] was completed and a new era in the history of Wythenshawe was about to begin.' Whilst this statement, taken from the last paragraph of *Wythenshawe: to 1926*, was essentially correct, there were to be another five years of wheeling and dealing within Manchester City Council and between the councils of Manchester, Bucklow and Cheshire before the building programme of Wythenshawe could make any real progress. At the time many people thought that with the purchase of the land Manchester had control, and only the practical problems of embarking on the scheme remained. Over fifty years later this was still the view of some who had witnessed the events. A retired police officer, recalling the annexation, asserted in 1980, 'I know it was 1926 when Manchester took over because we walked down to the river and said between ourselves, We're in Manchester now'.

Wythenshawe was unquestionably in Cheshire in 1926 and sent three councillors to Bucklow Rural District Council. But to Bucklow R.D.C., which met at Knutsford, Northenden was a distant outpost. A police sergeant and his constable were especially isolated as his orders came, effectively, from Chester. The Inspectors of Schools came from the same city. The Fire Service for Northenden and Baguley was at Sale and for Northen Etchells at Cheadle, though in practice Manchester's Withington Brigade generally reached Northenden first.

In one sphere, the hospital service, Manchester had already established a legation. Its embassy was the Baguley Sanatorium, which had been built in 1902. In 1912 its use had changed to help patients suffering from tuberculosis. Baguley residents objected to paying for dealing with sewage from Manchester's sanatorium and in 1926 the plans were passed for the building of its own sewage works.

At this time residents in Wythenshawe relied for their medical treatment largely on their own doctor, the General Practitioner or 'G.P.', even to the extent of having some operations done at home. To cover the cost of this, working men were insured under the National Insurance Acts, but to cover their families they became members of Friendly Societies. The 'Oddfellows', for instance, had their local headquarters at the corner of Royle Green Road and Church Road, below Miss Richardson's school.

For hospital treatment patients went to South Manchester, the Royal, St Mary's or Withington. The Medical Superintendent of Baguley Sanatorium was aware of this and suggested in his annual report for 1926 that consideration should be given to using Baguley for acute work in view of the huge population increase about to take place in Wythenshawe.

Northenden was large enough to suggest independence and self-sufficiency but at the same time small enough for many characters, such as the schoolmaster or mistress, the doctor, the vicar and many shopkeepers, to be known by everyone. Its atmosphere is suggested in the recollections in 1980 of a schoolboy of that time.

In 1926 I was nine years old. I had been born on what was then twelve Palatine Road, opposite the present Mobil Petrol Station, in 1917. So in 1926 I was at Miss Richardson's Private School, over the Oddfellow's Lodge. The school in the upper room contained three large tables, the little class, the middle class and the top class. My recollection of this particular upper room was a large certificate granted to the Northenden branch of the Oddfellows and which contained a large number of coloured flags. The other memory is the smell, the musty smell which met you as you opened the door. I think it had something to do with the gas fire, as when we came in on a winter's morning the gas fire would be on with a large bowl in front of it containing water and it gave off this peculiar smell. We left our outdoor clothes in the downstairs room before going into the classroom. The school had art from Miss Richardson's sister, downstairs. I remember quite clearly gazing out of the window at the lamp-post that stood in the middle of the junction here, a circular curb and the fancy wooden porch from the house next door to the Spread Eagle.

Dr. Munro was a large Scotsman and he travelled round the village on an overlarge bike with a crossed cross-bar. I used to see this bicycle leaning against the cast-iron fireplace in the waiting room, that same fireplace was arrayed with rows of bottles of various sizes, patients being expected to call and take them away. Dr. Munro had a small dispensary next to his surgery in this same building where he made up all his own medicines.

As far as groceries were concerned, John William and Son (whose shop was in the middle of the south side of Palatine Road), was a beautiful grocer's shop with a strong smell of coffee as soon as you walked in, with one counter on the left covered in marble and one on the right made of wood. At the entrance was large tall desk in which a young lady could peer at you as you came through the door.

Prominent in the schoolboy's recollections were the chairs for customers, the contraption on wire for shooting money from the counters to the cashier, and the loose sugar and raisins that were made up in blue bags. Privileged customers had their orders collected.

The first shop from the river, was the Gem. It was run by Mrs. Williams and was a sweet shop. The window was filled with samples of chocolates and sweets and just by the doorway where the window sloped in was a special place for items costing ½d. or 1d. Inside the shop on the left was a counter, each end filled with glass cases in which things were displayed and you could also get ice-cream sodas in a bottle which had a ball in it and could only be opened by Mrs. Williams by putting a wooden contraption on top and striking it sharply with her hand. She also sold you toffee from big slabs which she broke with a small hammer.

Next to the Gem was the Creamery of Mrs. Haseldon, where we bought cream and such groceries as we needed and hadn't ordered from John Williams. The great thing about the Creamery was its ice-cream. Before they had a freezing machine I have a faint recollection of the wooden tub in which the cream was turned by a handle and cranks inside a mixture of ice and salt.

Nearby was the fish and chip shop, with a counter so high you just couldn't see over it, but always in the window was something in the way of tripe laid out and possibly a few cold pieces of battered fish and faggots or savoury ducks . . . Next was the undertakers, usually with a silver urn in the window and little else, then Mrs. Norbury's little shop — part stationer, part sweet shop, very dusty and dear Old Mrs. Norbury, a very old lady even then, white hair in a shawl, who was always so happy to see us, and where we could spend pennies or even halfpennies. A funny dusty little shop Mrs. Norbury's, we wonder how she ever made a living.

After the furniture shop came Doris and Winny Campden's big shop with a café to take advantage of the week-end and Easter trade. They were the daughters of Mr. Campden, who was a horticultural-ist in Kenworthy Lane where he had an old cottage next to Cow Lane and a large area of greenhouses where he grew chrysanthemums.

Next, on the corner of Mill Lane, was the off-licence. I first went in there as a teenager for cider; [it] always smelt of paraffin because they had to keep it at the right heat. Part of what is now a car park was used for the fair — you would come to this bit before you came to the fair proper, and for some time there was almost a permanent fair with horses and roundabouts on the site near the *Tatton Arms* on the site where the caravans were sited. Later after there was the fair held on the old café-site (opposite Mill Lane) — it was a ruin so long as I ever remember.

I remember the fête when Wythenshawe Park was handed over to Manchester and the advertising gimmick, which was to drive a coach and horses through Northenden.

The fête he had remembered was held in June 1926 to mark the opening of Wythenshawe Hall, Park and Gardens to the public after they had been given by Ernest and Sheena

Simon to the city. The pageant depicted the siege of Wythenshawe Hall during the Civil War (*see* Chapter One) and was performed by members of the Northenden Amateur Dramatic Society, the Comrades Club and the Music Society. Colonel Duckenfield was played by Arthur Royle, Robert Tatton by R. A. Jackson, Henry Vawdrey by Captain Jackson and Captain Adams by W. R. Hampson. The script was written by Archie Rawson, a total of about fifty people took part and the spectators included R. H. G. Tatton and the Lord Mayor and Lady Mayoress of Manchester. The apocryphal tale of the shooting of Captain Adams by Mary Webb, the maidservant, in revenge for the death of her fiancé stirred the *Stockport Advertiser* to explain that the 'hot feeling' between the rival factions was 'because the heroine was a courageous English girl'.

St Wilfrid's parish church in the 1920s was enjoying a relative boom, with other churches in Britain. The church itself was well attended and the main village functions and meetings took place in the Church Rooms in Kenworthy Lane. The annual garden-party in the Rectory grounds was one of the highlights of each summer. The daughter of the head gardener in the 1920s recalled later:

> The whole village seemed to turn out for the Rectory Garden party. Great times these garden parties were. Most of the events took place in the paddock away from the house. There was fishing in the pond by the lane and pony riding and all the other games. No-one went on the lawns, they were sacred. They were kept for tennis and we weren't allowed on them. Mr. Hamilton was a Wimbledon player and his brother was a Wimbledon champion. There used to be tennis parties at the week-ends and Fred Perry was one of those who came to play — that was before he was famous. In Mr. Allen's time Douglas Bader, the one who lost his legs, and his brother used to come.

12. The Rectory, Northenden, *c.*1885. The conservatory and servants' quarters have gone, but church garden parties are still held in the otherwise unchanged setting.

There was a considerable gap between the life-style of those in the Rectory and many in the village itself, but the *Parish Magazine* tried to bridge it. The magazine tells us not only of the church officials but, for example, that the District Nurse was Nurse Diamond.

Excerpts from Rev. Chignell's editorial matter convey something of the prevailing concerns of the parish. The August 1926 issue discourses about the Wythenshawe fête money and also reminds us that tithes at that time were still a reality.

> The calf and pig were kindly given by Mrs. Shenton and Mrs. Faulkner as prizes for the Bowling Competition. The cake given by Mrs. Henriques was a work of art. It will be wiser not to put off too long the pointing of the church pinnacles, lest a strong wind should blow one down . . . as everyone in the Parish is keen on the exterior of the Church, even if they are indifferent to the interior!

Mr. Chignell explained that by a new law tithes had to be paid twice yearly. 'To those who have to pay tithe . . . I am sorry if anyone should feel aggrieved at the change, and at the same time hope that payments will be made, or else I shall get into debt!' Four years later there was the same concern about money when the wayward contributors to the Free Will Offering Scheme were chided.

> . . . it is surely much easier to give, say 6d. [2½p] a month . . . than 25 or 30 shillings, [£1.25 — £1.50], at the end of the year . . . Too often people miss a few weeks or months . . . and so give up altogether. That is hardly playing the game, is it?

There were brighter spots in the year, as the Parish Notes in the same issue record. In July there was a collection for the Diocesan Quota and a special service. 'The Choir excelled itself and the soloist Miss Phyllis Williams, delighted us all her sweet voice and beautiful singing . . . O for a closer walk with God.' The December 1930 issue includes an acknowledgment of a beaten silver communion set from the departed Tattons and, significantly, the first reference to the new inhabitants of the village. 'Now that the Parish is growing so rapidly we need more Magazine Distributors and I shall be most grateful if some ladies will offer for this work.'

The advertisements in the magazine tell us more about the Northenden of the 1920s.

> T Tomlinson, 40 Church Road, French Buns our Speciality.
> J Hudson, 47 Palatine Road, Standard Supply Stores — The Shop for the finest Bacon, Butter and Cheese in this District — Agent for Karswood Meat and Spice Dog and Poultry Food.
> M L Heywood, 22 Church Road — Butcher — Customers requirements courteously considered — Orders delivered anywhere.
> E H Liles — Family Boot Dealer and Repairer of 35 Palatine Road.
> Miss Coulson, 42 Royle Green Road, Teacher of Pianoforte — Success guaranteed.
> T Steele, 34 Church Road, Newsagent — Books on approval — dealer in smallwares.
> T Passman, St. Hilda's Road, Soot is a fertiliser not a food — then why buy BREAD made in the congested areas of Manchester and Stockport — trade with the local man.
> F Chapman, 36 Church Road, Family Butcher, all meat killed on the premises.
> G F Swindlehurst, Cycle Maker, Prams re-tyred.
> J Holt, Post Office, Circulating Library, Whist and Sport Prizes, Wedding presents — at prices cheaper than town.

One advertisement was that of F. S. Price, who stored his building and funeral materials at the top end of Ford Lane. The floor above his works was used by the dramatic society for rehearsals. The area around the church was regarded as picturesquely suitable for film-making by local Manchester magnates. 'I remember a carriage and horses, all dolled up for a film there and another Northenden film was Dick's Fairies which was shown at Peter Leigh's.'

The upper end of Ford Lane, round the church, was the ancient focus of activity in Northenden, but at the other end of Church Road a cluster of buildings, the Church Rooms and School, the Social Club, and on the opposite corner, the Post Office, made a second

13. The youth club in the Church Rooms, Kenworthy Lane, during the 1950s. This was the venue for all village activities for half a century from 1913.

village centre. The Church Rooms were effectively the village hall and were used for public meetings, banquets, whist drives and stage shows. It was from here in 1921 that the curate had the painting of *Icebergs* taken back to Rose Hill, its true value to be undiscovered for over fifty years. From the Church Rooms across a playground with outside toilets stood the Church 'National' school, which was also used for meetings. The Head at the time was Nellie Hargreaves. The nominal capacity was 250 children, but only a fifth of this total attended in 1926. The council school, similarly unfilled, was built to take 400 children and stood in Bazley Road. Its Headmaster was Percy Webber. 'It contains Cookery, Laundry, Housewifery and Manual Instruction Centres' states Kelly's Directory of 1926.

Entertainment and education at this time tended to overlap in Northenden. The Literary Society, whose aims were 'to provide social and intellectual intercourse amongst its members by means of Lectures and Discussions . . . and visits if sufficient support is forthcoming . . .', was popular in this and the next decade. The annual subscription was 1s. 6d. (7½p). Topics included:

14. *Church Inn* and the *Spread Eagle Inn*, before 1898.

15. Church Road, the church and *Church Inn*, 1903. On the right are the Reading Rooms of 1866, now a nursery. Opposite the inn stand shops and Miss Richardson's school.

Peeps at Parliament, with Lantern Views, Mr. W Henry Brown,
The History of Elephants, with Lantern Views, Rev. G H Carpenter, B Sc, MRIA,
The Wonders of the Mind, with Lantern Views, Rev. F Paton-Williams.

The Chairman of this last meeting was an exuberant personality of the time, Dr. Muriel M. Edwards.

Transport

Bus links with Manchester became increasingly important and were provided both by Manchester Corporation and by private firms. Prior to 1920, Manchester Corporation buses made few excursions over the Mersey as Wythenshawe was under the aegis of Bucklow R.D.C. The only service was a horse-drawn omnibus from the terminus at West Didsbury on Palatine Road to the *Church Inn* on Church Road, Northenden, where the vehicles turned round. In June 1906 Manchester Tramways bought three Crossley motor-buses to use on this route. Because of objections by West Didsbury people to the fumes of the new-fangled buses and the shaking of property foundations, the service was discontinued in September 1908 and the horse buses returned temporarily.

Manchester Corporation Tramways (M.C.T.) acquired some Ryknield buses in 1906. In 1909, when a service from West Didsbury to Cheadle began, the Ryknield buses helped to operate it. Motor buses were permanently used on the service from October 1910 onwards. Before the 1930 Road Traffic Act permission for bus routes had to be obtained from each local authority into whose area they ran. 'N' was used on number blinds for buses venturing into Northenden, which was not part of the City of Manchester for the purposes of M.C.T. until later. That meant that even M.C.T. might be required to apply to two or three local authorities for one route.

In February 1930, the North West Traffic Commissioners — the new licensing authority — granted a licence to M.C.T. for Princess Road Tram Terminus (Southern Cemetery) to Baguley Sanatorium. In January the following year another licence was granted to M.C.T. to run a service from Piccadilly to Wythenshawe, morning and evening, but there is no record of these routes ever being operated.

There were three private bus companies operating services around Northenden and Wythenshawe in this period. Two, Samuel Bailey, and Organ and Wachter, were based in Withington and Didsbury. The third and largest, North Western Road Car Company (N.W.R.C.C.), was originally based in Macclesfield, then moved to Stockport.

Samuel Bailey had a garage-depot on Upper Brook Street, Manchester, but was licensed from Cotton Lane, Withington. The earliest known reference to 'Bill Bailey's' bus company was on 5 September 1929 when Sam Bailey was granted a licence by the Manchester Watch Committee to operate a seaside coach service. Early in 1931 he applied to the North West Traffic Commissioners for a licence to operate a Manchester-Styal service via Moss Nook, with morning and evening journeys, which was granted. Until 1931 he was licensed from Bucklow. In 1932 or 1933 Organ and Wachter took over Samuel Bailey's Styal route. Mr. John Organ said of Sam Bailey:

> ... Bailey had only one vehicle, a very unreliable vehicle, and eventually he had to leave it on Upper Brook Street. He had a sawdust business. When he packed up we got permission from Bucklow to take it over. This is when we come to go up there [Styal] and by then we had these Gilfords. They weren't new but they were only one year old when we bought them. We used to get more people on them and then we used to go up to Styal and then come round. But it was a mistake really. It was too thin up there, you know.

Organ and Wachter was very much a family firm, owned and worked by Adrian Wachter, Mr. Organ and his eldest son, John. They kept buses behind the *Tatton Arms*. In an interview recorded in February 1980 Mr. John Organ, now a retired inspector from Greater Manchester

Transport, gave an account of his family's bus company.

> We started in 1927. We bought the business off a man named Fred Corkhill. We lived in West
> Didsbury in those days . . . Mr. Corkhill had his coach business and his garage in Lapwing Lane,
> West Didsbury. We bought it and two coaches off him and ran the service from the Church Inn into
> Manchester. We used to go straight down Oxford Road, up Moseley Street into Piccadilly in the
> morning when we took them in. And then in the evening we picked them up in Chepstow Street,
> because you weren't allowed to stand anywhere near Piccadilly. From Chepstow Street, straight
> out, then Upper Brook Street, alongside the Catholic Church in Ackers Street, down to Oxford Street
> by the University and out. We could stand there without getting mithered or getting booked for
> obstruction. The main thing was, to get back with us . . . people had to have a return ticket. We
> were not allowed to pick up once we crossed the river bridge and take money, and Manchester
> Corporation went to no end of trouble to catch us. But we had a very loyal set of passengers. If a
> stranger got on . . . they'd come and tell you, 'There's a stranger on, John'. You politely told them
> they couldn't have a ticket. 'But I can pay when we cross the river.' You knew then it was a trap.

Organ and Wachter also ran a service to Ringway and Styal. Their single-decker, two-
door buses had a yellow and green livery with 'Travel Ideal' on the side. Their third Gilford
bus had a toilet. 'The first time I emptied it, it went all over me!' They got a Bucklow
licence through the local councillor, Sam Price, but Manchester always turned them down.
A sergeant would wait in St Peter's Square to catch them out.

There was a warm relationship with the ordinary M.C.T. drivers, who took it in turn

16. Manchester's first motor bus at the *Church Inn*, a bus stop from the 1860s.

with Organ and Watcher to be first to leave the *Church Inn*. M.C.T. would send down a divisional inspector to stand in the chip-shop doorway to stop this practice, but he got a sharp answer from the M.C.T. drivers. 'This is the way we work it and this is the way it's been. We were the best of pals.'

The five-year war for Wythenshawe — 'Naboth's vineyard'

Manchester had been building up hopes of acquiring more *Lebensraum* from north Cheshire from the end of the First World War. Professor Abercrombie's report of 1920 had enthused about Wythenshawe's 'charming country lanes and country roads and the general air of rusticity'. Encouraged and cajoled by Jackson and Simon, the Housing Committee and most of the city's departments, except the Waterworks, had been in favour of purchasing Wythenshawe. The government was handing out cash for municipal housing at the beginning of the 1920s but, as already mentioned, it was not until T. E. Tatton died and his son wanted to sell that negotiations could go ahead.

The first Labour Government actively encouraged municipal housing in 1924. Ernest Simon asserted that the decision to buy Wythenshawe, or not, was the most important to be made for the next twenty years. When that decision was taken by the Conservative council on 3 February 1926 the go-ahead was given for the purchase of Wythenshawe by a quirk of the proceedings close to an error. After a three hour debate, the Conservative amendment, clearly refusing to entertain any purchase, was passed and the matter seemed at an end. The majority of Conservatives had left the chamber when William Jackson, already known as the 'father of Wythenshawe', put forward a further amendment. This was in order, since it was only an amendment that had been carried, and not the proposal itself. The remaining Liberals and Labour members were joined by those Conservatives in favour of purchase, and what might have been the final opportunity of a bulk buy was not lost. The second amendment was passed and purchase authorised.

The council backed the decision of February 1926 by the purchase in May of the same year of 2,569 acres at £80 sterling per acre. To top the transaction, as has been mentioned already, Simon bought Wythenshawe Park and presented it to the city 'as some return for all that we owe to Manchester'. A few sceptics were quick to make dark hints and, in one instance, a pointed accusation of bribery, corruption and, of course, simony. But, to the majority, the gift seemed a crowning gesture that provided a focal point for the planning of the new Wythenshawe. It was understandable that many now thought that the land south of the Mersey was 'in Manchester'. In fact the problems of building Wythenshawe were only beginning.

The situation was now that Manchester owned part of Wythenshawe, but only in the way that any John Smith can own land. It still had to get permission to build on it. It would have to go cap and plans in hand, a suppliant Goliath at the feet of David — Bucklow Council. To change this would need an Act of Parliament to incorporate Northenden, Baguley and Northen Etchells within Manchester. The first move to prevent this came from Manchester's own camp at a meeting in January 1927 of ratepayers who, under the Borough Funds Act of 1872, challenged their own city council.

While still coping with this grass-roots objection from its own ranks, Manchester had to face the united councils of Cheshire, Bucklow and, although not involved, the other urban and rural district councils of north Cheshire. Birkenhead and Wallasey were also striving for municipal boundary extensions, so that the Chairman of Cheshire County Council remarked that the county 'had become Naboth's vineyard'.

Swift action was taken by Cheshire to mobilise and demonstrate the opposition of the various parishes and councils to the takeover bid by Manchester. A joint petition was organised and the *Guardian* report of the manoeuvre indicated the strength of feeling.

The opposition to this plan is led by the Cheshire County Council and the Bucklow Rural District Council. At a meeting held at Crewe of urban authorities lying to the south of Manchester, decisions to join in the opposition movement were taken by Ashton-upon-Mersey, Sale, Altrincham, Bowdon, Hale, Cheadle and Gatley, and Handforth.

The report included the comments:

It is apparent that the purpose of the opposition is to set up an impenetrable wall between Manchester and the southward expansion she desires. It is a wall composed of the eight urban authorities already mentioned and the district of Bucklow, which includes the intervening parishes of Timperley, Ringway and Styal . . . At the meeting of the Sale authority one councillor, defending the reasonableness of Manchester's desire for air, accused some among his colleagues of a desire 'to build a wall along the Mersey, with a gate through which they could come and go, but through which Manchester was not to pass.

To demonstrate its capabilities, Cheshire now planned to build its own council houses. Bucklow Drive, off Royle Green Road in Northenden, was built by the county, as were houses in Yew Tree Lane and Rackhouse.

A poll was taken in the three parishes and showed that 82 per cent wanted to remain in Cheshire, in spite of the fact that nearly half of them worked in Manchester. At Sharston Hall Mr. Henriques, a member of an old Spanish-Jewish family of merchants, voiced his objection to higher rates. The report of the ratepayers' meeting in Northenden Church Rooms on 17 January 1927, with its 'not a square inch shall be taken' rhetoric, indicated the strength of feeling on the subject:

Mr. T. Hewlett presided and said he took the strongest possible objection to the proposed bill because he was of the opinion that if the Manchester Corporation obtained the necessary powers it would mean a very large increase in their rates, which at present were 18s. [90p] in the pound . . . Mr. Harold White referred to the scheme as fantastic and idealistic and contended that the people of Northenden would be acting extremely contrary to their interests if they did not oppose it by every means in their power. Lieutenant Goudie, Mr. W. Pland and Mr. G. W. Hewlett spoke in vigorous opposition to the bill and a resolution to this effect was passed with only two dissensions.

Cheshire's last audacious argument was that it might put in the roads and sewers only to find that Manchester could not go ahead with the houses.

As a result of Cheshire's fight, Manchester's Bill was rejected by parliament. This was a stunning blow for the giant that had produced 'damning evidence' by Manchester's Medical Officer of Health that disease was endemic in the congested areas.

Manchester saw that if it was not to be left with one of the most expensive cabbage patches in Britain it must box more cleverly. The city set up the Wythenshawe Estates Special Committee (the 'Wythenshawe Committee') to guide, control and assist with all planning and development in Wythenshawe. Leading proponents on the committee were Ernest and Sheena Simon, Lt.-Col. Westcott and Alderman Jackson, its first Chairman. The W.E.S.C. has been called 'a corporation within a corporation' and it was the nearest that Wythenshawe would get to its own council. It had now to fight in earnest.

The Wythenshawe Committee first met on 15 January 1927 and within a month had eight members: Chairman Alderman Jackson, Alderman Box, Councillors Cunliffe, Davy, Melland, Mellor, Sheena Simon and Lt.-Col. Westcott. The subjects of their deliberations ranged from the lavatories in the playground of Shadow Moss School to the negotiations about land with Bucklow Council.

After preliminary correspondence with Barry Parker and visits by Alderman Jackson to Letchworth, the architect was approached. Not only was Mr. Parker 'the most eminent town planner in Britain' at that time, but he had long associations with Manchester, going back to his own apprenticeship in Altrincham, and he was a fellow traveller, politically, with Jackson and Simon. With mighty Manchester behind him, Barry Parker could build the garden city of his dreams. The committee asked him to produce development plans for Wythenshawe.

Little time was wasted and discussion meanwhile proceeded on the plans for the main link road, Princess Parkway, the bridge over the Mersey and the widening of the Sale to Altrincham Road. The striking feature of Parker's Wythenshawe plan, the Parkway, was the first in Britain, and it boasted free-flowing traffic segregated from the houses and minor roads. Parkways had been suggested in Ebenezer Howard's schemes and now it was an obvious way of linking Wythenshawe and Manchester.

Three earlier reports on Wythenshawe conditioned Barry Parker's thinking about the design of the area. The Abercrombie report in 1920 saw Wythenshawe purely as a garden suburb with little or no industry. The second report, an independent survey in 1922 by Captain R. L. Reiss, had considerable influence on Parker's ideas of social integration. Although committed to a mixed-class estate, Parker had at first seemed to be segregating the classes by expanding private development on the boundaries of the area, in Northenden, Brooklands, Styal Road, Moss Nook and along the Parkway. Captain Reiss suggested that houses should be allocated initially to building workers, then for workers in local factories, which should be 'engaged in clean industry using gas and electricity'. Barry Parker accepted his ideas of a self-contained socially-mixed development and the city council, too, was happy at the prospect of higher rents and an enhanced estate.

The third report was made in 1926 by Sir Theodore Chambers and C. B. Purdom. They were considering floating a syndicate for purchasing and developing Wythenshawe. Their conclusion was that 'it would be wrong to turn it into a purely working class residential district' for Manchester. Although not an obvious influence, there were certain truths in each of these reports that can be detected in Parker's schemes.

The economic planning of the body of the new housing area generally fascinated Parker and he saw the finance available to Manchester as allowing heavier capitalisation and more rapid growth than had been possible at Letchworth. Thus the town could grow in a logical sequence, with some ten neighbourhood units of schools and shops being ready before the arrival of people. The parkways were to combine with the neighbourhood system, so that local cycling and walking trips could be made in safety. Parker was most concerned to keep the beauty of existing natural features, such as ponds and groups of trees, but to do this and still keep to 12 well-designed houses per acre costs had to be pruned elsewhere, particularly in respect of the cost of access and service roads to the houses themselves.

The principles to be applied to the development roads, those being the roads on which the bulk of the houses would be built and which would lie between the through-traffic roads, were given in a report to the Wythenshawe Committee by Barry Parker in May 1928. Extracts from this report tell us much about Parker's underlying strategy.

Ladies and Gentlemen,
    The positions and directions of the proposed 'Through Traffic Roads' in Baguley, Northenden and Northern Etchells have now been laid down, and it has become necessary that careful consideration should be given to principles by which . . . [we lay out] . . . the 'Development Roads' between . . .

Mr. Parker stressed that the main cost of housing development was not the cost of 'the cottages' but the 'acid test of the financial efficiency for housing schemes is the length of road per house'. He then went on to show that costs are effectively reduced by cutting out cross-roads as far as possible. 'It has now been proved beyond question that the introduction of these extravagant cross roads at intervals so frequent as to yield more than twelve houses to the acre is certainly unnecessary where land is not abnormally expensive nor traffic requirements unusual.'

Parker considered in a specific application the loss of 'frontage' which occurs wherever a

cross-road is introduced. With cross-roads, 'there are something over three miles of such
frontages', while without them 'something under two miles of such frontages'. With the then
costs of road construction, Parker estimated that without the cross-roads over £9,000 would
be saved.

> The use of the cul-de-sac is one means by which large savings in the lengths, and therefore in the
> costs of roads may be made. The cross road when carried through from one main road to the other
> only affords access to the same number of houses as it will afford access to, if that portion of it which
> is shown dotted were omitted, and the houses marked 'A' were built at 'B', and instead of a cross
> road a 'cul-de-sac' were thus created . . . In addition to the considerable saving of road, there is
> sufficient land on which to build 3 or 4 cottages . . . (*see* opposite)

The report then showed that development from a 'hub' road (as in iv) was much more
efficient that development from the 'rim' (iii). Further savings could be made, Parker
argued, by reorientating houses at the ends of a cul-de-sac.

Parker went on to castigate American planners for placing houses on cul-de-sac roads
opening onto main roads, so creating dangers and anxieties for the motorists on the main
traffic routes. He reminded them that the Town Planning Institute advocated that junctions
of other roads with main traffic roads should never be made at intervals less than a quarter
of a mile apart.

Lastly, Parker argued that housing estates had been conventionally inefficiently developed until the distinguished Canadian Town Planner, Mr. Noulan Cauchon, pointed
out that a saving of 10 per cent on the length per house and, therefore, on the cost of road
per house, as well as safer junctions, would be made by the adoption of the hexagon in
substitution for the rectangle as the basis of a lay-out. 'The use of two hexagons enables a
piece of land the same size . . . to be developed for the same number of houses with three
cross roads in place of four cross roads.'

Parker added that efficient planning not only cut capital costs and the costs of maintaining,
lighting, supervising, scavenging and draining, but also 'shortened the rounds of the rent
collector, policeman, milkman, baker, water-cart, doctor, road surveyor and our own visits
to shops, recreation and social visits'.

Mr. Parker's ideas, with a few modifications, were adopted. The Cauchon hexagons were
applied to the Roundwood Estate in Northenden, causing the area to be compared with a
maze. 'I've been living here for 20 years and I still get lost' is a typical comment.
Nevertheless, the principles of Barry Parker and his overall plan satisfied the Wythenshawe
Committee and provided the basis for a fresh approach.

With Barry Parker's plans in preparation, the Wythenshawe Committee could put the
Bucklow and Cheshire Authorities to the test. To call their bluff they submitted a plan,
which included 1,500 houses for the working class in Northenden, to Bucklow Council in
May 1928. A major road and bridge, and a large-scale sewerage system, were required to
open up the area. Cheshire countered by forming the North Cheshire Regional Planning
Committee, which submitted its own plans to Bucklow, but they were so hastily prepared
that the provision for sewerage was left out. Cheshire County Council dashed to Bucklow's
aid by suggesting that a comprehensive report on sewerage for the whole area was being
obtained.

Another fault in Bucklow's plans was the failure to ensure that Wythenshawe would
have an agricultural belt, trees and grass verges. To Parker, Jackson and Simon this was
the gravest of sins. Without the rural arcadian environment, Wythenshawe would not be a
garden city but merely another monstrous housing estate. In Manchester's own camp, the
City Engineer asserted, perhaps ingenuously, that 'grass could not be grown in the Manchester climate'.

In due course a North Cheshire Sewage Board set about the construction of a branch

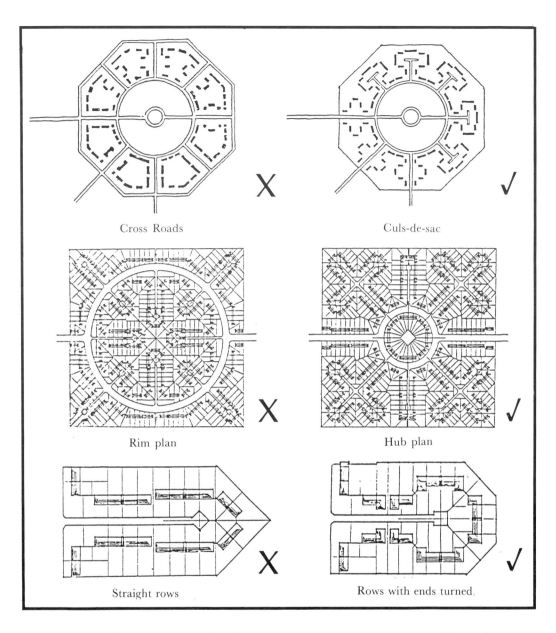

Cross Roads ✗

Culs-de-sac ✓

Rim plan ✗

Hub plan ✓

Straight rows ✗

Rows with ends turned ✓

17. (*above*) Ideas on efficiency from Barry Parker's reports — rights (on the right) and wrongs (on the left) of road plans for Wythenshawe. (*below*) The hexagons of Canadian planner Noulan Cauchon and their adaptation by Barry Parker in Wythenshawe.

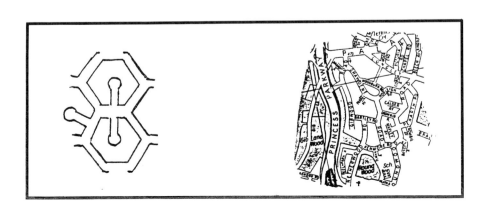

sewerage and main sewerage works. The first mention of the board to Manchester was in a letter from Bucklow Council in February 1929, written from the Union Offices, Knutsford.

Dear Sir

. . . I have to inform you that the same has received the very careful consideration of this Council who, in conjunction with the Cheshire County Council, have decided to obtain a comprehensive report upon provision of sewerage facilities . . . and it is therefore possible that amendments to your plans may be found necessary . . . time is necessary for the preparation of reports and plans . . .

Yours faithfully, W. C. Jennings, Clerk . . .

The Wythenshawe Committee asked the Town Clerk to express disappointment at the reply. It has been suggested that Bucklow's approach at this time was organised solely to cause as much delay as possible. With rates of £40,000 due from Northenden, Baguley and Northen Etchells (compared with Manchester's £6.8m) naturally progress was negligible and the rate of approval of Manchester's housing was correspondingly slow. By the autumn of 1929 only 142 houses had been approved. This figure, '142', was to become a symbol of stalemate between Manchester and Bucklow. Meanwhile Manchester's shortfall in housing was increasing at an alarming rate. The Housing Committee estimated that by 1936 the number of houses needed would be around fifty thousand.

The first tenants moved into the '142' in the summer of 1930 and were in the odd position of paying rent to Manchester, but having to register births and deaths in Cheshire. 'My parents were one of the first tenants of Manchester's 142 council houses in Kenworthy Lane but my father always called me a Cheshire "spiv" because he had to register my birth at Sale', recalled one early resident.

The situation could not continue. Bucklow Council was frustrating the will of England's second city (some would say first city) and, in real terms, was depriving thousands of its poorer inhabitants of decent homes. A second attempt to incorporate Wythenshawe into Manchester by Act of Parliament was undertaken and it was felt that the chances of success were much greater this time. All the political parties were standing on planks labelled 'slum-clearance' and when the Labour Party came to power nationally Ramsey MacDonald expressed great concern over housing. At the local level Ernest Simon, as Liberal M.P. for Withington, reinforced the pressure for new houses in the booklet *A Policy for the Slums!*

Opposition to incorporation was mounted by Cheshire, but by now a sense of the inevitable seemed to prevail. At a meeting of North Cheshire rate-payers in March 1930 the main argument, that 'Cheshire should be kept as Cheshire', had an emotive, desperate ring about it. Cheshire now proposed the incorporation of the North Cheshire Sewage Board. Manchester, however, needed nothing short of full control for effective viable working of its housing policy, so, in an effort to provide a settlement with honour for Cheshire, it offered differential rating, representation by an alderman and three councillors and, as the supreme prize, the sacrificial acceptance of Cheadle's and Gatley's sewage.

Much of Manchester's nail-biting on this occasion was unnecessary. In the event the Chairman of Cheshire County Council, Sir William Hodgson, was unbriefed and performed catastrophically when giving evidence to the Parliamentary Committee. The day at last belonged to Manchester. In the summer of 1930 the incorporation of Wythenshawe into Manchester was granted by parliament. Midnight on 31 March 1931 was to be the date.

While the negotiations for the incorporation of Wythenshawe into Manchester had been grinding on, the Highways Engineers had made a tentative start on Princess Parkway. Prior to 1930 Princess Road extended from the city centre to Barlow Moor Road, where it continued for a short distance as Christ Church Avenue. Section 16(9) of the Manchester (Improvement) Act, 1930, gave Manchester Corporation the authority 'to widen and improve Christ Church Avenue, Didsbury'. At the same time it was decided to take the Parkway across the Mersey to the Altrincham/Stockport Road. Sheena Simon, as Chairman of the

Wythenshawe Estates Special Committee, was very involved in the overall planning and conception of the landscaped Parkway designed by the then City Engineer, Mr. B. Meek.

The first act to establish the new route was the drilling of four bore holes in January 1929 to start the work on the new Princess Parkway Bridge. Because of the Great Depression grants were made toward Outdoor Relief Work for the unemployed (operated by the State, not the Poor Law Unions, which had been superseded in 1929). Considerable use was made of this labour in the construction of the road.

Although the motor-bus was fast becoming the most popular form of public transport on the roads, the idea of a tramway was considered in 1927 by the Wythenshawe Committee and was still alive in 1929, as the following minute shows: 'The Committee were of the opinion that a tramway would serve the transport need of the estate and that a sleeper track tramway should be constructed . . .'. It was not to be.

The new road, built from Barlow Moor Road to Altrincham/Stockport Road, was officially opened with the new bridge over the River Mersey on 1 February 1932 by the Minister of Transport and renamed Princess Road. The section from the Mersey to Altrincham Road was called Princess Parkway, after Sheena Simon's recommendation, in April.

Princess Parkway was a beautiful garden city road, the pride of the people of Northenden and Wythenshawe. A letter dated 17 June 1937 to the *Manchester Evening News* proclaimed what many people felt about this road and the landscaping of its wide verges.

> Allow me to express my grateful sentiment towards the Parks Committee for the informal planting of large clumps and masses of wild briar roses. The scent of the leaves in the warm spring evening is really delightful and never sates. The single roses are now in bud, and in a few days Princess Parkway will be a riot of pink and white colour, set off by the greenswards, that are cut daily by a small mechanised army.

In Barry Parker's original plan for Wythenshawe the Parkway was to be a pleasant road and a feeder to the garden city, not a way through. He wanted the Western Parkway to be the by-pass. But in October 1936 Manchester Corporation and Cheshire County Council were already thinking of extending the Princess Parkway to the city boundary in the north and through to Ollerton and Toft near Knutsford in the south. These plans were eventually incorporated in the 1945 Manchester Plan.

A new form of transport was considered by the Wythenshawe Committee at this time. In September 1928 Manchester Corporation, after much pressure from John Leeming of Bowdon, the Chairman of the Lancashire Aero Club and author of *Manchester and Aviation*, formed a special sub-committee to investigate the feasibility of an airport in Manchester. Barton, on Chat Moss, was chosen as the best site a month later. Since much work was needed on the ground and buildings, a temporary airfield was hurriedly prepared on land between Wythenshawe Park and Yewtree Lane at Rackhouse Farm, Northenden. Thus Wythenshawe had the first municipal airport in the country, and the airport would return to Wythenshawe in 1935.

Details of the City Surveyor's report reveal the makeshift nature of Britain's first city airport.

> The City Surveyor reported that . . . he has examined the brick built and slate roofed Dutch Barn at Rackhouse . . . [for conversion] . . . into a temporary hangar . . . For a plane to enter it will be necessary to remove two of the existing brick piers and to carry the roof on a steel girder . . . Some of the hedges will require to be grubbed up and the ground levelled and consolidated. The City Surveyor estimates the cost as follows:
>
> | | |
> |---|---:|
> | Conversion of Dutch Barn | £115 |
> | Grubbing up fences, etc | £30 |
> | Sundries, say | £5 |
> | **[Total]** | **£150** |

18. Croydon, Lord Mayor's Mission, 1929. City Council members arrive to collect the first airfield licence awarded to a municipal authority, for the airfield at Northenden — Capt. Kingswill, pilot; Sam Hill, airport manager; Warbreck Howell, Town Clerk; Bert Essen, mayor's attendant; Col. George Titt, Lord Mayor and keen Wythenshavian; John Leeming, director of Northern Airlines and prime motivator for the airport; Aldermen Davy and Carter; Capt. John, Pilot.

19. A passenger on a pleasure flight at Rackhouse descends from the locally-built Avro, an ex-RAF trainer.

The total area involved was about 54 acres for actual aviation fields. The rental for six months would be £100, which included all compensation to the quitting tenant, but not rates.

The Rackhouse airfield opened on 2 April 1929. The first landing was made by Captain A. K. Kingswill in a de Havilland 60X, owned by Northern Air Transport, in which the instigator, John Leeming, had a major interest. The first flights from this, the first civic airport, were joy-trips around Northenden given to members of the Airport Committee to whet their appetites for flying. On 22 April, the Lord Mayor of Manchester flew from Wythenshawe to Croydon, on his way to collect a temporary licence.

Some interesting aircraft landed at Wythenshawe during those few months of temporary licence. Ford's European 5-AT-C Trimotor demonstrator N84 12, a large aircraft for those days, and Gipsy-Moth H-AAAH, then owned by Air Taxis of Stag Lane, later to become 'Jason', the biplane that took Amy Johnson on her solo flight from Britain to Australia in

May 1930. The airport had a customs shed for the Dublin route. Most of the flights were joy-trips. Cobham's Flying Circus also used the field for their displays, after the airport licence had been withdrawn.

Barton Airport opened on 1 January 1930 and Wythenshawe closed.

THE DIE IS CAST
'Lancashire Bigger Tonight'
'First Municipal Garden City'

When the time came for Wythenshawe to change from Cheshire to Lancashire the tension and wounded pride of the past five years were put aside. Reports from citizens who remember the occasion suggest that the feeling of rapprochement was clearly tempered by a sense of the inevitability of the event. 'Of course they'd got it all fixed between them — both sides will make money and we'll have to pay the extra rates.'

After such protracted negotiations it is not surprising that years later there was confusion over the actual year, when the incorporation of Wythenshawe into Manchester took place (1926, 1930 or 1931). However, when the actual time came, Tuesday 31 March 1931, the journalists enjoyed themselves. The *Evening Chronicle*'s headlines were 'Lancashire Bigger Tonight. Wythenshawe Coming in at Midnight'. The report noted that Lancashire, and Manchester in particular, would be taking a slice out of Cheshire immediately after midnight when the new residents of the areas affected, Northenden, Baguley and Northen Etchells, 'will have the unique experience of going to bed in Cheshire and waking up tomorrow in Lancashire'.

Observing that the changeover would be a peaceful one marked only by a dinner, the writer then reported on a recent tour he or she had made in Wythenshawe. The older inhabitants were already full of reminiscences, thinking and talking about the Wythenshawe of old and its historical associations. Many, the reporter noted, seemed glad at the thought of having their affairs handled by Manchester, but most seemed reluctant to leave Cheshire. Miss Hannah Brickell, a 91-year-old of Brown Street, Northenden, felt especially sorry for the Tatton family. 'Old Squire Tatton would never have consented to Manchester taking over the district.' Her uncle had been his postillion rider, and 'there never was a finer man than the old Squire'. She concluded that she'd not mind whether she belonged to Manchester in Lancashire, or Northenden in Cheshire, but 'I shall always remember the beautiful place this was before your big ugly buses and motor-cars began to run through it'.

Mr. Charles H. Royle, 37-years headmaster of the Church school and 30-years clerk to the parish council, thought the change would take some getting used to and that 'many people would forego economic advantages in order to retain the rural aspects of their home'.

The reporter had found a number of residents giving their chimneys a final cleaning by firing them, as the practice was illegal in Manchester. The most vehement objector was a 76-year-old gardener-farmer, who also tended the war memorial — a job Manchester Parks Committee would now take over. He added, 'I came from Lancashire, but Northenden is too pretty to be destroyed by the City Octopus'. The *Chronicle* included the news that the likely new Alderman for the area would be Councillor T. E. Hewlett, whose 'we shall never surrender' declamation had so roused the meeting in Northenden in January 1927.

The banquet provided at the ratepayer's expense in Wythenshawe Hall to mark the changeover hour, was reported in detail on the following Friday by the *Stockport Advertiser*. Its dramatic headlines were 'Good-bye to Northenden. Parish Council's Funeral Feast. The Die is Cast'. Guests at the dinner were the Lord Mayor of Manchester, George Titt, the Town Clerk, F. E. Warbreck-Howell, Mrs. E. D. Simon, Mr. R. H. G. Tatton and Mr. R. Clarke, Chairman of the Bucklow Parish Council. Mr. G. J. Cooling, Chairman of Northenden Parish Council, presided and Clerk A. Barratt, Treasurer W. R. Hampson and all the members were present.

Mr. A. Hall proposed the toast of the 'The City of Manchester' and referred to the phrase on the menu '*Alea est Jacta*' — the die is cast -— the step is taken. They were bound to feel a little sad, he noted, but coming into one of the greatest municipal authorities in the country, they ought to feel proud. Hemmed in on three sides, it was clear that expansion was inevitable. Manchester would give them of its very best. Mr. Barry Parker was one of the finest town planning experts in the country. They did not like the slums but in many things Manchester set an example to other cities. In a few hours, concluded Mr. Hall, they would be citizens of Manchester and he felt sure they would accept the change with the good-will and determination to be loyal citizens, and that in the future they would look back on 1 April 1931 as one of the best days in the history of Northenden.

The Lord Mayor, responding, welcomed Wythenshawe as an integral part of the City of Manchester. This was a particularly historic gathering. It was historic in that some of them would go to bed in Cheshire and wake up in Lancashire. It was even more historic that a parish council, sitting at its own death-bed feast, should invite the undertaker along (laughter).

He had been round the estate with Alderman Jackson, who explained that every tree, shrub and hedge would be preserved for all time. Manchester, he believed, was the greatest city in the United Kingdom, and it was the city which had the most progressive civic outlook. All the experiments in garden cities in the past had been by public utility societies; this was the first garden city attempted by a municipality. In a few years' time representatives of every municipality in the country would be making pilgrimages to see what Manchester had made of this great experiment. He wished them all success.

Mr. G. J. Cooling proposed 'The Bucklow R.D.C.', which had fought hard to retain Northenden but lost. He was sure that Bucklow would agree that, after all, incorporation was in the interest of residents. Mr. Clarke, responding, said they were sorry to lose Northenden, for which Bucklow always had a great respect. Manchester needed more room but he hoped they would 'right about turn' and not trespass further into Cheshire. 'Northenden Parish Council' was proposed by Mrs. Simon, who apologised for the absence of her husband. She thought of the Lord Mayor and Town Clerk not as undertakers but murderers (laughter). To change farmland into a garden city was not an easy task and she hoped they would preserve the trees and green fields and flowers for those who at present lived far from them. Mrs. D. de Courcy Meade observed that it was the gift of the hall and park by the Simons that had encouraged the city to become owners of one of the most beautiful parts of Cheshire. Mr. F. S. Price proposed 'Wythenshawe'. As a boy he came to sing at the hall for Mr. R. H. G. Tatton's grandfather 'in the days when they looked up to the squire and obeyed the parson. We collected acorns from Mr. Tatton's trees, and sold them back to him at 4d. a peck!'

The Town Clerk reminded them that when Cromwell's forces were besieging Wythenshawe, they sent to Manchester for two pieces of ordnance. The recent five-year war for Wythenshawe had been quite as keen. Mr. Howell suggested a Friends of Wythenshawe Association to preserve historical Wythenshawe and advise the corporation. Mr. R. H. G. Tatton, responding to the toast of 'Our Guests' by Mr. J. C. Davies, said he regretted the absence of Charles Royle, his old schoolmaster. Mr. Barratt, Northenden's Parish Clerk, thanked the Squirrel Café of Manchester for the catering and Mr. Charlton, Mr. W. Bowden and Mr. F. M. Chappell for the music. Manchester's Town Clerk would make a good 'parish clerk'.

At midnight the gathering joined in singing Auld Lang Syne and the health of the new Ward was drunk.

Chapter Four

The Pioneers: 1931-9
'Tracks Across the Greensward'

After two bills in Parliament, ten years of struggle and some hard cash, Wythenshawe, including Northenden, had been taken from Cheshire and placed in Lancashire. Manchester's 142 houses in Northenden would pay their rates as well as their rent to the city from 1 April 1931. The Cheshire landowners could now resume their landowning and Manchester the preparation of its garden city.

New difficulties loomed ahead, however. A change of Whitehall policy crippled the initial building programme, but the city, veteran of battles with the Tattons in 1926 and with Cheshire in 1931, altered its tactics. In the next eight years a massive building operation went ahead. Homes mushroomed for 35,000 souls, more than in Canterbury. The Wythenshawe Committee had come to the point of considering where to site its cinemas and cathedrals when the Second World War stymied development.

At the start of the decade, however, there was time to check the dowry. With the fields, Manchester inherited a number of historically interesting buildings and sites. Wythenshawe Hall and Park were now owned and used by common citizens. Baguley Hall was owned by the City of Manchester but used by Direct Works as a depot and was in a sorry state. Sharston Hall, the mansion of David Quircano Henriques, would soon be let out as flats. Sharston Mount was let by Manchester to the Southern family, tenants for over seventy years. Interesting farm buildings listed by the Civic Advisory Committee in 1932 included Knob Hall, Newall Green, Moss Nook ('refused admission . . . little of value'), Chamber Hall and Peel Hall ('sound, fine stone bridge'). Sharston Hall Farm had losses in the Irish Republican Army fires of 1932.

The largest and most historically interesting prize inherited by Manchester was Northenden itself. A cluster of complementary gems rather than one sparkling jewel, the village was not a fossil but a community keen to preserve its past and yet serve the present. The older village centre, near the church, was now partnered by the area near the Church Rooms at the top of Kenworthy Lane, with its 142 new houses.

In April 1931 the church school had on roll 59 children. This rose to over one hundred and fifty in the next few years with the additional Wythenshawe children and fell back in April 1935 as new schools opened. The children were promoted according to their level of ability from Standards I to IV, which were shared between the two teachers, Miss Hargreaves and Mrs. Newry (later Mrs. Roberts and Miss Finley). On Empire Day 'Patriotic songs etc.' were sung. The morning was concluded with the singing of the National Anthem and saluting of the national flag. A holiday was given in the afternoon. 'Mr Royle, School Correspondent, visited re clay bin which was sold at a Rummage Sale and which is the property of the LEA.'

In March 1931 a 'Manchester Representative' checked the stock and 'the sanitary conditions' — the outside toilets. 'I remember the huge wooden seats and green cast iron cisterns which rarely worked. I never went if I could help it — they were so horrible', recalled one pupil. The entry for 1 April records a visit by Manchester's Deputy Director, Mr. Guest. The council school at Bazley Road was noted in its log-book as having left Cheshire and come 'under the Authority of Manchester'.

20. Sharston School *c.*1910. This school and its forerunners served most of Wythenshawe for over a century. It was a café from 1901 until 1934.

21. The replacement C. of E. school of 1901 in the centre of Northenden. Demolished in 1961 to make way for a supermarket, it was itself replaced by St Wilfrid's School in Patterdale Road.

The boy who in the first chapter was at Miss Richardson's Private School went on to South Manchester School in West Didsbury and Manchester Grammar School. In 1933, after one year, he joined his father in Manchester. In Northenden he attended a confirmation class, held in the dimly-lit St Wilfrid's church by Rev. Chignell, 'and a very fierce man he was. It was then I discovered that the clock in the tower really went — in the silence you could hear it tick. This was an opportunity to meet other children in the village'. The confirmation class, under Mr. Douglas Robinson, produced *A Midsummer Night's Dream*, a play often repeated. 'We rehearsed in one of the outhouses of the Rectory for weeks.'

Money remained a concern of the church. Typically, in 1937 Mr. Chignell pleaded, 'we need, badly need, more subscribers . . . whether people attend the Church or not.' Electric light was installed in 1935 and the organ blower then retired.

The coronation of George VI and Queen Elizabeth in June 1937 was marked by an ex-servicemen's parade, led by the Northenden Band, with representatives from the Oddfellows, the Chamber of Trade, St John's Ambulance, guides, scouts and cubs. The children of the village had a sandwich tea and there was community singing in the park led by Mr. Royle.

Rev. Chignell left a year later, after 18 years, a period that covered the metamorphosis of Wythenshawe. But the new incumbent, Rev. Allen, could still write:

> Northenden is a little cross section of England. We have in the parish the very old and the very new, town and country, industry and agriculture, the private and the municipal ownership of property. If we have many of England's problems, we have England's opportunities.

The church magazine advertisements are again enlightening.

> J. Brickell — Funerals and Cremations, 13 Palatine Road, All responsibility taken.
> A. W. Chantler — Funerals and Cremations, Boat Lane, Distance no object.
> Clifton Motor Engineering, 22B Palatine Road — Superior modern cars.
> Sanitary Laundry Ltd. — the 'Family Service' wash will interest you.
> The Magnet, 43 Palatine Road — Electric Lighting, Battery charging.
> Wm. Foster, 39 Palatine Road, Plumber — licenced to Manchester Corporation [Mr. Foster was also the reserve church organist].
> M. Chorlton, 63 Palatine Road — Wireless and Electrical supplies, gramophones and records.
> Woodside Café, Wythenshawe Road — For your parties, large or small.
> J. Holt, Post Office — Lending library — Constant change of books.
> Nora Furnival — Church Villa, Ford Lane — Happy feet mean happy faces.
> W. H. Buckley, 71 Church Road, Grocer — We . . . ask the favour of your patronage.
> J. & W. Davies, Kenworthy Farm — hygenic conditions — our own cows.
> John Burgess, 23 Palatine Road — Grocer, coffee fresh ground for each customer. A postcard to our Store — Our Traveller we will send Who's endeavour it is always — To please and not offend.
> Geo. H. Palmer, Bank Corner, Church Road — If you can make, you can mend — repairing over 60 years — oldest established firm in Northenden.

Northenden was now important as the middle-level shopping centre for Wythenshawe. There were 97 shops, three dentists, a lawyer, an estate agent, two music teachers, an optician, two doctors and two undertakers. 'Northenden was like Dodge City with traders nailing up the gaudiest signs to catch the passing traffic.' The Northenden, Wythenshawe and District Chamber of Trade was founded in October 1934, though in 1937 the Wythenshawe element broke away. That year the Chamber issued its free newspaper, which later became the *Wythenshawe Recorder*, and opposed the idea of a market-hall at the corner of Palatine Road and St Hilda's Road.

The village was sometimes dubbed Royle Northenden at this time, as the leading figures in so many ventures, including the Chamber of Trade, the Rosemary Fund and the Dramatic Society, were Arthur Royle of the District Bank and his father Charles H. Royle.

The building of the Forum Cinema in 1934 consummated Northenden's role as the

temporary heart of Wythenshawe. The first lessee was E. M. Burns of Cheadle, but the
A.B.C. chain bought the lease in 1936. Thus Northenden had the only two Wythenshawe
cinemas, the Coronation and the Forum.

Most of the private development of houses in the 1930s, almost all with the city as
ground landlord, took place in Northenden and Northen Etchells. There was piecemeal
development of individual houses along Styal Road, some in Spanish style; between Styal
Road and Northen Etchells' Recreation Ground appeared the semi-detached houses of
Halstead Grove Square. In and around Northenden houses appeared on Longley Lane,
Elmfield Avenue, Chretien Road and around Lingard Road, whilst Princess Parkway was
growing west of Northenden. Along the length of Wythenshawe Road that reached to
Princess Parkway (now Palatine Road) houses sprouted, with a garage on the corner, to
add to the existing cottages, the Woodside Café and shop. On the north side were the
Princess Mansion flats, the new cinema and an embrionic Homewood Road. North and
south of Wythenshawe Park a variety of larger houses, some with flat roofs, jostled with
council houses.

Most private house building in Northenden was on the Roundwood Estate, the vacant
space between the Parkway and the village. By 1934 a half-dozen larger houses had
appeared in Gibwood Road near the Parkway, and about a hundred semi-detached houses
had ventured down Corda Avenue, Roundwood, Norleigh and Penarth Roads. Soon Dron-
field, Kenmore and Shawdene Roads would be added. These houses (some let at first by
the corporation at £1 a week) were created from a few basic patterns. Few had garages and
many corners were cut, quite literally, but the estate was noted for the beauty of its cherry-
blossom lined roads.

Barry Parker controlled all planning at first and he was particularly disenchanted with
the plans for some of the larger houses, as this letter to the Wythenshawe Committee
suggests.

> Letchworth, 21st August, 1931
>   . . . For Dr Abercrombie, Messrs Potts, Hennings and Tipping sent a design to be built . . .
> overlooking the park . . . only slight advantage of the view taken . . . some very surprising things in
> the plan.
>   . . . a maid cannot answer the surgery door-bell . . . without passing through The Study and The
> Consulting Room . . . For the doctor, his family, patients, his servants and . . . the man looking after
> the garage, car and garden, there is only one W.C. and that is upstairs.
>   I know the importance you attach to the attainment of a reasonable architectural standard . . .
> this house will fall far short.

Later there is a reference to another architect complaining that the standard of house plans
had so deteriorated that the whole effect was 'detrimental to the attraction of good clients'.

Away from the building sites, one item of news from this era made the national headlines,
the flooding of the River Mersey and the rescue of a Mr. and Mrs. Pegge and baby John
from Didsbury Golf Club in January 1932.

> Six policemen and others dragged and carried a boat half a mile. Nearly 10 feet of water surrounded
> the clubhouse, and it swirled in a veritable whirlpool . . . Mr. Price, his sons and other helpers,
> managed to put a ladder to the top window of the house and to-day they brought food supplies . . .

South of Northenden, Wythenshawe Garden City began to grow at last. Manchester now
controlled Wythenshawe and owned most of it, but new problems appeared. One difficulty
centred on the land Manchester controlled but did not own. Local landowners, market
gardeners and small farmers continued to resent the invaders, and at a public meeting in
January 1931 they expressed their concerted will to resist more purchases of land — except
at the right price. The 'right price' rose to over £80 per acre as Manchester attempted to
buy by compulsory purchase the 1,307 acres, valued by some at £250,384.

To borrow the necessary money 'The City of Manchester Purchase of Land at Wythenshawe Scheme 1931' had been submitted to the Minister of Health, who in 1926 had actually encouraged Manchester to buy more land. By 1931, however, a financial crisis had hit the country and in August a National Government was formed. The aim now was to concentrate on building 'houses within the means of the poorer members of the working classes' — poorer-quality council homes. A report in November 1932 urged that the normal provision of working-class houses should be by private enterprise.

The Wheatley Act of 1925 was repealed. Without its subsidy the 8s. (40p) a week council houses for rent could not be built. At the same time guarantees were given to building societies. Ernest Simon appealed to his old enemy, Hilton Young, the Minister of Health, for a loan to buy the final 1,000 acres — in vain.

The city decided to buy some 129 acres for immediate use. But, linked with a demand for compulsory pasteurisation of the city's milk, it met combined opposition in December 1932. Councillor Harold White, at Crumpsall Constitutional club, described Wythenshawe as a white elephant and the bill for compulsory purchase as a 'Russian method of business without Russian honesty'. As a result of a poll, compulsory purchase was withdrawn; building slowed to a crawl but it never stopped completely. The Housing Committee thought to erect 75 houses for sale in Wythenshawe, but the Housebuilders' Association, Mrs. Simon and Alderman Jackson combined to prevent this. Four Housing Acts in five years, beginning in 1931, contributed to stop-go working and it was not until 1936 that full steam ahead could be ordered.

Guided by Barry Parker, every detail, from naming roads to telephone-pole stay wires, was decided by the Wythenshawe Committee. A few grand ideas faded, including the 'Wythenshawe Causeway' to link Didsbury and the flood lands of the Mersey to Wythenshawe, but most schemes became reality. By April 1932, when the committee noted that the ground rents for the first 5,000 houses would be £48 per acre, 684 houses were being erected north of Wythenshawe Park (Rackhouse) and 1,764 houses south of Altrincham Road. In Northenden the Piper Hill and Yew Tree area houses (behind Kenworthy Lane) were already completed, along with six shops of the new, now the old, parade at Moor End. Two months later the road names of Orton, Newhall, Nan Nook (subsequently changed to Lawton Moor), Lycett, Carloon, Daine, Pingot and Rackhouse were approved. The first roads and sewers were completed for the Rackhouse and Lawton Moor, Royal Oak, Benchill and Sharston areas and the first 400 houses were finished by December 1932.The number of completed houses rose to 3,363 by 1934, when Royal Oak was almost finished as the first full estate. From a population of 5,551 in 1921, Wythenshawe now had grown to 27,847 souls.

Dividing the pre-war progress into two phases, the numbers built in the early thirties — under the 1924 Act — were:

Baguley — Royal Oak and Northenden	880
Northenden — Kenworthy, Rackhouse and Royle Green	1,453
Northen Etchells — Benchill, Brownley Green & Heyhead	2,464

Built under later acts were:

Northenden — Piper Hill, Yew Tree	144
Northen Etchells — Benchill, Brownley Green,	
Crossacres and Sharston	3,204

Thus by 1939 much of Brownley Green and Crossacres was finished and the population had risen to nearly forty thousand people in 8,145 homes. Typical rent and rates figures for Wythenshawe council houses from 2 April 1934 were these:

Type of house		Rent	Rates & Water	Basic Electricity	Total
Non Parlour	A1	5s. 3d.	3s.	9d.	9s. (45p)
Non Parlour	A2	6s. 0d.	3s. 4d.	9d.	10s. 1d. (50p)
Non Parlour	A3				
Bathroom Downstairs		6s. 9d.	4s. 1d.	9d.	11s. 7d. (58p)
Non Parlour	A3				
Bathroom Upstairs		7s. 3d.	4s. 5d.	9d.	12s. 5d. (62p)
Parlour	B3	8s. 6d.	6s.	9d.	15s. 3d. (70p)
Parlour	B4				
Bathroom Downstairs		8s. 9d.	6s. 3d.	9d.	15s. 9d. (79p)

(A skilled factory worker would expect to earn £2 15s. a week.)

Rates for Northenden and the Rackhouse area were a few pence higher, for the Baguley area and Bucklow-built houses, a few pence lower.

Barry Parker's plans for better-class houses were followed and the earliest parts of Wythenshawe show an interesting variety of well-built houses, with boldly projecting gable fronts and striking ranks of tiles on the mansard roofs — roofs with two pitches. But the effects of the 1930s slump meant more and more little boxes making do as homes. As the standards of building declined so, judging from the complaints received by the Wythenshawe Committee, did the standard of behaviour of some tenants.

A few groups of garages were available but there was a general impression that cars were not for council tenants. In a letter to the Wythenshawe Committee in February 1931, the City Surveyor explained why garages were not allowed by the houses. They would, he argued:

    1. detract from the appearance of the estate,
    2. necessitate the widening of gateways, and
    3. lead to the formation of tracks across the greensward.

In spite of complications, Wythenshawe soon became popular as a housing estate. Up to 1932 the proportion of Manchester applicants requesting Wythenshawe, as opposed to other city estates, had been 24 per cent, but in 1933 this shot up to 48 per cent.

The fact that in later years Wythenshawe was sometimes spoken of as a refuge for people from slum areas was resented by many of the early residents.

We were given a house in the Royal Oak estate. Not anyone could get a house in Wythenshawe. Before we got one an official from the Town-hall wanted to know all about us: our parents had a nursery in Northenden and my husband had steady employment and a fair wage. We had to prove we would be good tenants; some people said they gave a priority to Northenden couples to placate the village. We also heard that some people were from slums but we never met any of them.

Another early tenant was a bus driver and he spoke in 1980 of the pioneering days.

We moved into a house in Button Lane in 1933 and we were the first there. They were good houses — just two sorts really, either a flat front or a bay window type — only the kitchen had plain brick walls and no plaster but I think that was general then. Two of the couples that came in then are still there today. Before they built the Moor Road houses we could see Bowdon Church from our bedroom window, and all round us were fields. We know they'd planted corn as we got little black flies all over the house. My pay as a driver with Manchester Corporation was £2 12s. (£2.60) and the rent was 11s. 9d. (58p) I think. The nine pence (3½p) was for electricity. Our neighbour came from West Didsbury like us. We never met the people from the next estate, they were in when we came. I don't know if they were slum clearance or not because we never came into contact with them.

A survey at that time carried out by the Manchester and Salford Better Housing Council showed that only one in five families had paid under 10s. (50p) rent before moving to

Wythenshawe, too high a sum to be found in slum quarters. The survey seemed to show that only 155 of the 430 families had come from slums in Manchester. Nevertheless, the mixing of people with differing backgrounds produced problems. The tenant of 7 Yew Tree Lane complained to the Wythenshawe Committee of the inadequate fencing around the houses, and protested that the open plan policy 'puts temptation in their path . . . fruit, plants and vegetables have been stolen'. In 1953 the booklet, *Wythenshawe, Plan and Reality*, announced that 'Open Development is under experiment, which means there are no front fences and no garden gates'. Although this did not apply to much of the estate, Walter Creese in *The Garden City* (1966) comments that there should have been alternative solutions to open fronts, since this 'evidently ran so counter to national custom'.

To keep up the appearance generally somewhat idealistic rules about conduct were included in the rent book. A reminder in April 1937 called for tenants to attend to:

1. the protection of grass verges and trees in the street,
2. the preservation and protection of the private open spaces. . ., particularly the protection of wild animals and birds,
3. the preservation of the Parkway particularly flowering plants and live hedges etc. and
4. prohibiting the outside drying of clothes (washing) at weekends (Saturdays and Sundays).

The school as a focal point for neighbourhood units was a basic premise of Barry Parker and it was specified too that they should be ready for incoming families. A complication to confound the local turmoil arising from the change from Cheshire to Lancashire was the change throughout the country from all-age schools to elementary, senior, central and grammar schools. In fact the schools were rarely ready and children who came to Wythenshawe before 1934, if they attended at all, either continued at their present schools, sometimes in the city, or travelled to a Northenden school.

The first elementary schools appeared at last in quick succession. Benchill opened briefly in January 1934 as an all-age school, re-opened with separate age departments on 8 April and made a third start in August 1937, when it shed its older children to Sharston Senior School. The head changed at that date from Mr. Boll to Mr. Ball. Jack Riley was a member of the staff from the start and for almost another forty years. 'The builders were still putting the floors in when we opened. The first thing you had to do if you were on yard duty was to clear the cows from the playground.'

There was a tie for second place. Rackhouse Elementary School opened on 20 August 1934 for juniors and infants, became an infants only school in January 1935, and became two separate junior and infant schools in 1936. It completed the cycle by becoming a combined junior and infants school in January 1977. The other half of the tie, Royal Oak, also opened on 20 August 1934 and became a junior and infant school two years later, as did St Johns, the first Roman Catholic school — 'with 350 children, six teachers and no books'.

Haveley Hey School was opened by Councillor Annie Lee in July 1935, so completing the elementary schools built pre-war. One of the first children had wistful memories of the period:

I attended Royal Oak School from 1934 to 1936. Most stayed there until 14 years. I left at 11 to go to Whalley Range High (first from Royal Oak) . . . Mr. Bryce, Headmaster. School built in 'new' way round quadrangles of grass on which we never set foot. Lots of fresh air as classrooms opened to cloister-like corridors.

Scholarship exam was taken at 10+ years. Some of us likely ones were pushed a bit; everyone took it but few thought seriously about it. I suppose most people were too poor to consider taking up further education. We took exams at Lingard Road School [the Council School, Bazley Road], Northenden. Most children treated it as a day out from school routine. The year I took it 2 of us girls 'passed' and 4-5 boys. In subsequent years several went to 'central' schools.

22. Haveley Hey School, 1938. This was the last elementary school to be built in pre-war Wythenshawe. Typically, it had open corridors and there was much emphasis on formal physical training.

23. Yew Tree School, 1934, on Sale Road leading out of Northenden, is now Arden College. The foreground houses are also of the 1930s.

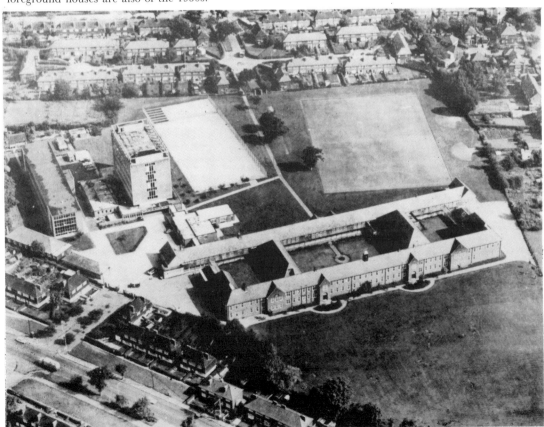

Though families were poor in the 30s, most children were well-behaved and I don't remember any vandalism. (Perhaps I was too naive). From time to time we had our heads inspected and saw the school doctor and dentist. School Clinic was in Lingard Road. I suppose treatment was good. It was always free.

Yew Tree Secondary School appears in 1934 as a municipal school, a senior school in August 1936 and the following year saw a selective central school open on the same site. Sharston School was opened in 1937, with its own adjoining primary school. Brownley Green School on Woodhouse Lane came into action later in the same year.

Further Education in Wythenshawe also had its origin at this time. Dr. Winifred Hall wrote in 1980:

When I moved to Wythenshawe in 1936, it is difficult to imagine what a cultural desert the estate was. Some of us decided to try to remedy this. A general meeting was called by Winifred Lewis, a teacher on the estate, and myself. Classes were started in music appreciation, drama, needlework, and later, languages. The Northwerthen Guild was formed (Northwerthen being the name in the Domesday Book for Northenden). The first chairman was Mr. John Blackie — an H.M.I., resident in Wythenshawe, supported by Miss Winifred Lewis, myself as treasurer, and a committee.

The Northwerthen Guild met at Yew Tree Central School in 1937 with 155 students. Benchill Night School commenced too in the 1936-7 season, with between 150 and 200 students per evening studying vocational and recreational courses.

24. Shopping parade, Altrincham Road. It was one of the first in Wythenshawe Garden City. Opposite is the garage hut that served as the police and fire brigade headquarters. The parade was demolished in 1970 to make way for the M56.

Shopping was as difficult a problem as schooling. The Wythenshawe Committee tried hard, often in vain, to match the progress of the neighbourhood units and the first parade to appear was a block of six shops at Moor End, Northenden, in 1932. Benchill shops followed shortly, and the Sale Circle and Royal Oak shops appeared in 1934.

Traders looked for a boom and by May 1932 there were 392 applicants for shops. They covered 40 trades, from newsagents and tobacconists, with 43 bidders, to that of cutler with only one bid. The committee considered the correct balance of trade and went into considerable detail about such matters as whether a chemist could sell white gloves or a grocer could sell toothpaste.

First-time residents especially found shopping a problem.

> When we moved into Button Lane in 1933 there were no amenities or shops within reach. The Co-op came round with milk — but that was all — that and George Leigh with wet fish on a hand-cart. He came round twice a week — we've never eaten so much fish but my wife couldn't have done without him. Sale Circle wasn't really a shopping place until 1935, so we had to go either to Northenden or Sale Moor. Then the Co-op came round once a week with a little van you could walk in — [that] went on till about 1964.

Street traders were ready to seek out new areas of operation. One coal merchant had left his engineering job and recalled:

> I'd seen the traders do well in Rackhouse so I bought some scales, took them for checking to Weights and Measures in Newton Street, got a hawker's licence for 1s. 6d. (7.5p), and some coal. As soon as the first tenant moved in at Benchill, 2 Boothfield Road off Greenwood, I was at her front door.

At first new Wythenshavians had to come to Northenden to shop and, while the new parades were settling in, they continued to come. But by 1937 the tenants of the Moor End shops asked the Wythenshawe Committee to reduce their rents, as they had lost trade to the new Wythenshawe parades.

The Wythenshawe Chamber of Trade separated from Northenden in 1937. Almost all the members shared the same landlord, Manchester Corporation. Worries ranged from vandalism and autonomy for Wythenshawe, to rents and the cost of plate glass window insurance.

More than once the Wythenshawe Committee flirted with the idea of a central market area. A 1931 minute records 'The first development in Northenden will produce in two or three years a population of about 10,000. The proposed layout of marketing facilities near the village should form a quadrangle and cover three quarters of an acre'. The report noted that as the Civic Centre would be further south and might not be developed for some years (thirty in fact) 'an unique opportunity is afforded'. No action was taken.

To the casual client there was little change in the running of police and fire protection when Wythenshawe became part of Manchester in 1931. The Police Station at Moor End continued as before, though no longer under Cheshire Constabulary, but directed from Platt Lane, Manchester. Police control of the spreading Wythenshawe was initially by police boxes, which had telephones and were also used as a shelter where the officer ate his sandwiches. Barry Parker's concern for high standards extended to these boxes, though he had to defend his approach, as his letter from Penarvon, Cornwall, in September 1931 shows.

> This police box is successful because it frankly expresses its method of construction . . . a real sense of design. For the Wythenshawe which is to be, I think it is suitable . . . I recommend only the original drawing bearing the name 'the Concrete Unit Company' should be used . . .

As more houses were built a few, with a flat above, would be used as police offices, where a report could be made and advice given. 'Tell us what you want and we'll tell you where to go' proclaimed a notice at one office.

Objective comparisons between the standards of law and order in one era and another are difficult. Typical of newspaper letters in the 1960s was one writing of the idyllic pre-war days, 'when not one window in Brownley Green School was broken in four years'. Against that there were the reports, minuted in the Wythenshawe Committee records of the mid-1930s, that 'due to wanton damage by vandals and hooligans various farms and unoccupied houses will have to be demolished'.

The Fire Brigade serving Northenden until 1931 had been that of Sale and Ashton, while Altrincham had served parts of Wythenshawe. After the change in 1931, cover came from the Manchester Brigade at Withington, a station already accustomed to attending Northenden.

The Police and Fire Services came together in 1934 to share a temporary building on Altrincham Road. This was little more than a large hutted garage, which stood on the eastern side of the junction of the Cheshire Lines Railway and Altrincham Road. When at last a permanent fire station was built on the fringe of the civic centre site in 1957 the *Wythenshawe Express* recalled the past.

> It was the early hours of a morning in 1934. Wythenshawe showed raw in those days. Roads were rough, muddy and unlit; pavements unmade. But the estate had its own fire station.
>
> Perhaps there are residents who remember hearing that fire engine race to answer a call to Sharston Mount Farm, where a barn blazed fiercely.
>
> The Fire Brigade and Police shared a temporary building on Altrincham Road — then named Stockport Road — which is now being used as an ambulance depot. In charge there at the station was Station Officer George Baron who had ten men working with him. All were provided with houses in Mullacre Road and Alderue Avenue, Sharston. Mr. Baron recalled, 'It wasn't until machines from London Road arrived that the local people told us there was a pond nearby. We pumped a well absolutely bone dry on that job. Rats streamed from the barn with all the smoke'.

Mr. Baron said there were no pavements or street lights at that time. Emergencies were only confined to a few house fires and there was little danger at Ringway. 'It was just a playground compared with today. We didn't have to turn out once.' Mr. Baron finished at Wythenshawe in 1940 and so missed the move to the coach house of Sharston Hall in 1941.

Hospital provision was the one service that did not need to be transferred. Like the Trojan horse, Manchester's Sanatorium had waited at Baguley since 1902 for the day when Manchester would take over Wythenshawe. From that year, 1931, onwards Withington Hospital took some tubercular patients to ease the pressure on Baguley. Three years later the Wythenshawe Committee allocated land for extensions and in 1935 a scheme first mooted in 1926 to increase the capacity of Baguley by the provision of 84 beds for females and a home for 91 nurses on the south side of Floats Road was approved by the city council. The cost, eventually approved by Ministry of Health, was £85,600 including furniture and fittings.

Staffing problems occurred in 1936 and 1937, perhaps because of the hospital's isolation, made worse by the reduction of nurses' working-hours from 48 to 40 a week in 1937. Questions were asked as to how the nurses would spend all this spare time and should a swimming bath be built. It was considered reasonable for domestic staff not to have any extra time off 'because they had a week-end off every other week'.

Wythenshawe Hospital, which would in time absorb Baguley Sanatorium, was first aired as an idea in July 1939 as a result of two decisions made by the Manchester Public Health Committee to change the status of Baguley Sanatorium. The first thoracic surgery (heart and lungs) was to be done at Baguley. Secondly, an emergency hospital of 900 beds was to be attached to the hospital for the receipt of expected air-raid casualties from Manchester. To meet this development, the sisters' home was converted into an operating theatre. An improved X-ray block was provided and the nurses had extra bathrooms and gas fires in their home. Baguley Sanatorium was ready for war.

Transport and industry
Northenden Station had come into existence with the Stockport, Timperley and Altrincham Railway Act of 22 July 1861 as part of the Cheshire Lines Railway or, to give it its official title, the Cheshire Lines Committee. These eight miles of line were opened in December

1865. It had a junction with the Manchester South Junction and Altrincham Railway, (M.S.J. & A.R.) at Deansgate Lane, Altrincham (Skelton Junction) in 1865 and another with M.S.J. & A.R. at Timperley (beyond West Timperley Station and later taken out) in 1879. At the same time Baguley Station came into existence.

The Cheshire Lines was the brain-child of Edmund Watkins, who lived at Rose Hill (*see* Chapter One), of the Manchester Sheffield and Lincolnshire Railway, and an attempt to break into the west and south-west of Manchester, formerly the preserve of the London and North Western Railway. It was built mainly between 1869 and 1880, the starting points being at Liverpool Central, Stockport and Woodley, Manchester Central and Chester Northgate. Allied with the Great Northern and the Midland Railway, the Cheshire Lines was the premier joint railway in Britain and the only one to retain its own management up to 1947.

An odd railway, it had 300 passenger coaches, but no locomotives, on 150 miles of line. These were originally supplied by the M.S. & L.R. and later through trains on the Cheshire Lines were hauled by L.N.E.R and L.M.S. engines. In the 1930s, the Cheshire Lines became involved in 'pooling' schemes with other companies to save money.

'Direct railway communication from Wythenshawe will become an absolute necessity and it seems a curious omission that no railway developments have been made in the general plan for the layout of the estate.' This comment by the Manchester and Salford Better Housing Council was published in the *Evening Chronicle* on 3 July 1935. In September 1935 Councillor W. P. Jackson said he wanted an electrified rail link for Wythenshawe but, after negotiations, the railway companies said it was expensive and impractical.

On the roads more buses appeared. In 1932 the Manchester Corporation Transport (M.C.T.) service 45, Wythenshawe Park to Southern Cemetery, came into existence and was extended to Sharston the following year. This was the first attempt by M.C.T. to provide the new garden city with public transport. In September 1934 a service to Piccadilly began. In the 1920s M.C.T. had envisaged trams running along Princess Road into Northenden and Wythenshawe, but by 1930, with a change of General Manager, it had been decided that buses would be better. Tram tracks had been laid as far as Southern Cemetery, a turning point in the middle of nowhere. Nineteen years later M.C.T. scrapped all their trams, their demise being delayed by the war.

By 1934, there were three service routes to and from Wythenshawe: 43 Lawton Moor/ Southern Cemetery via Wythenshawe Road, which extended to Nell Lane, Withington in May 1934; 44 Royal Oak/Southern Cemetery, also extended to Nell Lane and six months later to Piccadilly via Princess Road; 45 Wythenshawe Park/Southern Cemetery, by the end of 1934 running from Piccadilly to Wynyard Road via Broadoak Road, serving the newly built Benchill Estate.

According to a M.C.T.D. guide dated June 1938, there were six bus services operating between Wythenshawe and Piccadilly: 41 (later renumbered 50 in December and extended to the *Vine Inn*, Washway Road, Sale) and 42 (renumbered 64 in December); 43, now running from Orton Road to Piccadilly; 44, routed from Baguley Hospital to Piccadilly; 45, extended in April the following year to run via Hollyhedge Road to Benchill Road. There was also a work's service bus, 70, Wythenshawe to Trafford Park. The return fare along the Parkway to Manchester was 8d. or 9d. through Northenden.

In May 1933 M.C.T. acquired the service which a small private company, Organ and Wachter (*see* Chapter Three), ran from Parker Street, Piccadilly Bus Station, to Styal. They operated it jointly on a sixty-forty basis with North Western Road Car Company (North Western) and it became 41 to Ringway and 42 to Styal.

John Organ, of the private bus company Organ and Wachter, recalled an occasion when a council flatbed lorry tried to pull a double-decker bus, minus its rear wheel, out of a ditch near Ashton's pond by the golf links.

> A driver of one of Leggit's steam waggons arrived. 'The bloody fools!' he says, 'They'll never get it up!' And he stalked into the middle of that road and he said in a very loud voice, 'Who's in charge of this?' So some Corporation bloke came and said, 'I am'. So he said, 'Well, take that thing away and lose it,' he says, 'And I'll get it out for you.' So he came up, chuff, chuff, chuff and got this thing backed up to it. They never said anything. Never asked who he was or anything. But he shifted it for them.

This bus was probably the ill-fated No. 64, Manchester's first double-decker with pneumatic tyres.

The Organ and Wachter depot was first at Fred Corkhill's by West Didsbury Station, then at Kaye's by the *Tatton Arms*. On 23 May 1933 Organ and Wachter ceased as a bus company. Adrian Wachter and John Organ became employees of M.C.T.

> At the last gasp Manchester Corporation got an order from the newly formed Traffic Commissioners, and we were forbidden to pick up from the corner of Sharston Road and Longley Lane. I mean, there was nothing, very little, up there (Styal). Manchester Corporation, the North Western . . . the railway . . . all opposed us. There was not a railway link from here to Manchester but they opposed us just the same. Everything was against us.

The North Western began in Macclesfield in 1923. It was owned by the British Electric Traction Company (B.E.T.) and Thomas Tilling Limited. The buses were painted in the company livery of red and white. Over a year later North Western moved its registered office to Charles Street, Stockport. In 1933 it took over Organ and Wachter's Manchester-Styal route, its first incursion into the area of Northenden and the new garden city. Later Wythenshawe/Northenden services operated by North Western were the 71 Altrincham to Stockport via Sharston, 80 Altrincham to Stockport via Didsbury (established routes), and 79A/B/C Stockport to Ringway/Wythenshawe. Service 50 was entirely M.C.T.

The North Western continued for a time as part of the National Bus Company, then with Selnec (S.E. Lancashire and N.E. Cheshire), but ceased to exist in 1972. It had taken forty years for the 1930 Road Traffic Act to kill the company. Ironically, in 1980 a Transport Act designed to encourage private operators was passed (and came into force on 26 October 1986). Come back Organ and Wachter, and North Western. All is forgiven!

Barton Airport took over from Rackhouse Lane in 1930, but in 1934 when K.L.M. Royal Dutch Airlines reviewed the possibilities of a Holland-Northern England service and said that Barton was not suitable, the Airport Committee recommended Ringway as the best alternative site. The land was bought with compulsory purchase orders for £80,000 after a public inquiry and a High Court case brought by Cheshire County Council in May 1935. On 28 November 1935 the Lord Mayor of Manchester opened the site.

Eighteen months later, on 8 June 1937, Fairey Aviation Company held their own private opening day to celebrate the completion of their hangar for the final assembly of Fairey Battles. The Lord Mayor of Manchester had officially opened the hangar six days before. Fairey acquired the old National Aircraft Factory No. 2 in Heaton Chapel and they were given the western side of Ringway to use for the test flights.

On 25 June 1938, the whole of Ringway was officially opened by Sir Kingsley Wood, the Air Minister, and he inspected many visiting aircraft including a Hurricane, Demon, Harrow, Anson and Gauntlet. Services began on Monday 27 June 1938 with a Railway Air Services de Havilland Rapide, leaving at 9.06 a.m. for Liverpool's Isle of Man route. A K.L.M. DC-2 left for Doncaster and Amsterdam at 10.52 a.m.

When Ringway opened it had a control tower and administration block on the northern edge of the airfield, housing a passenger reception area and restaurant in the western half, and with a public viewing area on the roof. The whole eastern side of the building was a

25. Manchester Airport and staff, 1947. The airport moved from Northenden to Barton and then to its present site at Ringway in 1938. From the left are the reception building, control and administration, immigration and the main hangar.

large hangar. In front of the tower was a small concrete and tarmac area with petrol pumps along the eastern edge. Apart from the apron of the two Fairey hangars there were no taxiways and the whole landing area was grass.

At first, in 1938, the revenue from the airport was very small. The fee for housing a plane overnight was 2s. 8d. (13p); landing fee (depending on size) 1s. 6d.-14s. 3d. (7.5p-71p); a return fare to Belfast £4 15s. (£4.75p), to Blackpool £1 5s. (£1.25p), to the Isle of Man £3 6s. (£3.30p), to Liverpool £1 10s. (£1.50p).

Another facet of Ringway started in July 1938 and caught on — joy-riding operated by various airlines, mainly Isle of Man Air Services (I.o.M.A.S.) and Railway Air Services (R.A.S.).

In 1938 it was obvious that war was imminent and by February 1939 No. 613, City of Manchester, Auxiliary Air Force Squadron was formed. By May hangars had been built at Ringway for the units. On 20 May 1939 there was an 'Empire Air Day' with a three hour flying display. It was the Squadron's first public appearance. Planes there included Avro Anson, Armstrong, Whitworth Whitley, Handley Page Heyford, Bristol Blenheim, Fairey Seal, Fairey Battle, Hawker Hind and a new Supermarine Spitfire. Army and artillery detachments were also on public view.

The civil air services in the summer of 1939 were more numerous than the previous year. Great Western and Southern Airlines joined K.L.M. and I.o.M.A.S. in serving Ringway. The last pre-war non-service civil aircraft was a Percival Vega Gull, G-AFAV, owned by a Mr. E. Thomas, which returned to Ringway from Le Bourget on 1 September 1939. It flew to Woodford on 14 September, where it was stored until the end of the war.

The war would in time have a big impact on the newly established Wythenshawe firms. Barry Parker saw local industry as a service to provide local employment. Three industrial sites were planned for Wythenshawe. The Eastern Northenden, or Sharston, Industrial Estate was approved in January 1930 and development was confined to lighter industries with little smoke and with electricity, coke or oils as fuels. The proposals included a major road, 60 feet wide, to link with Cheadle, but this had to wait forty years. Otherwise the plans were carried out largely as drawn up. Manchester owned all the land, leasing sites for 99 years to developers who built their own factories to a design approved by the city. One incentive was a ground rent of only 3d. per square yard per year. Manchester had paid £300 per acre, which was 1s. 3d. per square yard.

The Sharston Estate would eventually take about fifty firms, centred on Northenden Station. Further west on the same railway line would be, in time, the Western Estate. The Southern Estate would be in Moss Nook. Loans of many thousands of pounds to firms to help them start were granted, but every effort was made to check potential nuisance. Permission for a potato-crisp factory was twice granted and withdrawn before a final refusal was given. Screens were planned of 200 willows, elders and rhododendrons. Development at the junction of Longley Lane, known as Winking Light Corner because of an early traffic light there, was shelved after local residents campaigned against it.

Some of the earliest firms setting up in Sharston in 1933 were J. Cramptons of Paxo Stuffing, Leyton Studios, Rushworth's Knitwear, Mays' Hosiery and Royle Green Motors. Firms setting up in 1934 included Wylex Electrical Products (established 1897), which in time took over Mays' and Birkbys' buildings, Brooks Bakery, which became Kipling's Cakes, Sowden Art Embroiderer, Moor End Underwear and a confectionery works. French's Rufflette Tapes came in 1935 with Gallacher's, tobacco merchants, and Pioneer Telephones. Rollinx Plastics and Brookside Clothing began at Sharston and later moved to the Round-thorn Estate.

Negotiations were being made for the bus depot, eventually sited at Bradnor Road, and for a crown Post and Sorting Office on Altrincham Road when the Second World War broke out. The Co-operative Society, too, were bargaining with the Wythenshawe Committee about their Super Dairy with its 'super economic coal fired boiler': the dairy would pump its own water from its own well — but it still had to pay for it.

Before the 1939 war halted most development, tenants and critics had started to take stock of early Wythenshawe. Mr. and Mrs. McGrath came to Wythenshawe in 1933. 'The only shop within reach was the little general stores. For other items one had to walk to Northenden or trek along Altrincham Road to Sharston where there were two shops.' The depression of 1929 put Mr. McGrath out of work and the building society foreclosed on his Didsbury house.

> At this time the Corporation were very fussy about letting their houses. No one who hadn't a job was ever granted a tenancy. Late in 1933 my husband was taken on engineering . . . expecting our fourth child we moved into 629 Altrincham Road, Royal Oak. It was the best Christmas present I ever had. Rent was 11s. 7d. (58p). His wages after stoppages were £2 7s. (£2.35p). The roads were literally 'dirt roads', the paths around the houses were of soft, red shale which caused havoc when little feet brought it into the house. We felt very cut off from everywhere since the bus to Royal Oak only ran about twice a day.

Helen McGrath wanted a 'parlour' house but these were 12½d. (5p) more rent — too much, but after their fifth daughter was born they got an 'exchange' to Benchill. They could use the Catholic school from 1937 and the Catholic church.

> A trip into Town was a real treat — eight pence return (3p). We often walked to our relatives in Moss Side and walked back pushing the pram. Before we left Altrincham Road I recall the old Royal Oak, a little country pub, being pulled down and the new monstrosity built. I wonder what happened to the old polished black oven with a flower design on the door? We were proud of our gardens. The horses along Altrincham Road often left manure behind which was eagerly shovelled up. Presently a row of shops were built on Royal Oak Road. They had a grand opening with 'special offers'. Three pounds of self-raising flour for eight pence (3p) (it was usually ten pence).

This verdict of satisfaction of a tenant can be matched by an open letter from 'Christopher Wren' to the *Manchester City News* in July 1935 when Alderman Jackson was seventy-one. After detailing the obstacles he had had to overcome the letter goes on:

> But you won! Wythenshawe is in being. Wythenshawe is the cynosure of all those in Europe and America who study housing in the light of civic ideals. Opposed by little men in your term of office, big men will praise you in the days to come. No public servant can ask more.

William Jackson's comrade, Ernest Simon, was painting on a wider canvas and, although he had been knighted in 1932, the city would wait for the sixties before bestowing its freedom upon him.

Ironically, the reward for Lady Simon's work for Wythenshawe was the loss of her seat on the city council. Lady Simon was probably the strongest socialist of the Wythenshawe proponents, but the juxtaposition of socialism and her title perhaps created suspicion with the electorate. She was defeated in Chorlton-cum-Hardy in the municipal elections of 1933. Standing next as an Independent Liberal for Wythenshawe, she failed to gain the seat. Her influence, through her husband, through letters, personal contact and co-option on committees, particularly in education, was to continue.

A more critical examination of the situation was made in a book written at the time, *Manchester Made Over* by Alfred P. Simon with a foreword by Barry Parker. A. P. Simon showed concern for the inability of Wythenshawe to 'throw off the swaddling clothes that Manchester provided'. 'There should be without delay some preparation made for administrative buildings in the projected Wythenshawe civic centre, from which local government can as far possible be administered, and where, in case of need, the Wythenshawe Committee could meet.' He warned of the need to preserve the green belt, not only by the Mersey but between the neighbourhood units. 'Benchill and Holly Edge already merge as do Rackhouse and Lawton Moor.' He also attacked the 'Fantastic excrescences' of the private houses and praised the 'contented socialisation' of the municipal homes.

Contemporary surveys suggest that the pioneers themselves were well-satisfied with their lot. The report by the Manchester and Salford Better Housing Council in 1935 showed that while there was concern over the lack of local employment and a third were overawed by their gardens and shop prices, over 90 per cent expressed contentment with life in Wythenshawe. A pressure group grew in 1934 out of the three community associations of Benchill, Rackhouse and Royal Oak, the Wythenshawe Residents Association. With the help of Lady Simon and the *Wythenshawe Gazette and Weekly News*, it successfully opposed rate increases on the grounds of costly travel and complaints about the lack of churches, post offices and shops. The association went on, under the leadership of Harry Lloyd, to be a powerful mouthpiece for Wythenshawe, population now about forty thousand, during and after the war.

The start of the Second World War in September 1939 came at a most unfortunate time for Wythenshawe. The first onslaught of house building was nearly completed and the W.E.S.C. was beginning to discuss the provision of amenities and better communications.

The problems of the Wythenshavians seemed over-shadowed by the impending war.

A.R.P training had commenced in Sharston Hall in 1938, but the first record in the W.E.S.C. minutes that war had been declared was a letter from a Mr. Cave requesting allotments, as 'men desire to get busy for 1940 crops if the present disastrous war continues . . .'. The letter was passed to the Agricultural Committee. The use of a garage at Sale Circle for an A.R.P. post was approved and potential shop and factory tenants withdrew. At the same time 35 acres of Poplar Grove Farm were compulsorily purchased for the airport.

Plans to extend Sharston Estate roads at Longley Lane went ahead, more houses were approved for Gibwood and Netherwood Roads and tenders for the extension of Shawdene Road went out in September 1939. Shopping facilities were discussed at length, after a report that Royal Oak Estate was complete with 860 houses and nine shops, but 'hosiery is being sold at a newsagents'. The Co-op Super Dairy, too, was about to be commenced.

Two projects, the building of a cinema and the extension of Princess Parkway, were being discussed when the war began. Negotiations for a Wythenshawe cinema on Hollyhedge Road, to add to the two in Northenden, had been going on for some years, chiefly with Associated British cinemas (A.B.C.). Early in 1939 A.B.C. wanted to build a cinema costing £16,000, while the council demanded one costing at least £20,000. After months of haggling A.B.C. lowered their offer down to £15,000, but stated they would not be able to begin building until 1940. For a shortfall of £4,000 the opportunity of getting a cinema was effectively lost. For the next forty years campaigners were able to complain that Wythenshawe had no focal point, no heart.

The other project under consideration by the Wythenshawe Committee when war approached was the extension of Princess Parkway to the airport, together with other estate roads. In July 1939, in a conciliatory mood, Cheshire agreed to the Parkway extension and to an east-west link to Altrincham and Stockport. The committee resolved that action should come about forthwith, if possible, but war intervened. For thirty years the Parkway ended at Northenden, and when at last it extended south as a motorway it would divide rather than serve Wythenshawe.

Chapter Five

'Leisure, Pleasure and Spiritual Treasure in the 1930s'

During the 1920s and early 1930s Northenden retained many of the characteristic features of village life. Most of the community activities were still church-based, as will be seen later. There were well-established, flourishing churches, dedicated to the Anglican, Roman Catholic and Nonconformist faiths. Many of the residents worked locally in the shops and offices of Northenden and Didsbury, but some found employment at the firms on the new Sharston Industrial Estate, which was being established in the mid-1930s, and others travelled on the bus, which now ran a more frequent service, into Manchester. The surrounding countryside was relatively unspoilt, the area south of the village was still dotted with farms and old halls, such as Chamber Hall, Peel Hall and Baguley Hall, some partly decaying, but others in a good state of preservation and forming part of the picture of rural Cheshire. Just before the boundaries of Wilmslow and Altrincham were reached, there were the landing strips and huts being built at Ringway. Before the war, however, it was still possible on a Sunday morning to leave Northenden on foot, travel south across the Altrincham-Stockport road, wend your way through the new houses at Benchill, and from then on the vista was of open fields, broken by the occasional farmhouse and outbuilding, until the grey temporary huts, and later the barbed wire, of the airfield was reached. Alternatively, you could leave Northenden via the Parkway, cross into Gibb Lane, a twisting tree-lined path (a popular spot for local lovers), through a copse which abounded with wildlife, and on, through the newly-built Royal Oak housing estate, following the lane which eventually passed Baguley Sanatorium, continuing through fields and nursery gardens until another point of the developing airport was reached.

This was the setting of Northenden from the late 1920s until the war, and to this quietly thriving village people came from outlying areas for their fun, entertainment and worship. It had been the custom for many years for travelling fairs and circuses to visit the area at Easter and Whitsuntide, and this arrangement continued, as one resident, a boy at the time, recalls:

> I remember visiting a circus which was held on a piece of land now occupied by Heyridge Drive. I also saw a circus on the car park opposite the Tatton Arms. I was also there one fantastic week-end when I saw a gentleman extract himself from a straightjacket, quite fascinating . . . but my main memories I have are of our visits to the fair at Easter, we would watch the arrival of the crowds on foot passing over Northenden Bridge and turn left down Mill Lane. So the fair would arrive sometime before Easter and those of us coming home from Miss Richardson's made sure that we did a detour in order to see the sideshows being put up and to marvel at the way Noah's Ark and the roundabouts were put together . . . down Mill Lane there would be people selling little imitation birds on strings with tails that twirled round and round in the wind, and Easter was the first time that ice-cream sellers appeared, particularly the tricycles run by Messrs. Walls — 'stop me and buy one' — were very much in evidence. We walked down Mill Lane towards the fair, the noise was deafening and the tunes they played stuck in my memory. Father, who prided himself as being something of a shot, would shoot at a sideshow and we would be given little gollywogs to pin on our chests. Fathers always won the gollywogs first. We would then roll pennies and the bravest of us would go on the roundabouts. I have seen at the fair the Wall of Death with motor cyclists cycling round inside a large wooden palisade. I have seen helter skelters, it could be anything higher than a house, and roundabouts of prancing horses.

Apart from the visits of fairs and circuses, most of the other festive occasions of the village were centred around the churches. Each year St Hilda's Roman Catholic church ran a big carnival procession from the Forum site to the Boat House by the river. This was led by the Northenden Prize Band and was a very gay and colourful affair, well-supported by all the people of the locality. On that day the organisers were given the free use of the boats on the river. Boating was then a very popular pastime. These festivities usually raised about £100, which went towards paying off the debt on the church. There were many side-shows, competitions and other events, and one in particular drew the crowds. This was a football competition in which local teams competed on a friendly basis, to the extent of sharing the tea rooms next to the *Tatton Arms* as a changing room.

Although this was a grand and colourful affair, another event just as popular was the Parish Church Garden Fête, usually taking place in June or July and having for its venue the Rectory garden. It was always very well attended and in 1938 the Rector, The Revd. Hendrick Chignell, was moved to write a poem as a means of advertisement:

> Have you heard of our Church Garden Fête?
> Come in crowds through the Rectory gate,
> If you cannot attend
> Please do not fail to send
> The cash you can spare little or great.

Most of the villagers, of all denominations, heeded this demand and became part of the following familiar scene, which was recorded in the *Parish Magazine* in July 1938.

'The Garden Fete'

Can you picture the scene? The Rectory garden looking fresh and lovely, the tea tables all set, the stalls fitted up, tents erected on the lawn, the games arranged and the Band prepared to play sweet music, everything ready for a great effort, and only a fine afternoon wanted to give success to all the work done. And then the rain which had been threatening all morning began to fall steadily about 2 o'clock. It soon appeared that there was little chance of the weather clearing, so with the help of those who had already braved the weather, everything possible was moved into the Rectory. The stalls were erected in the Conservatory and Hall, the tea tables placed in the Dining Room and study, and the Band crowded into the servants hall. The big kitchen was of course already occupied by the ladies who were preparing the teas ... The gentlemen who had kindly offered to help with the games had no chance of displaying their ability but some made themselves useful in helping to move tables and clearing up at the end of the day. The Band did its best in its restricted quarters and at least did help to keep everyone cheerful under the circumstances.

After reading this and similar reports of parish events, it is easy to understand how the Church became the seedbed for many of the societies that developed in Northenden in the 1920s and 1930s. Here we have the example of the band which was highlighted in the two foregoing events and when we look for its beginnings we find that in May 1929 the Rector wrote in his monthly letter:

'Band and Hand-Bell Ringers'

Mr. Peers is anxious to form a Brass Band in connection with the Church. He is an accomplished player of many instruments, and it will be a great opportunity for some of our young people to learn how to play. The band will be composed of Church people entirely and Mr. Peers has already enlisted a number of young men willing to learn. The question of obtaining instruments may present a difficulty but there are a few here at the Rectory, which apparently belonged to the Band which existed here years ago, to judge from their present condition. These when cleaned will be useful to begin with, and doubtless money will be forthcoming to purchase others.

Later that year there was some controversy over the membership of the band, for the parish church obviously felt that it should have ownership, so the Rector stated, 'I would like to make our position clear. It was never intended to form a Village Band'. His reason for asking for the financial support of the other denominations was 'simply because Mr.

Peers felt our Nonconformist brothers ought to have an opportunity of helping an object which later on they might be very glad to avail themselves of . . .'.

St Wilfrid's Band continued as such for another couple of years. At the same time the ladies of the church became involved in musical activity. 'A keen musical spirit peering into a box in the Belfry discovered a grand set of handbells and there is every reason to believe that soon handbell ringing will be heard in the land.'And indeed it was, for at the Northenden Allotment Holders Annual Show in 1930: 'The band led the procession through the village afterwards playing selections on the show ground. The handbell ringers under the direction of Mr. E. Price looked very charming arrayed in white, and rendered selections to an appreciative audience'.

26. Young wives keep fit at Beech House. There were many similar groups active in the 1930s. Centre is an arch taken from Manchester Cathedral during rebuilding, the architect Crowther had rebuilt Northenden church and superintendent Thomas Lings lived at Beech House. The house became a hospital in the First World War and is now a retirement home.

Throughout this period the Church provided the conditions and the atmosphere for aspiring musicians, athletes and thespians to meet and explore their interests. But always the development and growth took place in the wider community. For example, the band, at a meeting in October 1931 presided over by Mr. Tatton, passed a resolution: 'The Band hitherto known as St Wilfrid's Church Band be known in future as Northenden Public Subscription Band'. This same pattern of conception, birth and development of various groups was to be seen frequently up to the outbreak of the war in 1939.

The solely church-orientated groups included the Sunday School, the Choir and the

Mothers' Union, and we read of many bright moments in the life of their members in the records of the church outings.

The Sunday School Summer Picnic was one of the most popular events of the year and it was one to which many people in the parish and further afield contributed, so that the children could have an enjoyable day. Motor coaches were fairly expensive and not too readily available, but local farmers and tradesmen willingly lent their lorries and waggons to transport the children to the site where the picnic was to take place. Amongst these people were Mr. Leigh, Mr. Mayers, Mr. Shenton and Mr. Simpson. Others offered their premises as a venue for the event. In 1926 the outing to Kenworthy Farm was recorded thus:

> This year we did not go far from home, but accepted the very kind invitation of Mr. J.C. Davies to visit Kenworthy Farm. In order to give the children the leisure of a ride on the lorries a circuitous route was taken, via Royle Green Road, Longley Lane, Sale Road and Yew Tree Lane, with the result that the Shadow Moss contingent arrived at the farm before the St. Wilfrid's Children. As soon as the living freight was unpacked, and safely escorted to a large field, games of various kinds were indulged in until the tea was ready. This was served in the field and thanks to the excellent catering of two of the teachers Miss Dennison and Miss Walkden, who seem to know exactly what sort of cakes are appreciated, the children had a sumptuous repast and apparently enjoyed it to the full. The teachers then sat down in two relays to an excellent repast to which full justice was done.

So there was no shortage of offers from the owners of outlying farms and halls to use their fields and barns for this annual event. The occupiers of such properties expressed their pleasure in being part of such a happy day and over the years the organisers of the treats arranged visits to Sharston Hall Farm, Peel Hall, Royle Thorne Farm, Chamber Hall, Baguley Hall Farm, and in 1936 they travelled further afield, for the first time, to Old Hall Farm, Woodford. This farm lay miles away in Cheshire and was the new home of Mr. and Mrs. Mayers, who had accommodated the Sunday School previously when they were living locally. Sadly the long trip was made necessary by the closure of many of Northenden's neighbouring farms. As the tide of houses swept across the fields and farmlands the vista changed from green to the red brick of dwellings and for a time some of the farmhouses and halls were left islands of the past and no longer suitable for a country 'treat', hence the report of the 1936 trip:

> On July 18 this annual event [the Sunday School Treat] took place. It is becoming increasingly difficult to take the children to any farm in the parish owing to the large number that have had to be given up. This year we were fortunate enough to receive an invitation from Mr. and Mrs. Mayers to visit their new home at Woodford. The acceptance of this kind of invitation entailed the hiring of buses at the cost of £8. This is an additional expense but it was impossible to use lorries, so kindly lent in the past, for a journey of 16 miles. The children however seemed to enjoy the ride as much as usual. About 150 left the Church School at 2.30 p.m., and on arriving at the Old Hall Farm, most picturesquely situated in a very beautiful part of Cheshire, they began to scamper over the field, and appeared to be going to have a very enjoyable time. Unfortunately, however, the rain began to fall, and although the boys playing cricket refused to take shelter, most of the children retired to the cover of the barns, where later they managed to enjoy their tea. By that time the rain had ceased and the rest of the afternoon was fine, so that the sports were carried through, as soon as the teachers and helpers had done justice to the excellent tea so kindly provided by our hostess. After the distribution of the prizes the party left the farm and reached Northenden at about 9 o'clock at night having spent a most enjoyable outing despite the rain which certainly did not dampen the children's spirits even if it did their shoes.

The Sunday School Teachers' Picnic was usually a sober, more relaxed event, as might be expected, and, again, various places were visited over the years. Southport, Rudyard Lake and Buxton were chosen venues. The trip to Rudyard Lake in 1926 was full, and strenuous for the more energetic:

Thanks to the excellent weather and organising abilities of Mr. C. H. Royle the Sunday School Teachers' picnic on July 10th was a tremendously successful affair. For once, thirteen was a lucky number and those teachers who were unable to be present were deprived (or deprived themselves) of a most enjoyable outing. The charabanc left Northenden shortly after 2.00 p.m. and brought the party safely to Rudyard Lake at about 4.30 p.m. An interval profitably employed in exploring the amenities of the place though none had the courage to join in the dancing, was followed by a most enjoyable tea. Then boating on the lake, the more ardent spirits in rowing boats, the more sedate in a motor launch, occupied our time until unkind fate compelled a return. After an uninterrupted journey, Northenden was reached about 10.45 p.m. Surely a vote of thanks was due to Mr. Royle for his foresight and care if no-one proposed it. Was it because of the aforesaid uninterrupted journey?

The Choirboys' Outings were the largest single inducement to young boys to join the choir, and there was a goodly monetary reward given in the form of a 'tip' to spend during the day. The amount received was dependent on the number of attendances throughout the year. These outings were not without their incidents, as a trip to Blackpool in the late 1920s shows:

The boys found no difficulty in filling in the time before partaking of an excellent dinner at 12.30 p.m. After this a visit was paid to the Tower and then the rest of the afternoon on the Pleasure Grounds, at least for most of the party, though one or two preferred the Boating Lake, and as they each had been given a good 'tip' to spend as they liked they all enjoyed themselves thoroughly. Two or three of the boys were 'lost' for a time but all turned up punctually to tea and only one member of the party really disappeared for the whole afternoon and afterwards it was found that he had been quietly sitting on the front enjoying his book and the sea breeze all the time, and had been 'overlooked' by several who had searched for him. After another excellent meal at 5.30 p.m, a move was made for the chara., and we left Blackpool at about 6.30 p.m, though it was difficult to get some of the party away from the motor-cars, which were a source of great pleasure. After a pleasant ride we reached Northenden before 10 o'clock.

It was in this period between the wars that the Northenden Branch of the Mothers' Union was begun. Negotiations had started in 1930 but it was in February 1931 that the first members were enrolled. This was reported in the rector's letter. 'It was a great pleasure to see such a good beginning to our Branch of the Mothers' Union. Twenty-one members were enrolled at the service on February 5th.' Twelve new members were enrolled in June and from then on the Mothers' Union went from strength to strength. It was a very lively group of people, as the Parish Notes show, holding jumble sales, whist drives, garden parties, dramatic shows and American Teas, the name given at the time to what was later called a Bring and Buy. They invited visiting speakers, held regular services and gave the church continuous financial and moral support.

In October 1927 a social club was opened, St Wilfrid's Social Club, for the benefit of the boys and girls of the bible class and communicants of St Wilfrid's Guild (the membership of the club was confined to those two groups). However, this restriction did not appear to inhibit their inventiveness, for at their Christmas Party later that year a Fancy Dress Parade was held and although 'The first prize went to Miss F. Price who wore a beautiful gown over 60 years old — the gentleman's prize went to Bob Rowley who wore a most ingenious costume made out of Birkett and Bostock bread wrappers'.

For a short time this club flourished, holding dances and highly successful variety concerts, American Teas and other social events, but quite soon after its inception the venue for the meetings changed to the Woodside Café opposite the Forum Cinema site, and it can only be assumed that a breakaway from the church was beginning to take place. A similar sort of schism happened with another church group, also started in October 1927. 'A club has been formed in the village for the purpose of fostering athletics, its membership at present being confined to members of the Boys' Bible Class and St. Wilfrid's Guild.'

This body was called 'St Wilfrid's Athletic Club' and it held its first meetings in the park of Sharston Hall Farm. The events were flat racing and high jumping. In their first contest St Wilfrid's Athletic Club secured first place in every event. They were competing against Toc H Rovers and R.N.V.R. Sea Scouts. During the next three years the club entered many competitions and did well. In the *Parish Magazine*, under Parish Notes, we read about the 'Norcross Athletic Club (late St Wilfrid's Athletic Club)'. The change of name did not in any way seem to have affected their prowess, as the results recorded then were 'Norcross A.C. 35 points — Hans Reynolds 10 points', and that was an away match! But in 1931 there was reference to the 'lagging enthusiasm of the senior members' and the club seems to have been in a state of decline. Little further reference is found.

The church tried again in February 1937, publishing an open letter to young men of 16 years and over. This appeal came from the Assistant Curate of the time, A. Merchant, who spoke of the forthcoming meeting, saying there would be talks on different topics and then he introduced the bait. 'I have had requests about the formation of a soccer eleven. This might grow out of the meeting so that next season we may have a local team.' Later in the year: 'Next season we shall be entering a team in the new Wythenshawe and District Amateur Association Football League'. And eventually, in 1939, success: 'Our congratulations to St Wilfrid's Football Team on being runners up in the Wythenshawe and District Amateur Football League Cup'. Here is an example of the emergence of serious organised football in the Wythenshawe area.

The Whit Walks, which were to become such an important occasion in the life of Wythenshawe in the 1940s and 1950s, did not warrant much notice in the early 1930s. There is a *Parish Magazine* reference in 1935 to the occasion.

Whit Sunday Procession and Service
Once again we were fortunate in having a fine afternoon and everything passed off successfully.

However, by 1937 the estates at Benchill and Lawton Moor had been built and most of the people housed there had come from the inner areas of Manchester where for many generations importance had been given to these acts of witness. In Manchester and some Lancashire towns it was the custom for the Protestants to hold their Parade on Whit Monday, while the Roman Catholics held theirs on Whit Friday, and the pioneers of the estate continued this tradition, but the established churches in Northenden were at pains to show their different attitudes to these 'walks':

As in former years a large number of our Sunday School children accompanied by a goodly number of children from the Methodist and Mission Hall Sunday Schools, and headed by the Subscription Band processed to the Parish Church by way of Kenworthy Lane, Lingard Road, Palatine Road, Brown Street, Albert Road, and Church Road. The object of this combined procession to church is not a 'walk' in the sense in which 'a walk' is regarded in Manchester, but rather as a witness of the unity of Christian children, and of their desire to worship together at least once a year in their own parish church. Of course, it is pleasing to see children, especially the little girls, prettily dressed, and provided this can be done inexpensively there can be no objection to it but it is not right to spend money which is needed for more necessary things simply to make a pretty show, for our Procession is not a show but a witness.

Again, the different philosophy of the immigrants and the inhabitants is seen in sharp contrast when we read through the recollections of one living on the Lawton Moor Estate in the 1930s.

However, as the slums were cleared during the 1930s and the housing estates developed round the suburbs more local processions of 'witness' took place. The new outfit was kept a closely guarded secret until the great day. Mothers must have scrimped and saved for weeks to ensure that their children were as well dressed as their neighbours — for money was tight in the 30s. Afternoon Sunday School was well attended in those days and the new clothes were kept strictly for Sundays . . . Whit Sunday arrived at last, and, in the morning the children called on their neighbours and relations to parade their finery.

There were many other activities in Northenden apart from those fostered by the church. Prior to there being official and organised games, boys and young men had always kicked a ball about in the streets, but in the early years of the century it was illegal to do so as one 'player' told:

> In those days you couldn't kick a ball in the streets, so one lad used to watch out and shout 'copper coming', and we used to pick the ball up and run . . . we used to kick a casey ball about on Boat House fields because the Northenden copper wouldn't come over the bridge as that was the boundary and he usually just used to laugh . . .

There was some legal football, however. Manchester Amateur League Footballers played in this area on Saturday. They used an enclosed ground as described:

> . . . it was canvassed all around from Didsbury Golf Club up to the weir and there was a turnstile on 'Old Vic's Field'. It cost fourpence to go in and that was a lot of money in those days, but you used to have a programme, this was in the 1920s, and for a good many years after. Many teams played but when we played Didsbury — well — Didsbury Brass Band came and played so we got about 1,000 spectators, when we played Didsbury. Ladybarn was another 'Derby' game, it was good football — all the family came, people from as far away as Baguley and Shadow Moss, well there was nothing else to do . . .

Another place used for team football was the strip of land between Marigold Cottage and Peascroft on Longley Lane, the site now of Lee Court. When this was sold for house building the team transferred to Vic's Field. Also playing on Vic's Field was a team managed by a Captain Workman for 'the youth of the village'. It has been said that this well-used 'Vic's Field' took its name from one of the many teams that played there, the 'Northenden Victoria'.

An eye-witness account of the boxing bouts in the stadium by the river, which were taking place in the late 1920s, makes interesting reading:

> There was a chap called Stonewall Jackson. His name was Jackson, Stonewall Jackson. People used to hit him, and hit him, and hit him and nothing would happen. Nobody ever knocked him down or anything like that, and there was a chappy lived on Royle Green Road named Rees, Billy Rees. He did it. He'd been in the army, and he was a very big fellow. He used to be a heavyweight. He used to box but he never got far with it. He'd turn up there regularly. Sometimes he'd win and sometimes he wouldn't. There'd be several fights on, as you'd call them. There would be one or two local people. You know Heald's Dairy? One of their boys used to go down there and box . . . There'd be about 150 watching, something like that. Then for some reason or other, I can't tell you what year, the boxing just seemed to fade away and they started wrestling for a while, but that didn't last long. When there was a good fight, they'd throw pennies in the ring . . .

There were plenty of outlets for physical expression and also for outdoor entertainment in Northenden before the Second World War, so the people of Wythenshawe came into Northenden frequently to partake in sport or witness the fun. Another outdoor pursuit was sited on the outskirts of Northenden, chiefly because of the availability of land which was not building land, such as the river flood plain. This was the game of golf, and in time three golf clubs were founded in the area, one having its clubhouse on the south side of the river, the Northenden Golf Club.

This club was founded in 1913 under the captaincy of Mr. G. E. Baskerville. At the outset it was a makeshift three-hole golf course on the fields bordering the gardens on Chretien Road, but an irate farmer, demanding that the men attempting to play golf there cleared off his land or paid a deposit of £1 a head, caused the would-be golfers to gather at the Riverside Tea Gardens and make a formal proposal that a golf club should be established on the adjoining land by the river. Notice of this intent was sent out to 150 interested people and 95 replies supported it. An entrance fee of £1 1s. was set and the first flag of the Northenden Golf Club was hoisted in January 1913. The real hard work then commenced. The Silver Jubilee brochure of 1938 reads:

The task which faced the men was no light one. They had undertaken the formation of a golf course over a landscape which time had made anything but mellow. Where No. 1 tee now is there was a large allotment, No. 2 fairway was partly swallowed in a ploughed field. No. 4 green carried a piggery. No. 14 fairway was embraced by a pond, and together with Nos. 12 and 13 greens it presented all the appearance of a swamp . . . Hedges abounded and a refuse tip near No. 16 tee spoke of emptiness and abandon.

It was at this stage that the energy and resource of Mr. G. E. Baskerville were invaluable and it is scarcely an exaggeration to say that without him there would have been no Northenden Golf Club.

The lease of land had been arranged with the owners and a conveniently sited house rented for the purpose of a clubhouse. This had once been the 'Riverside Tea Gardens', and the slogan was still emblazoned on the roof. Until the new tenants were able to eradicate it, it became the duty of one of the members to repel foraging couples, hopeful of a cup of tea after a long and dusty walk.

Less than ten years after the foundation, the club bought land for more fairways from the railway company. These were seven, eight, nine and ten, land which had been used for the grazing of horses. Then, in 1935, a splendid new clubhouse was erected. When, during the war, the Lord Mayor of Manchester opened his sportsmen's appeal in aid of the British Red Cross Society, the Northenden Golf Club rose to the occasion and on 18 February 1940 an exhibition match was arranged. Famous players, such as Henry Cotton and Dick Burton, gave their services entirely free, combining with Northenden Golf Club to help the war effort.

Founded in 1876, the Wythenshawe Cricket Club continued to flourish throughout the early part of the century and into the 1920s. One resident spoke of how his grandfather had played in an inter-gentlemen's house game for the 'Hall'. These matches were held on a private ground in Wythenshawe Park, 'still distinguishable between the main path and the Hall, although it is now grassed over'. Teams from houses in outlying Cheshire, such as Capesthorne Hall, competed. The Lord of the Manor, R. H. G. Tatton, had been so keen on the sport that he hired a private cricket coach. This then was the background to cricket in Northenden and Wythenshawe. At a later date they played on a field bounded by Longley Lane on one side and, roughly, Harper Road on the other. This land was only rented and eventually the strip bordering Longley Lane was sold for housing and the pitch had to be moved back. The changing hut also had to be moved, but as it was made in sections it was easily handed over the hedge into the adjoining field. This change of venue was not a new experience for the hut, as it had previously stood on the lawn of Beech House in Yew Tree Lane, doing military service as a hospital ward during the First World War. All this was happening at about the time that Manchester Corporation was stretching out its tentacles to catch in its net as much land as possible for the promotion of its garden city, but when it attempted to buy this particular piece it was strongly opposed by concerned members of the village, although the club was very short of funds. To raise funds, a company was floated in 1932/3 and this enterprise was helped with the gift of land from the Hewlett family, on condition that £25 was given annually to the Wood Street Mission.

Manchester continued to negotiate for the land and, knowing that eventually an irresistible offer might be made, the club decided to offer the land to the National Playing Fields Association, with a proviso that while there existed a Wythenshawe Cricket Club that club should hold the ground. If it went out of being then the land would revert to the National Playing Fields Association. On this ground three tennis courts were also marked out and in the winter a lacrosse team rented the area. On Wednesday afternoons the Northenden Wednesday Cricket Club used the pitch, being a group of local traders 'who liked to knock a ball about on their afternoon off'.

The lacrosse team eventually became amalgamated with the cricket club and used the site as their permanent winter home. This team was a combination of two local groups, the South Manchester and the Wythenshawe lacrosse teams. Until the coming of the war both cricket and lacrosse teams played regularly and had good followings, but by 1940 the ranks were much depleted as all the fit young men were called up, and so for the youths of the village play was postponed indefinitely. The field was taken over by the War Office and was used by the local Home Guard to perform their manoeuvres. The lacrosse players who were left were undaunted, and found a new home on the playing fields near Kenworthy Hall, now covered by the motorway. The daughter of a referee at that time recalls: 'The players got changed in our garage, we had large tin baths which they filled with cold water for a quick wash after the game, and my mother would make them pots of tea to warm them up . . .'. In view of the coldness of the season in which lacrosse is played, this must have been much appreciated!

Also in this area at the far end of Kenworthy Lane, behind Guest's Nursery, where the lacrosse men had their spartan baths, and down Tom Tit Lane was the Northenden Methodist Tennis Club. This club continued to be used during the war and for some time after it.

The Northenden Social Club began after the First World War as an ex-servicemen's club, 'The Northenden Comrade's of the Great War Club'. It later widened its membership and in 1923 changed its name to 'Northenden Comrades and Social Club'. Eventually it acquired larger and more splendid premises, fronting onto Palatine Road by the side of the church school. This was in 1926. Throughout the 1920s and 1930s the club continued to flourish and grow, fulfilling the words of a President of the Club in the 1920s, Mr. Hampson. In one of his speeches, referring to a criticism that, at various times, the club had been called a station, a picture house and a factory, Mr. Hampson said:

> Well, the club is a station. It is the terminus for members who after a day's work go there to have a pleasant time in the company of their fellows. As for a picture house, the only pictures that could be supplied were the very pleasant ones of the lady members playing tennis. Factories are places where something is made. The Club is a place where friends are made and good comradeship found and enjoyed,

and he went on to say he hoped 'it would be of great use and service to the village'.

As the club expanded, it became obvious that living accommodation on the premises was needed for the steward and his family. It was built in 1929 at a cost of £670. These living quarters were built above the clubhouse. A resident, who was a child at the time, records a view from the extension during the war.

> The living quarters were reached via some steep, dark stairs at the top of which was a passage with doors opening off it, and at the end of the passage a large, light airy room. The end wall in this room was composed almost entirely of windows from which you could see across the bowling green, the tennis courts, past the air raid shelter, which was used by the school, to Parkfield Road.

Among the members of the club in the 1930s and 1940s was Wilfrid Pickles of ''Ave A Go' fame. Although a radio star, his face became well known to the children of St Wilfrid's School, the girls mainly, for the Billiard Room of the club was high above the girls' playground. Often he would lean through the window of the club with friends, watching the children at play.

Through the years many of the trophies for competitions were donated by club members encouraging the various sports. There was the Hampson Cup for tennis and bowls, and the Hewlett Shield for billiards. In 1938 a resolution was adopted to drop the word 'Comrades' from the title and the club became known as the Northenden Social Club. To quote once more from the souvenir handbook of 1941: 'It is safe to say that many hundreds of friendships had been formed in the club and not a few of these have led to the life-long comradeship of marriage'.

From 1921, when the Northenden Amateur Dramatic Society — the N.A.D.S. — was formed from what had been the bible class run by Mrs. Herald, the curate's wife, into the 1930s, the society continued to develop and grow, usually producing about six plays a year, which were sometimes performed in the Church Rooms and sometimes in the open air of the Rectory garden. As time went on it amassed a large amount of equipment, which it found difficult to store. Over the years there were several rehearsal places, one of which was an old stable off Palatine Road (now used as a store room by Geoff Holmes, plumbers' merchants). On the upper floor (the loft) actors rehearsed in a steaming aroma of fish glue. This pungent liquid was constantly bubbling in a pan on a small gas-ring for use by Bill Roper, who was constructing and repairing the scenery in the area below. On the Sunday before the play opened all the properties and scenery were transported the short distance up Palatine Road to the Church Rooms, where actors, painters and producers alike would feverishly set to and enlarge the front of the stage by means of trestle tables, and erect a proscenium arch and scenery in preparation for the dress rehearsal on the following Monday night. After playing for five nights, usually to packed houses, similar feverish activity would remove all traces of their world by lunch-time. Matins, however, had depleted congregations on those Sundays. Many of the local community were involved in these activities, as a stage electrician of the 1930s said: 'I managed at the time to get biscuit tins from Brooke's Bakery which was on Sharston Road, and I went to see Frank Hatton the blacksmith who made the arches to fasten onto the biscuit tins so that I could make these into floodlights'.

One memorable occasion for this group occurred in January 1939 when the N.A.D.S. shared second place in the *News Chronicle* Amateur Dramatic Contest, which was staged at the Fortune Theatre in London. One member reported the event:

> It was an excited group of amateur players that entrained for London on 9th January, their destination was the Fortune Theatre, where five teams were competing in the *News Chronicle* Amateur Dramatic Contest. The first prize was a silver trophy and the N.A.D.S. meant to win it for Northenden. The *News Chronicle* provided excellent accommodation at the *Waldorf Hotel*, Aldwych, and spared no expense in entertaining their guests. The Fortune Theatre, tucked away behind Drury Lane, is small but very cosy, although members of the cast found its backstage passages somewhat confusing. Tuesday was devoted to intensive rehearsals, during which several hitches occurred, but only served to key the players up to concert pitch, and make them all the more determined to give the performance of their lives. The man in the box office assured a member who was booking tickets that an excellent company was playing that night, and this was retailed to a very gratified cast. The great evening arrived, the house was packed even to the boxes, the curtain arose and the show was on. Two hours later the players felt it had been a good effort, but they were quite unprepared for the splendid ovation given them by the audience, the curtain rose at least a dozen times before the thunder of applause ceased. A tired but happy company left the stage for their dressing rooms to take off their grease paint, but on the way they were met by a crowd of friends who literally mobbed them and there was a glorious reunion with lots of old members of the society who now live in London and had come to see the N.A.D.S. perform. The excursion was voted a never to be forgotten experience by the fortunate members who formed the cast of *The Letter Box Rattles*.

So the N.A.D.S. continued to flourish until the war came. When many of their numbers were called up or became engaged with war work, the society decided to close down for the duration of the war. There were, however, one or two people who had been members of the N.A.D.S., who were willing to try to carry on with the youngsters still in the village. So a few people, including Bill Roper and Frank and Joan Whitehurst, took it upon themselves to gather together a few drama enthusiasts, who produced a play, the proceeds of which (£4) went into the Rosemary Fund. They borrowed the N.A.D.S.'s equipment and performed under their name at first. It seemed, however, inappropriate to use the society's title for this young group of amateurs, so they put their heads together and came up with the decision to call the new group 'The Younger Generation'. Under this heading and very enthusiastic leadership, they went from strength to strength. There were many improvisations in equipment, make-up, lighting and heating because of wartime restrictions. But one of the advantages of the war regulations was the large Morrison shelter in the back room of the Church Rooms that so comfortably held so many trays of tea for refreshment time.

The war ended and the old members began to return. Now it was going to be a question of whether those old members of the N.A.D.S. who had ruled the society with a rod of iron before the war were going to get back into power or whether the whole thing was going to change.

27. Rosemary Petal Festival, Yew Tree School, 1938. The Northenden charity made use of Yew Tree School for its summer festivals.

Another significant body of the 1930s was the Rosemary Fund (rosemary for remembrance), set up as a local charity in 1934. The primary object of the fund was to see that no child in the district went without a holiday in the summer because of adverse circumstances, and old people, too, were to be cared for by receiving coal in the winter and food parcels when necessary. Knowing that this sort of deprivation could be found in and around Northenden, the local shopkeepers, members of the Rotary and a few public-spirited villagers got together, rented some committee rooms over a shop on Palatine Road, and, with Arthur Royle, the local bank manager, as treasurer, they set about raising money. By 1939 the *Parish Magazine* reported: 'During the past three years something like 800 children from this area have had a holiday who otherwise wouldn't have had one'.

By 1939 the Wythenshawe estate had been growing for a few years and then had the problems that usually go with a working-class housing area: large families, low-paid jobs and lack of money for 'luxuries', such as holidays and substantial clothing. The people who ran the fund were well aware of this and, while acknowledging that the Manchester Education Authority were beginning to make provisions for children in need of holidays, they felt that:

> This will allow the Rosemary Fund to extend the scope of its benefactions in other directions. Many of the children on these new estates suffer from the lack of suitable clothing during the winter months. The Fund has decided to make this their main avenue, in the disposal of its charities, at the same time making sure that no child misses its holiday, and also providing one in the case of convalescence.

Amongst the fund-raising activities was one that became very popular, the regular dances, which were held in the Church Rooms on Kenworthy Lane on Tuesday nights. The entrance fee from these dances, 6d. during the war, went into the Rosemary Fund for a time. These dances were known as the Fellowship Club or, as a youngster of the time recalls, 'The Tuesday Hop'. Other groups ran whist drives, football matches, bowling matches, performed plays, or held jumble sales, and as a result of their efforts money flowed into the fund.

Another source of revenue was the annual Rosemary Pageant, for which a young girl was chosen as Rosemary Queen. Tradesmen loaned and furnished floats on which children, appropriately dressed, performed tableaux while the vehicles processed slowly through the village and out to a pre-arranged venue. In 1939 it was Yew Tree School's Playing Fields. Here they were met with a gala atmosphere, there were stalls, competitions, races and many other entertainments. This was a red-letter day in the life of Northenden and people from the surrounding estates flocked to join in. The theme of the Rosemary Fund was one of caring, as we read in the rector's words:

> Its aim is not to patronise the lot of those whose life is cast in unpleasant places but to uplift, not so much to help as to enable people to help themselves, to leave no section of the community in a position of isolation through poverty, but to bring them within the community circle. The Fund knows no sects and no sections.

Community and Church in the new Wythenshawe

The people on the growing Wythenshawe estates had to travel to Northenden, Gatley or Sale for most of their entertainment in the early years. No provision of community halls or cinemas was made when the houses were planned. There were one or two existing pubs; for instance, the two-up-and-two-down cottage pub on the site where the *Royal Oak* now stands, and the *Gardener's Arms* on Wythenshawe Road. The *Benchill* and the *Sharston* hotels were erected near the beginning of the project, but there was nowhere for families to get together and socialise. Rackhouse started a community association (C.A.) in 1935 in a large, old converted house in Daine Avenue and, as the Royal Oak estate grew, across the other side of the park, members of this Association contacted the Royal Oak residents with offers of help. They had heard the people were collecting pennies in the hope of building a hut on Pitfield Gardens. One resident, who was a child at the time recalled:

> ... the Royal Oak people were collecting their pennies each week to get their little hut ... and Rackhouse contacted Royal Oak but they all worked independently and got together for Rose Queens. Then one Rose Queen would invite the other Rose Queen to their functions and all the Association would go ...

These Rose Queen events, as well as being a method of developing good community feelings, were also a source of revenue. Royal Oak residents, however, were more fortunate than Rackhouse financially, for they had on their committee a cobbler who worked for Noel Timpson, the shoe manufacturer and well-known philanthropist. Through this employee Mr. Timpson heard what the people were attempting to do and he said that he would build them a proper centre. A site was purchased right in the middle of Royal Oak and a

28a and b. Carnivals, pageants and parades of 1937. Displays involving children were popular with emerging community associations. These pictures were taken in the Sale Road area of the Rackhouse Association, one of the first to be formed along with Royal Oak and Benchill.

community hall, costing £4,000, was built. A group of trustees were appointed and a constitution was drawn up, which stated that there must be no alcohol in the building, no political meetings and no religious meetings. These rules were strictly adhered to and Mr. Timpson always took a keen interest, attending the A.G.M. and helping out if a large item was needed. The Royal Oak Community Centre flourished, holding dances, putting on pantomimes, plays and other dramatic entertainment, and offering other more sedate pastimes, such as whist drives and handicraft circles.

A third community association developed about this time in Benchill. Like Rackhouse, it too held its meetings in a converted house, 'The Cedars' on Woodhouse Lane. Here the same type of activities as those at Royal Oak took place and, of course, they too had their Rose Queen.

The interest of the local residents of Northenden in the activities at Benchill and Lawton Moor was great. Many people were sympathetic towards them and wished to help with their problems, as can be seen in the work of the Rosemary Funds. The Church, however, sounded less welcoming, for when the Diocesan Conference of 1932 discussed this new entity, Wythenshawe, feelings were mixed. The Bishop of Manchester stressed that Manchester must not avoid its responsibility in this matter, but one speaker at the conference said, 'We are ready to marry a beautiful bride, but ought she not to bring a dowry with her?'. The annexed Christians of the garden city were later to prove more than adequate in raising money to build their own churches.

The planners had catered well for the physical needs of the people coming to live in Wythenshawe. The philosophy underlying Barry Parker's dream manifested itself in light, airy homes set in pleasant rural surroundings, yet there were those who were well aware that there was a spiritual need that could not be filled by the existing churches in Northenden: St Wilfrid's Church of England, St Hilda's Roman Catholic, the Northenden Methodist Church and the Mission Hall. The Bishop of Manchester, Dr. Guy Warman, had opened a £50,000 appeal fund for the building of new churches on the housing estates which were going up around the city in the 1930s, and in 1937 he declared that half the money collected was being spent in Wythenshawe. This was revealed during his address at the consecration of St Michael's and All Angels, Lawton Moor, the first Wythenshawe church to be built.

People in the newly-built area of Rackhouse had previously worshipped at a Mission Hall on Altrincham Road, built in 1934 as a temporary church and still standing (1989), opposite the *Royal Oak* public house. At about the same time a site was bought for a parsonage and church on Orton Road. The Bishop stipulated that no more than £10,000 should be spent on the building of this church, which was to be dedicated to St Michael, and almost as if by some magical power the cost was kept to £9,400. This was not without effort and scheming on the part of the builders and architect.

> Offers to tender the cost were carefully considered by the architect and the contract was finally given to Messrs. J. Clayton and Sons of Denton. This was an extremely satisfactory choice as verified later during the building, the firm worked with the architect in a close spirit of friendship, and it must be remembered that even for the day the church was extremely inexpensive . . . the builders must have drawn little or no profit but they took a great interest in their work.

The architect, Cachmaille Day, said in one of his letters to Rev. Nightingale, the Rector of St Michael's, 'I am fortunate in obtaining a tender for £9,400 for this church as the cost is only 8½d. per cubic foot . . .'. And yet, despite the necessity to keep down the cost, he later wrote, 'Of all my churches, this is the favourite for it has many interesting points and the construction makes it possible to express new ideas'.

It is an extremely interesting church and yet, when Cachmaille Day was approached to build it, he declared that he did not altogether favour a modern church. The church he eventually designed and built was unique and modern, so unusual that the only other similar design is in Canada. More important than this is the realisation that, although there arose, in practical terms, a beautiful building, in human terms there developed a group of dedicated people who worked harmoniously together with pleasure and satisfaction. This kind of outcome was soon to be repeated all over Wythenshawe. The foreman of the building operations in his spare time carved the Bishop's Chair from oak and offered it as a gift to the church. Each aspect of the church was given much care and thought. The star-shaped design meant that there was a large open area and the congregation could be as near as possible to the pulpit and the altar, so feeling truly united in the act of corporate worship. The east window was designed by Christopher Webb, a well-known stained glass artist. It shows '. . . numbers of heavenly hosts, Cherubim and Seraphim facing into the church, the blue ground of the glass which suggestes space being relieved by the red wings of the Seraphs . . .'. When the sunlight streams through this window, particularly the morning sunlight, the window glows and fills the sanctuary with red and blue patterns. The price of all the stained glass was only £375. The altar frontal, St Michael with outspread arms, was also designed by Mr. Webb, and embroidered by Mrs. Ozanne, well-known for her beautiful church embroidery. The builder, Mr. Clayton, gave the gold cross, which hangs centrally in the sanctuary. The architect, who had desired himself to donate the cross, instead gave the two Italian Renaissance candlesticks and also asked to be allowed to contribute to the church's Two-Year Plan.

St Michael's church and rectory, along with the next church described, St Luke's church at Benchill, was to be listed as of special architectural interest, though the roofs of both buildings were in time to give trouble.

Throughout the building of this concrete and glass temple there is a theme of care and love shown by the experts, and it continued to be there in the congregation, as the community of St Michael quickly flourished and thrived. The Bishop of Manchester, Dr. Warman, in a dedication speech as he laid the foundation step of the Mission Hall, said:

> . . . some homes are like heaven but it is the people and not the place that make them so. You can have the best house in the world with every contraption to make life easy. Our task is to try to plant heaven in every home in Wythenshawe.

It seems that at Lawton Moor they had got the best of both worlds.

A similar development of spiritual life was going on in another part of the newly developing Wythenshawe estate. By 1934 houses were springing up at the south end of the parish, in the Benchill area. At that time there was no Mission Hall. The only available building for worship was Hollyhedge Farm and into this house the incumbent, Rev. Colin Lamont, moved in March. He announced that there would be Church and Sunday School the following Sunday and a notice to this effect was stuck on the farm gate with a drawing pin. He recorded in graphic detail the response:

> The farm was like a rabbit warren. I packed the Church rooms with children, then the second Church room (both the size of ordinary sitting rooms) and still they came. I turned the maid out of our kitchen and I packed that. Some sat on the hearth rug, then the kitchen dresser and table, then the window ledge; then I brought in bricks, bit of old timber, odd rugs, laid them on the store floor and made the children sit on those; still they came; I looked round and noticed the farmhouse outhouse and loft. I filled both these places with children and still they poured mercilessly in. I asked my wife if I could put some on our bedroom landing upstairs. She consented, and I trailed a party of children up to our private rooms. (I wish you could have seen them when the children had gone, the curtains were upside down and it was chaos with toffee papers.) Still the children came.
>
> I dashed down to the Church room to find the place a bedlam. Some children were frightened by the crowd in such a small place, and were crying; half a dozen were sitting on the Altar rails and as I moved forward to get them off, the rails collapsed with a crash and precipitated the children

onto the floor; I had visions of broken arms and legs but thank goodness, nobody was hurt. I turned from one packed room to another like a hunted animal — not knowing which way to go. To my amazement when I looked at my watch it was time to close and there was no time for a Lesson.

This show of enthusiasm made it obvious to the ecclesiastical authorities that there was need for a purpose-built church in Benchill, so a site was obtained. As this was on undeveloped land, without roads or drains, it was decided to buy a temporary hut costing £27 10s. Unfortunately, this hut was in such poor condition that it cost £40 to be erected. At first the hut was the answer to the problem of overcrowding, but as Rev. Lamont wrote:

> Unfortunately the hut was neither soundproof nor weatherproof. Every sound made in the hut was heard by the people in the houses around and as young people are not the quietest of creatures, we became somewhat unpopular in certain quarters. The trouble caused me many hours of uneasiness.
>
> The weather was another difficulty. I have been in the hut in the winter when the water in the flower vases on the altar has been frozen solid and I have been there in the summer when the altar candles have been melted over double with the heat. Rain and cold were our biggest enemies; mopping off pools of water on chairs and pews was a regular occurrence before Sunday services and two or three buckets and a large bath, under the weak spots in the roof, were always part of our interior fittings. To see our Church officers carefully manoeuvring them so that they could catch three or four or even five drops at a time was an inspiration.
>
> Frozen feet was a common characteristic of those days and we often advised our congregation to come in two pairs of socks rather than stay away. If people did stay away we told them they were soft and accused them of degenerate Christianity. We were 'up against it' and desperate circumstances meant desperate treatment.

Despite all these physical difficulties, the spiritual life of the Anglican community in Benchill continued to advance, as seen in the development of the Mothers' Union, the Church Lads' Brigade, the Girls' Friendly Society, the Men's Club and the St Luke's Players. In 1936, when the Bishop of Manchester dedicated the church hall, the church in Benchill was well established and growing. On 11 March the Church of St Luke the Physician was consecrated. Unlike the architect of the church in Lawton Moor, Mr. W.C. Young, the architect of this church, had not aimed at uniqueness in design. To quote his own words from his survey,

> The Church in the past has been the dominant feature of every town and village of England. Following such tradition, the Church of St Luke the Physican is designed to express outwardly the service to which it is to put and to be a lasting landmark. No striving after sensational effect is aimed at, but a feeling of strength and endurance has been the motif.

29. St Hilda's Roman Catholic Church, Kenworthy Lane. Built by Mrs. Ziba Ward in 1901 'for working class Anglicans' — who did not appreciate her largesse. It was bought by the Catholics in 1904. The Roman Catholic church of SS John Fisher and Thomas More was built at Benchill in 1935. St Hilda's was replaced in 1970 by a striking building reminiscent of Liverpool's Roman Catholic Cathedral.

The Roman Catholic Church of St Hilda's, on Kenworthy Lane, was a small wooden building and in the late 1930s was beginning to be inadequate for the growing band of Roman Catholic worshippers. Also it was not within easy reach of the two new estates and people looked around for more accessible places to worship, as a pioneer on the Royal Oak Estate recollects:

> As we were Catholics, Sunday Mass was a must. At first we trekked to St. Hilda's at Northenden or spent a precious tuppence going down the Parkway to St. Ambrose's. We had to walk back since two tuppences for bus fares was out of the question. Later a Mass centre was opened at the Sharston Tea Rooms and we attended here until the Church of St. John Fisher and Thomas More was opened in 1935. Our fifth daughter was baptised there only a week after the church had opened. We had a bus for the Tea Rooms (one penny and you could walk back), and as our church was built about the centre of Benchill it was difficult to get there and we began to think that we might move to Benchill and be ready when a school should open.

In August 1935 the Church of St John Fisher and St Thomas More was opened with a seating capacity of five hundred and fifty.

The Nonconformists, too, were very conscious of the need to provide a place of worship for their followers. During the early part of the building of the estate they had been allocated time for their devotions in the Sharston Tea Rooms, as had the Roman Catholics, who said Mass there on a Sunday. As the congregation grew these premises became unsatisfactory and the Methodists erected the first purpose-built church on the Wythenshawe estate on Broad Oak Road in 1934, the Brownley Green Methodist Church. On the other side of Wythenshawe, in Lawton Moor, a Methodist chapel was opened in October 1936 on Button Lane. Prior to this, worship had taken place in Mrs. Kilpatrick's house and later in a hut on the site of the present church. The Salvation Army built a meeting place for 100 people on Boothfield Road in 1937 and the Quakers were accommodated at Rackhouse Community Association Centre from 1935 until 1939, when their own Meeting House was erected at the junction of Wythenshawe Road, Sale Road and Palatine Road.

Northenden was never short of public houses, no less than seven lying within a mile radius, and four of these within 300 yards of the church. These four still exist, although in a changed form, and include the *Church Hotel*, the *Crown Inn*, the *Spread Eagle* and the *Tatton Arms*. The other two were the *Jolly Carter* on Royle Green Road, the oldest pub building, with foundations dating back to the 18th century (it was rebuilt about 1979), and the *Farmers' Arms* on Longley Lane, originally just converted cottages to which elaborate facades were added.

By contrast the public houses which were built in Wythenshawe in the 1930s were of very different construction. They were tall, rather imposing buildings, such as the *Benchill Hotel*, the *Sharston Hotel* and the *Royal Oak*, which itself replaced a picturesque cottage pub. At this time licences were not generally granted to social and community clubs.

Chapter Six

The War
'I Suppose We Got Off Pretty Lightly'

In terms of physical damage inflicted by enemy action, Northenden and Wythenshawe survived the war relatively intact. This was all the more remarkable when we consider that the great industrial complex of Trafford Park and the city centre of the regional metropolis were within a stone's throw of the district. For the A.R.P. wardens and fire-watchers in the early years of the war looking up at the enemy bombers droning overhead towards their selected targets the expression 'not far as the crow flies' must have taken on a new significance.

Apart from the proximity of established heavy industry and the city centre, Wythenshawe itself had recently acquired a new significance as a highly imaginative housing and planning venture not without its importance for civilian morale and the hopes for a more just and caring post-war society. Although the industries established at Wythenshawe just before and during the war became increasingly important to the national war effort, they were on a relatively small scale compared with their local big brothers. On the southern edge of the district, at Ringway, despite being the wartime scene of major aircraft development and large-scale paratroop training operations, the hastily-laid tarmac runway not only survived the war, and in particular a Luftwaffe attack in November 1940, but was still in use up to the end of the 1970s without any radical resurfacing work having been done in the interim.

Inevitably a number of heavy bombs did drop in the area. During an air raid on the night of 6-7 September 1940 a bomb fell in the Mersey near Ford Lane. Emergency work was undertaken to strengthen the embankments, which had been unsettled, the natural hazard of severe flooding being as great a threat as enemy action. Several Northenden residents recall another incident involving an unexploded bomb which fell on the land adjoining Homewood Road. Nearby homes were evacuated, one of which was put at the disposal of the police to allow a watchful eye to be kept on the bomb until it was successfully defused. One landmine destroyed The Poplars and Alderbriar House on Palatine Road, near the bridge. The German Luftwaffe also managed to score a direct hit on the toilets in Mill Lane. Several other landmines, probably intended for Trafford Park, were dropped in the area but, like the one which landed near Baguley Sanatorium, failed to explode. One landmine, however, which came down in Floats Road, demolished several houses and resulted in one fatality.

Incendiaries, however, caused considerably more damage to property, and compulsory fire-watching duties were soon introduced by the government, which required men of between 16 and 60 to put in a minimum of 48 hours per month. One resident remembers an incendiary on the Rectory Cottage roof and the damage that could be done if prompt action was not taken. A retrospective article in the post-war *Wythenshawe Express* refers to the hard work put in by the A.F.S.

> With the outbreak of War A.F.S. bases were set up at the Cedars, in the grounds of Baguley Hospital and at Henley Garage, Northenden. All stations were fully occupied by two successive raids shortly before Christmas 1940. German bombers ringed the estate with incendiary bombs using chandelier flares as markers. It is believed their objective was Ringway.

Assistance to the A.R.P. wardens, fire-watchers and the fire brigade was given by the

30. Styal Road, Gatley, 1941. When No. 44 was hit grandmother Dukinfield, with a fractured pelvis, cried as she was rescued, 'We are in the Lord's hands'.

local constabulary. On hearing the sirens all policemen based at Moor End had to report for duty to the station and were then deployed where necessary, giving what help they could to extinguish fires and evacuate occupants. In January 1941 four farms in the Baguley area suffered incendiary damage. At one of them, Newall Green Farm, two hay sheds were destroyed, while at another, Old Wood Farm, a large Dutch barn was lost. Both farmers saw their entire hay and straw crops destroyed (they could submit a claim under the War Damage Scheme).

Adapting to war

Schools figured prominently in the wartime domestic economy of Northenden, staying open for meals during holidays to allow mothers to work, and to work longer hours. Temporary nursery accommodation was provided throughout the area and the Church Rooms were used not only for lunchtime meals for school children but also as an emergency receiving centre for people made homeless through enemy action. During air raids children would be ushered to shelters where, equipped with lamp, first-aid box and gas masks, the teacher called a register and 'entertained' the gathering as best she could with the chanting of tables, singing and poetry recitations. One ex-teacher at St Wilfrid's remembers that the staff were instructed to summon the Home Guard in the event of an invasion by vigorously ringing the school bell. Needless to say, this mode of raising the alarm was, fortunately, never put to the test. School staff, along with many other citizens, regularly went to the Manchester Royal Infirmary and later to Nell Lane to give blood. One particularly interesting note in the Haveley Hey Junior School logbook for January 1940 tells us: 'Owing to the shortening of school life and the fact that needlework lessons have largely been devoted to knitting 'comforts for the troops', some modifications are being made in the needlework scheme'. One hopes that the 'shortening of school life' was not owing to direct enemy action . . .

The urgency of war brought renewed interest in Further Education. The one-time treasurer who had helped to found the Northwerthen Guild in 1936 reported: 'The Guild continued to flourish during the war and classes were held usually in private houses, under the great difficulties of blackouts and air-raids'. If the outward signs of enemy action were not extensive there were plenty of other reminders that Northenden and Wythenshawe were districts of a country at war.

Ringway, though never requisitioned by the Air Ministry, soon became a major service base, with over sixty thousand paratroopers passing through the training school in the course of the war. Over half-a-million drops were made from Ringway, especially over Rostherne and Tatton. For a time in 1940 the newly-formed Glider Training Squadron was at Ringway, before moving to Thame in Buckinghamshire. The airport and its immediate environs were also host to a number of important aircraft projects and test flights. A. V. Roe developed and produced the York transport plane at Ringway — 85 for the R.A.F. and some for B.O.A.C., including 'Ascalon' for Winston Churchill's personal use. But the more famous association was that with the legendary Lancaster, which, though not in production at Ringway, was developed and tested there in 1940-1. The A. V. Roe Lincoln bomber appeared in 1944.

All this activity meant that there were thousands of servicemen in the area. Many prefabricated blocks were built to house them on Outwood Lane, Woodhouse Lane and elsewhere in Wythenshawe. Existing premises were deployed where planning permission could be obtained. A vacant shop in Northenden, for example, was used by the Y.M.C.A. to provide recreational facilities for R.A.F. personnel, while the White House, Princess Parkway, was taken over for mess and officer accommodation. Nissen-type huts were also erected and we read in the minutes of the Wythenshawe Estate Special Committee that it considered planning permission for R.A.F. recreation and canteen facilities in the Parkwood neighbourhood. It was usual for the Wythenshawe Committee to lease land to the appropriate ministries at nominal rents on the understanding that land would be returned to its former state on the cessation of hostilities. At one point in 1943 such was the pressure on accommodation that even some of the precious houses in Wythenshawe were requisitioned for services' use. The sudden increase in the volume of traffic moving to and from Ringway necessitated various road improvements. Woodhouse Lane was widened, although work was delayed owing to the general shortage of timber for fencing, and later, in 1941, improvements were made to Ringway Road.

The long-awaited Northenden Bus Garage was completed in 1938. A year later it was commandeered by the Ministry of Aircraft production for A. V. Roe. For them the garage was ideally positioned, close to Northenden Station on the Cheshire Lines and providing connections with Manchester, Liverpool and all parts of the country, so parts for assembling into planes could be brought in by rail. It had another advantage, the closeness of Ringway. As has already been mentioned, A. V. Roe's prototype bombers were tested and developed at the newly-opened Ringway Airport.

Late in 1940 M.C.T., because fuel was in short supply, only ran its Wythenshawe buses as far as Southern Cemetery, to meet the trams, apart from some rush-hour journeys. At first the buses turned round at Nell Lane, but empty-running from Barlow Moor Road to Nell Lane was stopped by the building of a level crossing. Services 43, 45 and 46 were curtailed at Moss Side. Service 63 (originally the Organ and Watcher service) was withdrawn. At about this time there was a bus park on Lawton Moor, opposite Orton Road. It was a dispersal point to prevent loss due to air raids. A similar function was performed for the Princess Road Garage by a dispersal point in Alexandra Park, Moss Side.

The Cheshire Lines in the Second World War had a vital part to play, serving the ports of Liverpool, Birkenhead and Manchester. In addition to the port traffic, some very important government works were constructed at various points on the Cheshire Lines: the Ordnance factory at Risley, an R.A.F. Maintenance Unit at Burtonwood near Warrington, British Ethy Corporation Works at Plumley on the Northwich Line, and, of course, Northenden's own A. V. Roe aeroplane-assembly factory. Troop trains over the Cheshire Lines numbered 362 inwards and 881 outwards in 1944 (perhaps in preparation for 'D' Day), 509 in and 471 out in 1945. There was much war damage to the Cheshire Lines. The large goods warehouse at Manchester Central was bombed in 1940, the whole roof destroyed by incendiary bombs and the top floor also damaged. The nearest that bombs came to Baguley and Northenden Stations was when the viaduct carrying the M.S.J. & A.R. was breached at Castlefield and Old Trafford Junctions.

Complementing the full-time services in the area were the local, part-time forces which played such an important part in defence and safety on the Home Front. A.R.P. posts sprouted at strategic places, sometimes using existing premises like unused garages at Sale Circle. Fire-watchers' huts appeared, equipped with ladders and stirrup pumps, while the Home Guard not only had rifle ranges and drill areas — one of which was near the *Royal Thorn Hotel* — but its own band, the 47th Battalion, County of Lancaster H.G. This was to become the Wythenshawe Prize Band after the stand-down of the Home Guard in 1944.

On the domestic front allotments proliferated. The Wythenshawe Committee was careful to maintain a balance between encouraging allotments and home-grown produce, and the preservation of effective control. Great though the pressure was on the City Fathers to provide more and more land for cultivation, permission to plant unused land was given only where there would be no obvious destruction of some other visual or functional amenity. Several people and organisations were reprimanded by the Wythenshawe Committee for digging too zealously for victory! Grass verges and plots of naturalistic landscaping in Wythenshawe were carefully protected, an example of how conscientiously the committee tried to adhere to town and country planning ideals. Typical of the many allotment tenancies given during the war was one for a plot of land at the rear of Homewood Road of 340 square yards at an annual rent of 12s. 6d. Rates, where liable, would also be payable and land was to be used for the 'growing of foodstuffs' only. Many of these sites were temporary, granted for the duration of the war, since much of the vacant land available in 1939 was earmarked for development. After the war a good number of gardeners felt some bitterness at the new arrangements which the inexorable pressure of post-war housing needs forced on the council.

From the early days of the war permission was also sought to cultivate large plots of ground, which were unused or vacant. Permission was usually given, whether to farmer, smallholder or organisation, again on the understanding that such land would be wanted after the war for Wythenshawe development. In some cases, where the land was unsuitable for cultivation, the committee permitted livestock owners to graze their animals. Again after the war there was some resentment here, among smallholders especially, at having to give up, often at very short notice, land which had become valuable. This resentment, however, was mainly felt by families, who had farmed the land for a much longer period than the war years.

One particularly interesting and, at the time, unusual use of land was at Kenworthy Farm, where Mr. Davies obtained permission to reclaim land south of the Mersey and adjoining Princess Parkway which had been used for council tipping. He wanted to grow oats and, as there was very little experience of cultivating tipped waste, the City Surveyor recommended the scheme for its experimental nature. The results, he believed, would be of great interest and potential value to the country as a whole.

The war brought not always popular government involvement in the everyday lives of citizens: blackout, rationing and essential work registration, for example. Never before had so many aspects of daily life been touched by government bureaucracy and restraint. The blackout regulations, though essential, were far from popular. Many thought them too strict and limiting on easy or safe movement. One resident remembers the use of the Northenden Amateur Dramatic Society (N.A.D.S.) curtains as a blackout precaution on the East Window in St Wilfrid's, while another, an ex-police sergeant based at Moor End Station, described the difficulties encountered by night-time drivers. Moving in convoy through the unlit streets, motorists found it difficult to pick out pedestrians, who could often be moving swiftly to get out of the dark into relative safety. One accident recalled by the policeman involved a driver who failed to see the roundabout at the Princess Parkway-Palatine Road intersection, his car ploughing up the grass and shrubs before grinding to a halt on the central island.

The difficulties of getting about during the evening and at night did little to encourage social interchange and gatherings. Long hours at work and the gloomy effects of the blackout helped to foster home-based interests. Publishers, if they could obtain sufficient paper, enjoyed a minor boom, while the popularity of the BBC radio news, danceband and comedy series is well documented. It would be misleading, however, to suggest that there was no local social life outside the family and the gatherings of friends at home — on the contrary. The cinema, for example, played an important recreational role in helping to keep the Home Front going. Wythenshawe was without its own cinema and the lack of this valuable amenity continued to be one of the prime complaints of the residents throughout and after the war. For the time being Northenden and the city centre provided for the movie-going public.

Many local societies suffered, not only from the familiar privations and conditions of war, but also from the marked absence of men and women members! A combination of combatant and essential war work services soon began to take away large numbers of the most active members in all kinds of social, cultural and sporting bodies. In the immediate post-war years many societies tried reforming to attract old and new members and to pick up the often tattered threads of pre-war activities. The Northenden Choral Society continued with a ladies choir during the war, giving five or six charity concerts a year. In 1946 they were making attempts to attract ex-servicemen into their ranks but, as with other groups, they found that many men were still away from the district. Another group, which kept itself alive by adapting to temporary hardships, was the celebrated N.A.D.S. Closing down as such during the war, as has been mentioned already, it made most of its equipment and properties available to a 'small body of young people under military age', 'The Younger Generation', who kept the dramatic flag flying in Northenden. The Wythenshawe Cricket Club on Longley Lane, noted for its cricket and tennis activities, was another group whose members had been scattered all over the world but which was able to reform after the war (their premises had been kept warm by the Home Guard).

Other social and recreational needs were met by the three community associations (C.A.s) founded in the new areas of Wythenshawe in the mid-1930s. Their role as social, recreational and educational focal points in the new and inchoate communities of Benchill, Rackhouse and Royal Oak had had little opportunity to become defined and established before the war put an end to domestic building and scattered much of the membership, but they had begun to make their mark. According to their respective chairmen, the Rackhouse Association had 'flourished' pre-war, while the Benchill and District C.A. 'kept the flag flying' during

the war years. The chairman of the latter, Mr. H. Lloyd, was also chairman of the
Wythenshawe Community Council, founded in 1943 to 'unify opinion in Wythenshawe'
and, by representing as many facets of local life as possible, to give the Wythenshawe
resident and trader a voice in the city. The three C.A.s, together with a number of other
bodies, were federated to the Council. In retrospect it appears that the Rackhouse and
Royal Oak C.A.s all but petered out during the war, holding the occasional meeting but
struggling to keep together a nucleus of interested members. Benchill, with Mr. Lloyd at
the helm, seems to have provided more wartime activities at 'The Cedars'. There were, for
example, various activities for 14 to 18-year-olds. Moreover, Mr. Lloyd continued to stress
the importance of the C.A.s running their own affairs and managing their own premises if
they were to play a living part in the injection of new life and community spirit into post-
war Wythenshawe. More than once, however, during the war, the Wythenshawe Estate
Special Committee questioned whether or not the C.A.s were the best bodies to run these
centres.

Many social activities were directed towards helping the war effort. Potato-pie suppers
and fêtes were held, individual schools often adopting a particular ship or cause. One
group, the Happy Circle Club, founded in 1937 to help the local poor, turned its primary
efforts towards servicemen, sending 5s. postal orders to over a thousand men worldwide.
Prisoners of war from the Wythenshawe area were sent 200 cigarettes a month as a token
of friendship and support. The British Red Cross (East Lancashire County Branch) leased
premises in Northenden for 'bring and buy' work to help with the war effort. Activities like
these gave people a common, defined purpose, a meeting ground, and civilian morale, a
major aspect of total war, was kept from flagging too seriously.

'Queues, queues, queues . . .'
One of the more widely felt pressures of life in Britain at this time was food, or rather the
lack of it. Paradoxically, the introduction of rationing resulted in a speedy improvement in
the diet and health of many working people and, although money and the privileges that
went with it still called many tunes, shortages and the complete lack of certain commodities
were experienced across the social spectrum. Northenden, as a long-established township,
was well-provided with shops, but in Wythenshawe, where even before the war there was
an acute shortage of shopping and other local amenities, the war brought serious problems
for housewives. Travelling to other district shopping centres, like Gatley and Northenden,
became more difficult, especially on the regular basis required by rationing registration.
Housewives registered with what local traders there were and queues, a problem everywhere,
were particularly long. The council had agreed to build six permanent shops in Hollyhedge
Road and, although these had been started in 1939, work was delayed owing to the priority
use of building materials elsewhere. Approval was also given in December 1939 for two
sets of temporary shops at Panfield Road, Benchill and at Crossacres Road, Brownley
Green, the two least well-served neighbourhoods of Wythenshawe. This was several months
after the Estate Committee had received a letter from a local councillor asking about the
inadequate facilities and pointing out likely pressure on existing shops.

Complaints continued. Typical of these was a letter from the Wythenshawe Shelter and
Protection Committee in July 1941, again highlighting the difficulties brought about by
limited mobility, few and crowded shops and a lack of variety of potential purchases. The
City Surveyor promised to look into the possibility of further temporary shops and a little
later in the year a scheme for four more shops on Hollyhedge Road was sanctioned. These
were to be constructed from weather and plaster board on timber frames at a cost of £2,160.
By 1941 the council were beginning to appreciate the link between the war effort, morale
and adequate shopping facilities. At a meeting in April 1945 Mr. Lloyd, Chairman of

Wythenshawe Community Council, addressed the Wythenshawe Committee on the vexed, recurring question of amenities and community resources:

> ... the fact remained that although the Wythenshawe Estate has been in existence for a considerable number of years the Corporation have provided very little, apart from houses. They had built one public convenience and a cactus house, and the residents on the Estate did not consider it right that buildings should be erected for the preservation of plants, but that buildings required for human beings had not been provided!

By 1946 Mr. W. S. Shepherd, M.P. for Bucklow, was saying in the local press that Wythenshawe housewives were the worst off in the country in terms of access to food and clothing in local shops.

If shoppers in Wythenshawe had problems there were equally severe difficulties for the shopkeepers themselves. Some were unable to obtain sufficient supplies from distributors and were forced to relinquish leases or to turn down tenancies on shops vacant. The council showed considerable leniency during the war, deferring, where possible, rent and rate increases. One greengrocer was unable to meet an increase in rent because, in addition to the scarcity of fruit, many of his former customers were now growing their own vegetables. A butcher, pointing out that Wythenshawe residents were finding it difficult to buy conventional cuts of meat, applied for permission to add pork to his list of stock so that he could make 'brawns and cooked meats', for which there was a great demand. In February 1942 the Manchester and Salford Co-operative Society applied for further premises to rehouse their butchery department. The Assistant Secretary argued:

> Such a removal would undoubtedly be of material assistance in the reducing of the congestion which now occurs daily at this shop (190 Crossacres Road), and possibly this will be better appreciated when it is mentioned that there are upwards of 1500 family registrations for rationed commodities, both in the grocery and in the butchery sections, and in consequence there are queues being formed daily outside the premises.

The Society got its extra premises — a temporary shop up the road.

Of bricks and men — building and planning

Shopping, then, was one already difficult aspect of life in Wythenshawe aggravated by wartime conditions. There were other casualties. In fact, Wythenshawe, its conception and physical realisation, was the major casualty of the war. Within the first decade of the satellite town's development European hostilities meant an immediate Treasury embargo on all unnecessary expenditure, a massively broad category, including building and construction, which hit local authority housing. By November 1939 Manchester's committees were being asked to review all capital projects, completing only those necessary to the war effort or to the immediate welfare and safety of the population. A cash restriction was nationally enforced on local authorities. 'Consent [by the Ministry of Housing] to the exercise of borrowing powers will not be given unless the project is of pressing necessity either for reasons of public need or on account of war requirements.'

In the light of this Treasury requirement of September 1939, the City Engineer drew up a list of projects already or about to be begun. These included the purchase of land where the agreement for purchase had been completed, street and sewer works where adjoining houses had been completed or where there was likely to be significant industrial development, as in the Eastern Industrial Area, and the erection of shops. Until the problem of post-war housing became an urgent preoccupation of Manchester City Council (which it never really ceased to be, even throughout the bleakest early war years), it was the expenditure involved in industrial development which came up most often for approval by the council and government. In January 1940 the council had discussions with the Ministry of Health on the 'general question of capital expenditure which it may be necessary to incur in connection with proposals for the leasing of lands on the Estate'.

The emphasis placed on the restriction of borrowing powers for capital expenditure reflected the relative importance of borrowing in wartime conditions when a relative decline in the rate income could be expected. While the usual sources of local authority income dwindled, councils were faced with a heavy and on-going burden of civil defence work on top of their regular and manifold functions. It is not surprising, therefore, that by 1941 the Wythenshawe Committee was under great pressure to justify every pound spent. Amenities, such as community centres, swimming baths, libraries and the proposed civic centre itself, so essential to the integrated development of Wythenshawe as a town, were low down the list of priorities, except, of course, to the residents, who continued to feel these privations.

National and local government imposed such strict control on spending for reasons which conditions in the early war years dictated. With no comparable experience to draw on, the City of Manchester had to make meagre resources go a long way. Able-bodied labour was at a premium, especially as the government demanded a heavy commitment to civil defence work from local bodies. Building materials, especially timber and brick, became scarce and what was available was carefully directed towards essential work. Many builders in the area either had to abandon work already begun, leaving Homewood Road, Northenden, for example, partly developed, or if they had not begun the foundations, to relinquish the lease on the land. As with shopkeepers, the Wythenshawe Committee showed considerable flexibility. Some builders, unable to proceed because of lack of materials and labour, were given options on plots of land which could be taken up and further considered after the war. Knowing that it was unlikely that conditions would favour any substantial house-building programme during the war, the committee must have felt that it was a mutually convenient arrangement to let developers reserve land either for a nominal rent or no rent.

A further problem for builders was the completion of work for which estimates had been submitted and contracts drawn up before the war. Shortage of construction materials forced prices up and more than one developer found it necessary to submit revised figures to the committee. Early in the war a general guideline was established: 'In principle, the fact that war has broken out does not relieve a contractor from the terms of his contract unless it has become impossible of performance'. There were several ways around the problem, however, and one of these, employed as early as September 1939, was to build into a contract an additional payment clause which would allow the contractor to submit an invoice for 'unforeseen costs', subject, of course, to satisfactory accountability. This assumed that adequate resources could ultimately be found to finish the job, a big assumption indeed. In this, as in other areas, a readiness to adapt to new and difficult conditions was displayed by the Wythenshawe Committee.

In spite of these very real restrictions on wartime development, Wythenshawe continued to work hard at attracting suitable industry. Advertising on railway stations was not abandoned, although the posters were redesigned so as not to give the relative position of Ringway Airport. The Wythenshawe Committee and Supervisor received many applications for sites and, by 1945, 22 firms were established on the Eastern Industrial Area, with about sixty serious applications on the books. The immediate concern in 1939 was to develop the partially-occupied Eastern Industrial Area, Sharston, so construction resources were made available to continue the sewer and road works there. But as the war in Europe drew to a close extensive plans were being prepared to open up the Western and Southern Industrial Areas, with the City Surveyor and the City Engineer placing great emphasis on the importance of preparing the groundwork — both commercially and physically — for the expansion of post-war Wythenshawe industry.

Planning permission for factory development was usually given on the understanding

31. Sharston Industrial Area, 1940. Controlled development of factories continued in the war. The bus depot of 1938, with the largest single span roof at the time, was commandeered as an aircraft factory.

that available and temporary materials, like asbestos sheeting, would be replaced after the war by more permanent constructions. Some companies were allowed to take a site, develop part of it, but defer more extensive building until better materials were available. Throughout the war, however, there was no fundamental shift in planning standards. Relaxations of controls were to be seen as temporary expedients and even so new and existing firms were required to build acceptable front elevations with uniform forecourts. The committee, deciding that the industrial area still looked bare, had trees planted along the existing roads and asked firms to do what they could in the difficult circumstances to break up the monotony of their sites by planting shrubs and borders. Concern to maintain the ideals of garden-city industrial planning was always present during the war years.

Scrupulous attention was given to new proposals, especially to effluent-producing processes and office heating systems.

Commendable and remarkable though this environmental and planning concern was, there were growing misgivings about the type of industry attracted to Wythenshawe. Because of environmental constraints, most of the companies established before and during the war could be classed as light industry — food processing, electrical engineering, printing, clothing, soft-furnishing and so on. In the words of the City Surveyor, reporting to the Wythenshawe Committee:

> practically all the industry at present established at Wythenshawe employs a predominance of female labour, and unless a proper balance of male and female labour is obtained in the future, then the industrial areas will never fulfil their proper function — that of largely providing work for persons living on the Estate.

In the final year of the war the City Surveyor recommended two industrial applications, pointing out for one that, 'It is worthy of note that if this factory is established in Northenden 82% of male labour will be employed', and for the other commenting that, 'this particular industry employs 80% male labour which is a condition not generally met with on the Eastern Industrial Area as a whole'. If environmental considerations were too inflexible, he argued, then the objective of making Wythenshawe as self-sufficient as possible in terms of local employment opportunities could never be achieved.

As well as the concern to achieve a better balance between male and female employment prospects, there was a growing appreciation of the urgency with which facilities for new post-war industry would have to be provided if Wythenshawe was to have a chance of attracting sufficient and diverse industry to employ a large number of its new residents. It was estimated that only about thirty per cent of the industrial workers ultimately living in Wythenshawe could be employed locally, given the level of industrial development in 1943. A census for that year, taken for the City of Manchester Plan of 1945, indicated that the seven firms interviewed employed on average 63 per cent local labour. The council was urged to press ahead with further compulsory purchase orders for parcels of land in the Western and Southern Industrial Areas still privately owned. The road and services infrastructure for these areas ought be developed, so that firms could move in without delay. Apart from advertisements on major railway stations, such as Euston, Kings Cross and Crewe, newspaper advertisements were placed in 1945 exhorting local firms to act quickly! '. . . Sites at Wythenshawe are rapidly being taken up . . . Manchester firms who desire sites are advised not to delay their applications' — a good example of the old technique of making what you have to offer desirable by implying there's hardly any left.

The composition of the workforce reflected not only local circumstances, but also the various national arrangements and trends. The trade unions had reached agreements on the employment of women in traditionally male-dominated industries. By 1942, 6,311,000 women were employed nationally in the services and in industry. Bevin's 1941 Registration of Employment Order required all women of 20 and 21, later extended to all women of 18 to 50, to register for essential war work. Because Wythenshawe's factories were new and built with employees' welfare in mind, working conditions for local women were much better than in many of the older areas. But on what kind of war work were Wythenshawe's women and men working? Despite the relative infancy of industrial development at Wythenshawe, a number of firms made notable contributions to the war effort. Among these was Thomas French and Sons, Ltd., of Sharston Road. Founded in 1887, the Wythenshawe factory was built in 1935, and during the war 1,400 people were employed on a three-shift system, producing bullet clips and webbing for machine gun belts. The manufacturing processes were adapted from curtain-rail and curtain-tape production respectively. A post-war newspaper article reviewing the company's war effort commented on the composition of the work force — all but a handful lived on the estate and 70 per cent were women.

Another locally well-known firm busy at this time was George H. Scoles and Company. Founded in 1897, they moved from their city-centre premises to Wythenshawe in 1934, one of the first firms to take up a site in the 'countryside' of the Eastern Industrial Area. At the Wylex Works, Longley Lane, they worked on government contracts for aircraft switches and electrical control components. As in many other industries, war needs fostered change and speedy development. Components for bombers had to be small, light and highly efficient. Seemingly impossible deadlines were set for new and intricate switch designs. G.P.A., whose Wythenshawe factory was completed in 1940, were precision tool engineers, earning the wartime title of 'tool-room of the North'. The skills involved in making gauges and lathes were also employed in the manufacture of radar components and the gyrocontrols of gun-laying gear. The quality of many mass-produced goods depended on the precision tools from G.P.A. Victor H. Iddon and Co., Ltd., was another example of an enterprise playing a supportive role to other industry and the services. They turned out millions of lampholders and switches for munitions factories, aerodromes and military camps.

The quality and reliability of one particular company's products were very close to the hearts of thousands of men on active service. The Walmer Manufacturing Company were busy at their Longley Lane premises, machining parachute canopies for the Normandy landings. To enable them to expand their war work, planning permission was given to take over the adjacent premises of the British Fondants factory, a firm which had been forced to close owing to lack of sugar. Parachutes were folded with painstaking care on splinter-free, rubberised floors. Walmer also machined electrically-heated, kapok-lined flying suits and, no doubt, some of their work was put to the test at nearby Ringway and the Paratroop Training School.

The Wythenshawe Committee then was keen to attract new and environmentally compatible industry, with a view to providing adequate employment for men in the immediate post-war years. There was some discussion about the length of lease, 99 or 999 years, which was preferred by industry taking up new plots, and the importance of allowing subletting, to encourage small but essential enterprises to gain a foothold, was not overlooked.

But, in its keenness to develop the industrial aspects of Wythenshawe, the Wythenshawe Committee did not lose sight of the planning ideals it had set out with in the previous decade. This concern for maintaining the fundamental principles of contemporary town and country planning, and of Barry Parker's plans, in particular, survived the worst privations and pressures of the war. Although there was some relaxation of standards in the industrial sphere, dictated by the scarcity of certain building materials, heating and plant fuels, the city, through the Wythenshawe Committee, tried hard not to let the war bequeath an inheritance of poor design and workmanship. In December 1941, the City Architect brought to the attention of the Wythenshawe Committee a memorandum on standards of design and building on the Wythenshawe Estate. The memo, intended for potential builders, had been written and approved in 1939 but the war had interrupted publication (only one house had been begun in the interim). It recommended as the basis of future guidance to developers simplicity of design and avoidance of over-elaboration. Variety was to be achieved by interesting brick, variation of roof pitch and building lines, and by conservation of natural features. 'Good design,' the City Architect argued, 'is principally a matter of proportions and the proper use of materials'. Discussing workmanship, the memo insisted, 'All work must be of a lasting quality . . . Quality of work will be one of the principal recommendations for persons desiring to build on the Estate'. Especially where factories were concerned, potential developers had to have proven, high-quality work behind them.

This memo and other similar documents could do little more than recommend and guide once a developer had obtained a lease. In 1943, however, the Wythenshawe Committee approved the detailed architectural supervision of buildings: 'In the opinion of the City Architect it is essential in the interest of the development of the Wythenshawe Estate that the architects who design the buildings should be retained by the building owners to supervise their erection until the final completion'.

The nagging worry about standards of design and workmanship persisted. Early the following year, the committee were told about the Welwyn Garden City Company and its management of the different aspects of development. Mr. Rowe, the Estate Supervisor, had paid a recent visit to Welwyn and had discovered that the Garden City Company, as a parent organisation, owned subsidiaries which ran their own stores, brickworks, housing estates and factory areas. In Mr. Rowe's words, '. . . a unity of control is established which is not possible on the Committee's land at Wythenshawe'. Although some useful ideas could be gleaned from the Welwyn experience — it was suggested incidentally, that the committee should visit Letchworth and Welwyn — it was agreed that Wythenshawe, as a local authority-run major city satellite, had a more complex relationship with its potential residents and industry.

Further evidence of the city's unwillingness to sacrifice too much, even under pressure, was to be found in its reaction to a Ministry of Supply proposal in 1943 to use part of the Princess Parkway/River Mersey green belt for the open-air storage of cotton. Cotton had been in short supply but was now reaching Britain in large quantities. The Wythenshawe Committee adamantly refused to consider the Ministry's application, arguing that the temporary roads and other structures needed would do irreparable damage to the already scarce, 'near-natural' landscape. A few weeks later the Ministry made a further application, asking Manchester to reconsider its decision in the national interest. The Wythenshawe Committee, however, stood firm and confirmed its decision, although it was prepared to ask the City Surveyor to find an alternative open-air site.

Planning for the post-war years

Inexorable regional and national problems were, however, beginning to nudge Wythenshawe development along in certain directions, long before the war was over and the first domestic foundations laid. As early as 1943 the City Surveyor was presenting preliminary reports on post-war housing development, especially in relation to the proposed expansion of Ringway as a civil airport and the route of the Western Parkway. More and more emphasis was placed on Ringway as one of the economic keys to Manchester's and the North-West's post-war survival and prosperity. But good access to the airport was essential if it was to play a major part in the region's growth. Access to the city centre would be along Princess Parkway, which had been imaginatively planned — if not fully realised — to give Wythenshawe both a finely-landscaped, efficient route and a linear greenbelt into the parent, Manchester. Approval to extend the Parkway up to the Cheshire boundary had been given in 1940 and, together with the proposed Western Parkway along the southern and western boundaries of Wythenshawe, it was envisaged that the airport would be well-served. What this insistence on Ringway's economic importance did, however, was to shift the emphasis from Princess Parkway's role as an access route to Wythenshawe to its function as a fast and efficient link from the airport to the city centre. The lack of the Parkway extension, it had been argued in 1939, was impeding the development of the estate. By 1945, with a keen eye on the region's future, there had been some change of emphasis. Whatever the primary motive for extending this attractive roadway — and Barry Parker himself saw the need for this projection — any extension involved the bisecting of the Wythenshawe land, a division later etched in the landscape by the motorway of the 1970s.

As the country began to turn its thoughts to post-war reconstruction, plans for housing programmes gathered momentum. There was a feeling that the immediate dangers and gloom of the early war years were receding. With this feeling came a growing sense of urgency about the housing situation — a reawakening of the familiar problem. Although the Wythenshawe Committee retained its brief throughout the war to continue to purchase land for development, its job was made particularly difficult by the government's postponement of confirmation of a major compulsory purchase order, originally submitted in 1937. 1944 saw the committee working closely with the Ministry of Housing and the recently formed Ministry of Town and Country Planning, keeping government informed about Wythenshawe proposals and seeking smaller-scale compulsory purchase orders and borrowing powers to enable the groundwork for the first and second year post-war housing programmes to be started. Plans were submitted in March 1944 for the North-Western Neighbourhood Unit and existing tenants of smallholdings and farms were requested to vacate sites after their next full harvest. Mention has been made earlier of the resentment some of these tenants felt at the short notice given and, in some cases, at the upheaval involved in leaving land that had been intensively cultivated for many years. Clauses in the appropriate leases made it quite clear that the council could retake their land on the estate for sewerage and building purposes without notice. In giving up to four or five months notice the council believed it was easing the blow, allowing tenants to harvest their wheat, oats and potatoes.

Borrowing powers were approved by the council in July 1944 for advance preparations of housing sites on the North Western Neighbourhood Unit — mainly road and sewer work — and approval was sought in the same month from the Ministry of Housing for further purchases of land to enable the city to develop the South Western Neighbourhood Unit. Members of the council were informed that Wythenshawe would accommodate most of the city's first, second and third year post-war housing programmes, and that the government was prepared to allow contractors from aerodrome and other civil engineering projects to be diverted to the now pressing area of domestic building. By April 1945 the council were debating the need to press ahead with new compulsory purchase orders for 'the whole of the lands not owned by the Corporation, which are required to carry out the revised planning proposals', the revised planning proposals as embodied in *The City of Manchester Plan* (1945).

One particular consequence of the expected post-war spurt in house-building and industrial development was a reassessment of Baguley Sanatorium's role as a T.B. hospital. Land adjoining the sanatorium had been leased to the Ministry of Health at the beginning of the war for additional emergency hospital accommodation, including a plastic surgery unit for military personnel and civilians suffering from burns and injuries sustained in air raids and victims of industrial accidents. Although this unit continued after the war, Baguley remained primarily associated with T.B. work. Before the cessation of hostilities, the city's Medical Officer of Health had suggested in a report of October 1944 that, because of the likelihood of encroaching housing and industrial development, Baguley might be better suited for other than T.B. services. The open land surrounding the hospital would be soon little more than an ornamental garden and it was suggested that another site, outside Wythenshawe, be found for sanatorium purposes. The immediate post-war years saw many Manchester T.B. patients waiting for places at Baguley, so acute was the shortage of qualified staff. This waiting list was testimony to Baguley's importance and to the still-high incidence of the disease.

Another particular implication of the proposed housing programmes was the need to consider the suggestion for a Wythenshawe district heating plan. It was felt that no better opportunity than that offered by present circumstances would arise. If a scheme could be

32. Wythenshawe Hospital, 1947. The hospital developed from a T.B. unit by the addition of huts to receive air-raid casualties and a military wing with a plastic surgery unit. After the war it became Wythenshawe Hospital and Maternity Hospital.

agreed on now, then it would be an integral feature of post-war housing on the estate. A detailed plan, involving a central boiler and heat transfer system, was submitted to the Wythenshawe Committee in January 1945 and, in the interests of both domestic economy and environmental atmosphere, the committee agreed to share the costs of further investigation with the Housing Committee. A firm of consultant heating engineers was retained and in November of the same year a further, very thorough report was presented and debated. Action, however, was deferred, pending yet more discussion and investigation. The council were particularly worried about the capital costs falling largely on the post-war rates and whether or not it was possible to get such a complex scheme working in time to be applied to a 'significant portion of post-war Estate development'.

But what were these plans and programmes developing? What, physically, was Wythenshawe by 1945? The following figures appear in the minutes of the Wythenshawe Committee for November 1945:

Corporation houses erected	7,934
Corporation houses approved to 'complete development stopped by War'	218
Corporation houses 'immediately contemplated' (on North-Western Neighbourhood unit)	1,472
Private houses erected (on land leased by Manchester)	843
Shops erected, included temporary premises	103
Industrial organisations established (on the Eastern Industrial Area)	22
Industrial applications received (approx.)	60

As indicated earlier, a further compulsory purchase order was in the pipeline to permit the development of the South-Western Neighbourhood Unit, the Western and Southern Industrial Areas and the extension of Princess Parkway. Of course, these figures tell us very little about the actual environment and texture of daily life in Wythenshawe and about those local amenities like shops and community-shared entertainments, the relative sparsity of which the war only served to highlight.

Although house building was at a standstill, industrial development was not. There is plenty of evidence, too, to suggest that despite the restrictions and shortages of wartime Britain, planning and building standards were not radically upset. Where there was a falling-off the Wythenshawe Committee was quick to identify the problem and to insist on the highest standards being maintained in the circumstances. While there was considerable impetus from central government — pressure, for example, to develop industry towards the war effort and to prepare for post-war housing and reconstruction schemes well in advance — credit must be given to the City of Manchester for keeping alive the ideals of Wythenshawe, while being hampered in their realisation. Some of these ideals are discussed in the next chapter, in the context of the *City of Manchester Plan* (1945), itself an impressive achievement of wartime effort and commitment to the very notion of detailed and hopeful planning. If such a plan now seems a little unreal or remote, a vivid charter of post-war social optimism, it is perhaps because of its proposals for a comprehensive restructuring of the community. Its thematic continuity and integrity, its distant horizons, give it a visionary quality different in character to the 'nuts and bolts' of everyday planning and management. It may, of course, be more to do with the plan having played a less significant role in the shaping of the environment than other post-war economic and social factors have done. For in the closing months of the war the writing was appearing on the Town Hall wall — the driving force behind immediate post-war development in Wythenshawe would be the demand for houses.

Chapter Seven

'A Grand Adventure'

In March 1941 Barry Parker retired from his appointment as consultant architect-planner on the Wythenshawe project. The minutes of the Wythenshawe Committee recorded the unanimous warm praise for his achievement. Since his retention in 1927 the

> satellite town had grown from 5,500 residents to over 35,000, new industries had been established and Princess Parkway, the first road of its kind in the country, had been built. Moreover, much of the credit which is reflected in the achievement of the Corporation must properly be attributed to advice and guidance given by Mr. Parker.

In reply, Barry Parker referred to the great pleasure and satisfaction he had had in working on the project and pointed to the significance of Wythenshawe. For him it represented the nearest he had got to realising the perfect garden city, a satellite town in this case, closely and uniquely related to its parent city.

Historians of town and country planning in Britain agree that Parker's concept of Wythenshawe displays his maturity and authority. It anticipates many of the objectives and features of the post-war new-town developments. The realisation of the concept, however, depended on having the scale of financial resources only a city of Manchester's size could provide. These resources in turn would allow both the rapid development of the satellite town and the careful co-ordination of amenity with house building. But as Creese remarks in *The Search for Environment* Wythenshawe's misfortune was that 'it lay between two world wars and athwart a great depression — various emergency programmes and expedient adjustments would interfere with its systematic realisation'. By 1939 there was a growing debate surrounding the question of Wythenshawe's identity as a town, its lack of cohesiveness, social amenity and obvious focal point. There was also some concern, referred to in the last chapter, about house building standards and how best to monitor the individual developments of the future. Although Wythenshawe was still very young, this debate was not confined to the town's critics. Individual councillors, especially those representing Wythenshawe, were worried that wartime conditions would be more severe in the new 'estates'. Some of their fears were well founded, especially where shopping, nursery, recreational and travel facilities were concerned. The Wythenshawe Community Council, founded in 1943, offered a platform from which a number of affiliated organisations could direct their criticisms towards Albert Square.

A New Optimism and a New Start

Misgivings then, both within and outside the corporation, were beginning to be felt by 1939, not so much with the original concept but with the way in which the development seemed to be of the very kind of isolated, one-income group estate type which Barry Parker's integrated plans were designed to avoid. As we have seen in the previous chapter, the war brought an immediate embargo on house building, apart from the odd completion by private developers, and a restricted, though carefully monitored, programme of industrial development. Non-civil-defence amenities, other than the temporary shops and the occasional wartime nursery, were out of the question. But what did emerge from the wartime frustration of not being able to carry through the original plans was an opportunity to stand back after a decade's development, to reassess and to incorporate some of the more recent ideas of the growing town and country planning movement. This wanting to reassess and think about the social changes the war had encouraged coincided with, and was in part a reflection of, a much bigger, national will to look forward, to reconstruct and to entertain hopes for a more caring society than the one shattered by the war. Rethinking Wythenshawe was tied in with rethinking Manchester, and the influential document here was *The City of Manchester Plan*, prepared for the city council and published in 1945.

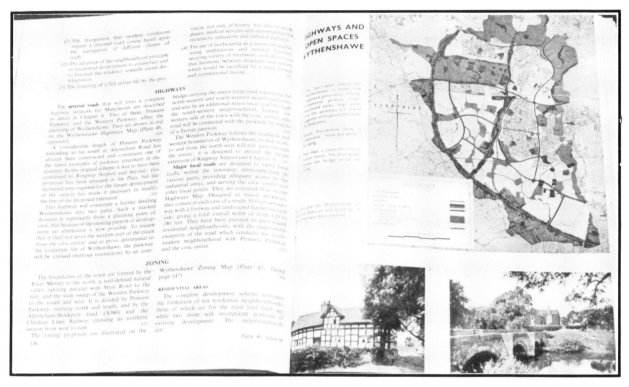

33. The Nicholas Plan, 1945. This was an overall plan for Manchester; the map here shows 'zoning' in Wythenshawe and below it South Poundswick Farm and the bridge, moat and 18th-century Peel Hall Farm, incorrectly titled 'Peel Hall, a 16th-century Manor House'.

The presiding spirit and author of the Plan was R. Nicholas, City Surveyor and Engineer, an influential and far-sighted man whose advice guided the council on its Wythenshawe development, particularly after the departure of Barry Parker. The Plan embodies his ideas:

> I have thus been given an entirely free hand, and I alone must accept full responsibility for the principles and proposals here outlined. This procedure has the advantage that the corporation can now approach its task (of post-war planning) with an equally unfettered discretion.

The Nicholas Plan (*The City of Manchester Plan*, 1945), reflecting the ideas of one man in particular and of a group of his city colleagues in general, is concerned with the whole of Manchester. It is a document remarkable for its depth of research, its commitment to producing a human-scaled environment and its detailed incorporation of contemporary planning concepts. The production of such a plan was all the more impressive when the wartime circumstances in which it was conceived, researched and written are taken into consideration. Manchester was not alone, however, in making resources available for detailed planning, responsible projections of likely needs. Other cities, such as Glasgow, produced plans inspired by the prevailing wartime spirit of community awareness and the revival of popular interest in social welfare and planning (witness the 'best seller' readership figures of the famous 1942 Beveridge Report).

Although war damage alone meant that there was pressure on local authorities like Manchester to plan for post-war housing, employment and public amenities, the optimistic tone of these reports suggests much more of an eager readiness to get on with the job, a wish to plan for ten, twenty and even fifty years ahead, than a war-weary need to make the best of necessity. Gordon Cherry remarked in *Urban Change and Planning*, 'In the trauma of war there had been urban devastation but this only seemed to renew a determination to work towards a new social order and to rebuild our cities to a new pattern'. This determination is certainly evident in the Nicholas Plan, although its author was wise enough to temper his enthusiasm by reflecting that the wartime spirit of neighbourliness might evaporate with the coming of peace!

> The question is now being asked whether peace will bring a reversion to the old order; whether comradeship and sociability will give place to selfishness and apathy, or whether the heightened interest in cultural pursuits and in local and national affairs will be maintained. The answer depends to a great extent on whether the structure of our cities is designed to foster or frustrate, to stimulate or stifle, our wartime consciousness of membership in a living social organism.

Wythenshawe and the future of the region

Apart from the country as a whole turning its thoughts towards post-war reconstruction and the kind of society it wanted, there were other underlying factors at work. There had, for example, been further developments in the town and country planning movement, reflected in legislation which paved the way for the new towns of the post-war years. The first Minister of Town and Country Planning was appointed in 1943, and it was to his new department, as well as to the Ministry of Housing, that Manchester submitted its revised proposals for Wythenshawe. Although the specific legislation, the New Towns Acts, came a little later, in 1946, the growing interest in the concept of the independent, self-sufficient town — an extension of Parker's and Unwin's much earlier vision — helped to fuel the local debate about Wythenshawe's status.

The new town concept had in turn been stimulated by an important report published in 1940. The Royal Commission on the Distribution of the Industrial Population (the Barlow Commission) had been appointed in 1937 and, working as comprehensively as possible, it collected evidence from many sources, including the Town Planning Institute. Its brief was to study the reasons for the industrial and commercial overcrowding of certain, traditional areas of the country, and to suggest remedies. The Barlow Commission recommended further spacing-out and redevelopment of congested areas. While this was an important influence on the Nicholas Plan as a whole, more significant for Wythenshawe were two further suggestions. Firstly, there should be some decentralisation and dispersal of industry and the industrial population, and secondly, the government and local authorities should try to achieve through planning control a balance of types of industry and service within each region. These policies were already a part of the Wythenshawe industrial plan within the Manchester conurbation, although establishing a genuine mix of industry and services, especially in terms of categories of employee, was proving difficult. Within the context of the Barlow Report it was important to consider Wythenshawe not as an isolated, self-contained industrial pocket, though the objective for the post-war years was to employ as many residents as possible in local factories and services, but as one aspect of the 'regional dispersal'.

Important though these national influences were on *The City of Manchester Plan*, there were more local and regional motives for drawing up a comprehensive programme for post-war Manchester. Throughout the 1930s there had been a growing concern about population movements. People of working age, young families especially, had been moving away from the north-west, from the heavy, staple industries, to the south-east where there was a rapid development of light industry. Freed from the necessity of being sited near traditional sources of fuel, the new, electricity-consuming industries of outer London and the Home Counties attracted men and women from the relatively declining, big-employing, heavy industries on which the north-west had depended. One of the most urgent pressures on the City of Manchester by 1945 was the need to stem this accelerating drift, to prevent the gradual decline of the whole region by consolidating 'its traditional strengths where possible, and, more importantly, by taking heed of the Barlow Report's recommendations on diversification and balance of employment'.

But Nicholas saw that more than the bread-and-butter of employment was needed. Manchester would need to be regenerated as a 'centre of excellence', the focal, regional metropolis, offering its citizens the best of carefully co-ordinated educational, health, artistic and sporting amenities. Although these facets of the Plan are not immediately relevant to the discussion of Wythenshawe, mention of them gives some indication of the bold scale on which the Plan is drawn and, more particularly, that metropolitan Manchester is the parent city to which Wythenshawe residents look. In the light of this need to encourage people not to leave the region and, indeed, to draw new residents from other areas, Wythenshawe's role as a potentially attractive domestic and light industrial satellite town was crucial. The net migration from the north-west was accompanied by a falling birthrate and Nicholas hoped that the prospects of a good house in a pleasant garden suburb and a job in a clean, local factory would encourage young families to settle.

In a Gallup Poll of June 1945 four out of ten people interviewed thought that housing would be the most important post-war problem. Cherry, in *Urban Change and Planning*, estimates that on the outbreak of war Manchester had sixty-eight thousand dwellings unfit for human habitation. This figure represented a third of the city's total housing stock. It might seem that the problem of rehousing tens of thousands of Mancunians would have been eased if the population drift was allowed to take its unchecked course. But what Nicholas envisaged was a growing, prosperous, regenerated north-west, not a region waiting for the expedient of families leaving the area so that their houses could then be demolished or re-let. Although there was a net emigration, people needed rehousing as soon as possible, not in some indefinite and arbitrarily-decided future. There was a need then for a Manchester plan to cope with the massive scale of house building required to ensure that the city not only got the number of houses it wanted, but of the design and type needed to accommodate the different economic and age groups. It was important that they were built to the highest contemporary standards and in those areas of the city where people would want to live. Without a plan developments might be piecemeal, out of step with the existing or proposed amenities and industry, and lacking in any fundamental social coherence.

Planning the ideal — Nicholas and Wythenshawe

But surely Wythenshawe already had a detailed and imaginative plan? Had it not been for the depression of the 1930s and the war, development would have been well advanced. We have seen that there were misgivings about how the original concept was working out in practice and the war, though disastrous for Wythenshawe in one respect, did give rise to a period of national stock-taking and social reassessment. Without putting Wythenshawe into the melting pot once more — 7,934 houses were already inhabited — it appeared to be a good opportunity to reassess the original Wythenshawe model in the light of the first decade's development and, if necessary, of shifting some of the emphases. Wythenshawe

34. Mitchell Gardens, built according to Parker's plans and recently restored.

35. Newall Green's 'Tin-Town', reflecting post-war haste and austerity.

would be accommodating the majority of the city's first, second and third year post-war housing programme. The responsibility was considerable. In Nicholas's words:

> The objects of the proposals submitted in this chapter [Chapter Fourteen], are to complete the development of Wythenshawe in accordance with the most advanced standards of modern planning and to remedy admitted defects in its already built-up areas.

It was acknowledged that Wythenshawe was something of a special case within the terms of *The City of Manchester Plan*. Not only had there been a significant amount of development already, but the very concept of a satellite town, a self-contained project on a large scale, gave Wythenshawe a unique status within the framework of post-war Manchester planning. The Plan stressed the need to be cautious when rehousing large numbers of people from older areas of the city. As few people as possible should be uprooted and moved away from the traditional areas, with their associations, communications and network of personal links, it said. But, on the other hand, new houses had to be built, net densities reduced and environmental conditions and amenities improved. So, while the original motives for developing Wythenshawe still held good, the Plan tried to look ahead and avoid the situation, perhaps in the 1980s or 1990s, where a large proportion of the population would have been resettled well outside the city while large areas of the inner-city were sparsely populated (which has happened). Wythenshawe's uniqueness was that it was the only large area of land available to the corporation for development, that it was still mainly virgin territory and that it was designed to be a town, self-sufficient in most of its day-to-day civic and community needs, not merely a dormitory adjunct to the city centre.

Allowing for Wythenshawe's special status, what were those features of the Plan as a whole which were most relevant to the reassessment of Parker's original concept? The surveys on which many of the later proposals were based were necessarily very selective, given wartime conditions. Though still relatively detailed in the range and number of questions put to Mancunians, Nicholas recommended that the findings be treated with some caution. Many of the people interviewed, living in older parts of the city, were worried about being moved away from the central amenities and from the major pockets of industry and employment, despite a widespread desire for better living conditions. Of the Wythenshawe residents questioned, 93 per cent liked their houses, but complained of the slow development of proposed and sought-after amenities. Coupled with the basic surveys were detailed analyses of population and population forecasts, and, as noted earlier, the city anticipated a falling population, a combined effect of a falling birthrate, a levelling off of the death-rate in the higher age group and the net migration to other regions of Britain. The composition of the population by age group was obviously very important in helping to determine the types of dwellings needed and preferred — an emphasis in Wythenshawe, for example, on the provision of houses for young married couples with or without children — and in planning the complexities of educational, social and other services.

Many features of *The City of Manchester Plan* as it affected Wythenshawe were really extensions or modifications of ideas already present in the original Parker concept. Drawing on developments in town and country planning, Manchester was trying to apply these ideas to the city as a whole, in some ways a much more difficult task than starting with a new site untouched by a complex of existing, historical and piecemeal development. But because of this newness and the overall planning control involved, Wythenshawe could be quoted as a model, a touchstone of environmental engineering. On the theme of industrial zoning, for example, the Plan cites Wythenshawe's grouping of industry into three areas. At this stage only the Eastern Industrial Area had been developed but there was sufficient evidence to show how zoning could work. (In March 1944 there had been some concern about the division between factory and domestic sites in Wythenshawe. Factories on Longley Lane were dangerously close to encroaching on domestic development and questions were asked

36. Eastern Industrial Area, Sharston. The grouping of Wythenshawe industry into three zones was used as a model for others by Nicholas. The picture shows the development by 1935, the railway in the foregound and Northenden in the distance.

in the Wythenshawe Committee about the adequacy of screening and spacing. Planning vigilance was required if zoning ideals were to be fulfilled.) Industrial zoning was of great importance in the heavily built-up, older areas of the city where heavy, dirty industry was often cheek-to-jowl with cramped domestic development. Although Wythenshawe was untypical here and would only have lighter industry, free from major noise, smoke and smell pollution, what factories and services there were would be grouped and well-screened from the residential neighbourhoods. Zoning was designed to keep incompatible uses of land separate and, through landscaping, soften the boundaries between these uses.

Encouraged by the findings of the Barlow Commission, the Plan recommended a greater provision of local employment opportunities. Too many people, it felt, were travelling long distances on relatively expensive transport to get to the traditional areas of industry and commerce. We have already seen that Wythenshawe, in particular, was conscious of the problem of attracting a sufficiently diverse and large industrial base to employ a good proportion of local residents, especially skilled men. If people had to travel to areas like Trafford Park or north-east Manchester, then a good transport network could do much to mitigate the hardships. People should be able to get to their factory or office cheaply and quickly.

Moreover, good transport was needed to convey people into the city, the centre of excellence and its many amenities. Towards this end the Plan proposed an integrated network of roads and railways, including an inner-city circular road, intermediate and outer ring-roads intersected by major radials, and a new station, Trinity, off Deansgate. The extended Princess Parkway would be one of these radial roads. Detailed specifications for parkway planning were given: 'It should take in such natural features along its route as spinneys, streams, banks, and should merge wherever possible into existing parks'.

The proposed Western Parkway was so envisaged. Local roads would be built according to their local function, major roads skirting, rather than intersecting residential city centre and recreational areas. Systems of field paths were planned so that people could walk more pleasantly through neighbourhoods without using the ordinary roads, linking open spaces, schools, shops and other amenities. The whole regional network was conceived of as an elaborate hierarchy, from field paths to inter-town parkways.

Imaginative landscape planning was a pervasive feature of the Plan. The influences of the garden city movement and the growing town and country lobby were strongly felt. The key emphasis was on the use of existing natural features, mature trees and shrubs, copses, ponds and the rises and falls of the land itself. Existing man-made structures, like churches, large public houses and historic buildings, should, where possible, be used as focal points and references for the eye. The object was to avoid monotony by breaking up the surfaces and planes along which the eye moved, to create a sense of depth and the integration of the natural and the man-made. There would be not only a mix of dwelling styles, both in type and design, but a variation of building lines. Front and back gardens played their respective roles, too. Occupiers were thought to have a responsibility to make their front gardens attractive, part of the local amenity, while back gardens were seen as private areas for more idiosyncratic use! The provision of larger open spaces was thoroughly investigated, analysis of the rather loose term 'open space' revealing a wealth of public and private use of land, parks, allotments, small-scale farming, golf courses and uncultivated grazing among them. The Plan recommended that wherever possible educational and public recreational facilities should be adjacent and commonly available, and that not less than seven acres of open space per 1,000 people be provided. This was the very minimum figure that could be recommended and was compared with actual figures for 1945 of 0.28 acres and 0.08 acres per 1,000 people in Ardwick and Collyhurst respectively. Children's playparks, organised-games areas and ornamental parks were seen as very important features of the urban landscape, planned for from the beginning and not merely provided as afterthoughts.

The fundamental principle at work in *The City of Manchester Plan* was very much to do with anticipating needs, industrial, social, recreational, etc., planning for these rather than providing for them as an afterthought or only when demand became embarrassingly vocal. The first decade of Wythenshawe development had shown how difficult it was to build more than good houses, to create a new town on a large scale which could meet many of its day-to-day requirements within its own boundaries. Nicholas stressed repeatedly the importance of co-ordinating house development with all the other amenities which the new residents were going to want. It was better, he argued, to build schools, shops, nurseries and community centres in advance of the people moving into the new developments, rather than leaving them to be started only when their absence was noticed. If the precise demand for a particular service was not yet known, leave more than adequate space for likely develop-ment. This kind of coordination was a delicate act of planning, of ensuring that people were moved to the new developments with care and only when there was a structure of civic and community facilities to support them. Particularly important here was the advanced provision of primary and secondary schools — the 1944 Education Act was very much in people's minds at this time — and of a good number and mix of well distributed shops. It was hoped that experience gained in the 'Wythenshawe experiment' could be drawn on if and when Manchester developed other satellite or overspill projects in the post-war years, albeit outside the city boundaries.

In one of the most interesting and central chapters of the Plan, Nicholas discussed the concept of neighbourhood planning. Hoping that something of the wartime spirit of community consciousness would survive and that peace would not bring social apathy, he developed a kind of hierarchy of social organisation, rooted in family life, where the consciousness of oneself as part of a larger 'organism' was fostered and extended to a civic awareness via school and work. Neighbourhoods would ideally consist of about ten thousand people, including all age and income groups, with a corresponding mix of dwellings. They should be 'small enough to function as a real social organism in whose life every individual can take a responsible share, knowing that his voice will be heard' . . . and yet be 'large enough to make an efficient social unit'. Nicholas put great emphasis on the need to attract a blend of public and private development, high as well as lower income groups, and not only young families but a much broader cross-section of the age groups already living in the older parts of the city.

Neighbourhood units were conceived of as 'modern urbanised versions of the traditional village', carefully planned as radiating developments around neighbourhood centres. These

37. Neighbourhood school. Brownley Green School, Infants' Department, is here acting out the May Queen ceremony. The Nicholas Plan suggests the grouping of neighbourhood units into districts.

villages, with the added advantages of city life, would have at their hearts the community centre, 'real peoples' clubs', containing a branch library, further education facilities, sports and social amenities, a canteen and small rooms for hire. Shops, adequate to meet most daily needs, would be sited nearby — about thirty at the central focus and several sub-groups of four on the outer perimeters of the unit. There would be a choice of small, cosy pubs scattered throughout, with several larger ones around the neighbourhood centre. Local roads were designed to lead 'naturally' towards the centre, while through and heavy goods traffic would be encouraged to use major, external roads. Nicholas conceded that neighbourhood planning of this nature was rather conceptual and that many factors, like existing pockets of development and the natural contours of the land, would 'tend to upset the theoretical allocation'. The idea, however, was an influential one, and was at the root of post-war Wythenshawe planning. It was in part a reaction to that first decade of attractive though socially-anaemic satellite development.

It was intended that individual neighbourhood units would be grouped into major districts, the ideal population for one of those being about fifty thousand. District centres were to have a district hall, major health centre, baths, main library, cinemas, large shops, residential hotels, police and fire stations among their attractively-landscaped amenities. Within the hierarchical pattern, neighbourhoods would look towards the district centres for their large amenities and civic services, much as the areas of the neighbourhoods were clustered around their smaller, more modest focal points. The planning of neighbourhoods would be seen in the larger context of the city as a whole: 'Detailed plans for each neighbourhood must conform with the overall plan for the district which in turn dovetails into the broad outline scheme for the City'. Wythenshawe could be viewed within this impressive, if theoretical, scheme as a 'district with a difference', a satellite which would achieve a greater independence and self-sufficiency with the realisation of its target population of eighty thousand.

The fabric of family and social life still depended, however, on the local conditions within the neighbourhood and on the quality of house design in particular. While the W.E.S.C. had done its best to insist on good standards of design and workmanship during the war years, it was *The City of Manchester Plan* which discussed in detail the standards recommended for post-war dwellings. Nicholas referred to the famous Tudor Walters Report of 1918, which had recommended a net dwelling density of 12 to the acre. He believed that criticism of this recommendation was unjust. If critics had said that 12 to the acre was too sparse it was probably more to do with poor landscaping and unimaginative building lines than the mere number of houses per acre. The example of Barry Parker's fine landscaping and sensitive use of building materials and existing natural features informed much of the local environmental planning undertaken by Nicholas and his colleagues, although it was appreciated that the pressure to rehouse would result in some, if not widespread, use of new building materials. Prefabrication was inevitable.

House design itself had been influenced by two wartime government documents, *The Design of Dwellings* (Dudley Report) and *The Housing Manual* of 1944. There was a growing concern to provide more space and more opportunity for privacy within standard family accommodation. Minimum standards for space were founded on the principle that there was a 'close connection between overcrowding and morale'. Patterns of kitchen and living-room use were changing and it was thought that, with the new, post-war opportunities in secondary, technical and continuing education, more quiet and secluded accommodation would be needed for individual members of the family. Because of the importance Nicholas gave to the social blend of age and income groups within a neighbourhood, detailed specifications also appeared for single persons' flats, maisonettes and for a number of types of special accommodation. Private developers would have to be attracted to build low-density housing if Wythenshawe was not to become a one-income-group town.

A new age and a new hope

In the final chapter of *The City of Manchester Plan* Nicholas allowed himself some general, perhaps more personal, comments on the social·climate that would need to prevail if the schemes outlined were even partially to be realised. One of the more technical criteria for success was a reformed local government system. He envisaged the formation of an elective regional planning authority, leaving services which are essentially of local concern to the smaller existing local authorities. He was not alone, then or later, in his views, as the eventual creation in 1974 of the Greater Manchester Council, with its brief to oversee the integrated structural planning of the conurbation, testifies (it was abolished in 1986). Of more immediate concern were his remarks on the relationship between Wythenshawe and its parent city:

> The task [of developing a new town] demands the most comprehensive and detailed — yet flexible — organisation at both ends, a precise but elastic timing of each stage in the creation of the new town and the loosening-out of the old . . . It is hardly conceivable that it could be carried out smoothly, and without serious hardship to the people whose lives it most transforms, if the authority responsible for redevelopment and dispersal had no direct control over the scale, pace, quality or character of the new development in the satellite town.

But: 'Nor incidentally, is there any reason why the new township, when fully developed, should not become an independent borough'.

Perhaps Nicholas may be allowed the stirring rhetoric of his final paragraph, for the previous two hundred pages displayed a blend of disciplined investigation, humane recommendation and cautious optimism. So he concludes:

> To bring such a grand adventure to fulfilment calls also for sterling qualities in the community that undertakes it . . . We are entering upon a new age: it is for us to choose whether it shall be an age of self-indulgent drift along the pre-war road towards depopulation, economic decline, cultural apathy and social dissolution, or whether we shall make it a nobler, braver age in which the human race will be master of its fate.

Chapter Eight

The Second Wave: 1945-64
'Houses, Houses and yet more Houses'

It is on record that an African bishop, touring Wythenshawe in the 1960s, exclaimed in bewilderment, 'Houses, houses, and yet more houses!' The same words had been the cry of the planners following the Second World War, but by the end of 1964 the original goal of homes for a population of 100,000 people had been reached. The relentless pressure of building homes on an estate barren of all but the basic amenities had meant a very difficult time for the new Wythenshavians.

As the Parker-Jackson-Simon era passed, and Northenden shrugged off what it saw as its misbegotten daughter, there was less pioneering exuberance to sustain the newcomers. But enterprise was not lacking and the Civic Weeks were 'carnivals of delight and cornucopias of resourcefulness'. Wythenshawe had its own councillors, its own M.P., while the Federal Council raved on all subjects from bus shelters to home rule for the new town. By 1964, however, the last Civic Week had staggered to a close and the Federal Council was disbanded. Manchester City Council's Parks Department began its Open Days and although the cultural centre would not be started for some years, at least the shops were going up in the Civic Centre.

Northenden survived with the façade of a peaceful but lively village in the post-war period, despite the bustle and feverish activity relating to the building of Wythenshawe on its doorstep. In the fashion of the neighbourhood units it acquired for itself a community association in 1947, and to mark the Festival of Britain in 1951 the Northenden C.A. put on its own Northenden Festival for three weeks from 21 May to 9 June, with an exhibition, the light opera *Merrie England*, plays, concerts, dance displays, ballet and sports (as further outlined in the following chapter).

Included in the programme of the festival was a comprehensive, if rather bland, description of the village, 'About Northenden 1951' and 'Before', supported by photographs of 'Northenden Village . . . Bygone Days' and 'Two Views of Northenden Today'. In spite of its assurance that 'any impression of insularity should be dispelled at once as a fallacy', the only hint of the new Wythenshawe in the 30,000-word piece is the phrase 'undisturbed by surrounding change'. Every club, pub and society, from the Junior Football Club to the Ancient Order of Buffaloes and the Lily of the Valley Lodge of Oddfellows ('under the guidance of its portly secretary Mr. Andrew Watson'), was presented as a flourishing concern. Arthur Hooley, the writer, concluded that '. . . our village is honoured and privileged by its own efforts and is proudly entitled to record its progress up to 1951 mark to mark with the British Nation'. The village atmosphere, however, was not always tranquil. Rev. Sockett had to fight vandalism with appeals in the church magazine for parents to control their children. At one time the churchyard had to be locked.

The two schools in Northenden, Bazley Road and the National School, new at the turn of the century, began to look old compared with schools in the new town. The municipal school had £80,000 spent on modernisation, while a rather smaller sum built a replacement National School in Patterdale Road, St Wilfrid's Junior School. Due to Mr. Sockett's efforts to refurbish the organ at the same time, the Education Authority had to take over the building of the adjoining Royle Green Infants' School. This unique set-up of a church junior and a county infants' school opened in 1961. The junior school had a fully equipped stage, but due to authority rules, the advancement of television and the acquisition of its own theatre by the local dramatic society, it was little used outside school hours.

The older brickwork of Northenden provided a welcome relief from the sterility of parts of new Wythenshawe. A survey in 1960 showed that shoppers on the new estates still regarded Northenden as their centre. Nevertheless, the Post Office, still at the northern end of Church Road, was seeking a new home. On the south side of Palatine Road new interiors were fitted into many old shop premises, often in the framework of an even older house, but on the opposite side a clean sweep was made.

Northenden's status as a shopping centre was enhanced by the building in 1955 of the new Parade between Lingard Road and Heyridge Drive. Traders and the local newspaper promoted the idea of Northenden as 'the Shopping Centre' with occasional 'Shopping Festivals'. Woolworth, Boots, Timothy Whites, MacFisheries, Granada, Timpsons and two banks joined a variety of local traders. Among the promotional openings, the late Pat Phoenix, 'Elsie Tanner' of Coronation Street, opened the new Co-op furniture shop in 1961.

The garages of Henlys (once Morgans), Barrows on Palatine Road, and Royle Green Autos were joined by a Merseyside brace, Lookers and Northenden Service Station. The latter, opened in 1963, proclaimed 'have a round of golf while your car is being serviced'.

Other landmarks changed, too. The *Old Spread Eagle Inn* in Royle Green Road was replaced in the early 1960s and the Church Rooms in Kenworthy Lane came down in 1964. The focal point of Northenden for the last 60 years, the Rooms had witnessed the plays, socials and musicals of that era, battle meetings in the five-year war for Wythenshawe and the arrival of the evacuees in the war. After a bitter fight they were replaced by a flat-roofed glass-and-concrete structure near the church on the site of Price's buildings. Also in Ford Lane, the Rectory lost its 19th-century outbuildings in 1958, including the servants' hall, conservatory and kitchens.

Further down Ford Lane, the Northenden Stadium, that had seen boxing, wrestling, roller skating, concerts and latterly gaming machines, was gutted in a spectacular blaze in August 1962. In contrast, the much older Northenden Mill near the river was allowed to decay, so that when it was levelled in 1965 its loss was barely noted. Other buildings took on new roles. The Fellowship House in Church Road became a School of Dance, Rose Hill in Longley Lane became a Remand Home and Beech House in Yew Tree Lane a clinic.

Land for new buildings was getting scarce, and when the British Legion wanted a club site they looked to the riverside but settled on the coalyard of Mr. Turner — whose horse and cart had been well known in Old Northenden. Founded in 1958 by Jack Secker, money for the new club was raised by bingo in the *Church Inn* and in the Ballet School. With the aid of a brewery, a hall with bar and rooms above was opened in 1965.

The schoolboy of the 1920s, after training for the A.R.P. at Sharston Hall in 1938, and after war service, had come back to Northenden and was entering social life again. He joined the choir and the reformed dramatic society — the N.A.D.S. — and represented them on the new Northenden C.A., which failed to get a community centre. In 1959 he took part in the Planned Giving Campaign of St Wilfrid's church when two double decker buses 'took the village to Belle Vue for a Parish Meal — and to pledge gifts to the Church'. 'During this time I noticed the arrival of the new Wythenshawe people to take advantage of the new shops in Northenden. They used the bus that was put on to bring them down here while the Civic Centre was being built.'

South of Northenden in the new Wythenshawe many smaller cottages, farms, market gardens and smithies surrendered to the builders, especially if the price was right. Some in better condition were renovated, notably in Gatley, and a few continued as before. The farms of Baguley Hall and Floats Hall disappeared with little ceremony. Mayer's farm at

Peel Hall remained for the time being and more than once did 'Peel Hall School sports have to wait till the cows agreed to leave'.

The two older schools in Wythenshawe, St John's at Northern Moor, where Moor Road joins Wythenshawe Road, and Shadow Moss School, had been effectively community centres for years. When closure was mooted committees were set up and petitions prepared but the use of Shadow Moss as a casualty centre in the Viscount disaster on Ringway Road in 1957 precipitated its closure. The axe fell and the children of both schools were taken to St Wilfrid's in Northenden. The parents of Shadow Moss kept the bus link with the new school for 20 years. Attempts were made to have St John's School kept for the community for the disabled — in vain.

The battles over Peel Hall and Baguley Hall were to come, but Wythenshawe Hall was almost lost on two occasions. In 1946 it needed £20,000 to beat the death watch beetle. Many said 'demolish' and, although repaired, the rear became a shell at one point. Dry rot caused further expense in 1960 and again 'landmark or liability?' was the cry. The stables only just survived the planners' spring clean of 1958. Further restoration work in 1983 for more dry rot uncovered a 400-year-old wall painting of a Bacchus-like figure, and workmen's graffiti from the same period.

Sharston's stately homes, the Hall and the Manor, were leased again by the Watch Committee in 1946 for use by the Police, Fire and Ambulance Services. Community associations, model aircraft clubs and the like shared the premises until vandals, lead thieves and the weather took over. By the late 1960s both buildings were boarded up, though in the grounds a temporary employment exchange and passport office arrived in 1952. A lesser stately home, Nield's Tea Rooms, 'Wythenshawe's only social centre in the war' yielded in the mid-1950s to Sharston Baths.

Manchester's lack of concern for its heritage was, with hindsight, understandable if not excusable. Wythenshawe's urgent need for its forty thousand people in 1939 had been civic amenities. It was urgent in 1945. Twenty years later the need was desperate. Without civic pride Wythenshawe 'could become another dreary new suburb full of impersonal estates'. Barry Parker's concepts of 1927 still held, but the Nicholas Plan of 1945 for Manchester as a whole and the 1946 Act's insistence on houses dominated. Each government boasted that it had built more houses than ever.

The Wythenshawe Committee still ruled as war ended, though in a few years it dissolved into a standing committee and finally vanished as part of the general Estates Committee. But in 1945, with the Civic Centre pushed further into the future, a few prefabs, very few bricks and fewer bricklayers, the Wythenshawe Committee resumed its building programme with zeal.

Immediate needs were satisfied by prefabricated houses, mainly at Royal Oak and in Wythenshawe Park. The agreement made with the Tattons when the land was sold, that the park should forever be retained in its original form, was broken as prefabs replaced trees in the south-west corner.

There were a number of estates to be completed in Wythenshawe but forward planning meant that the committee had immediately to set about the purchase of land for the South-Eastern Neighbourhood Units of Moss Nook and Woodhouse Park. In June 1946 the committee resolved to buy 493 acres for building as follows:

Houses	2,968
Cottage-flats and flats	550
Single/Aged Person and misc.	358
Total	3,876

The number of units to the acre would be 13, one outside Barry Parker's standard, and in July of that year, at a cost of £493,000, the layout of the two units was approved.

38. **Plan and Reality**, 1953. Manchester's leaflet told the story of 20th-century Wythenshawe so far and outlined future plans for it.

On a lower plane, the Wythenshawe Committee commended its officers for collecting scrap iron — to the value of £8.36 over three and a half years. The police, too, were praised for catching a 16-year-old stealing a 12-foot fence. The committee enjoyed itself at the city's expense in May 1945 when it visited Barry Parker's other protégés at Welwyn and Letchworth. One sorry saga in the annals of the committee was that of the District Heating Scheme, turned down by the government after years of expensive preparation.

In 1953 a leaflet, entitled *Wythenshawe, Plan and Reality*, was published about the new town. After a brief history of the area it went on to explain that Wythenshawe would not be a dormitory suburb or a satellite town, but that it 'will come near to being a true New Town, many of its people being able to find employment in its three industrial areas, its shops, offices and market gardens'.

Pre-war Wythenshawe was described as good, 'but not good enough', with main roads running through instead of round the area; 'there were not enough shops, cinemas and other public buildings — and the war prevented their building'. Nevertheless, it was claimed that Wythenshawe 'is regarded as an outstanding example of planning', where everyone can take an active part in the planned communities of 10,000 people, each round a hub of public buildings, such as shops and a school and the nucleus of a community centre sponsored by the city. For bigger enterprises a civic centre would be built.

The leaflet reviewed post-war progress and the post-war houses of Baguley Hall and Newall Green. Some of these, it explained, were of steel with aluminium or corrugated-steel-sheet cladding and glass-wool filling. Others were a mix of concrete and foamed slag made from glass rubble — good insulators — while some were of concrete made to look like stone. Culs-de-sac, the writer argued, 'give that precinctal feeling which can add charm', while the frontal greenswards of open development create a sense of space.

A revision slip, put out in 1956, revealed that the target figure for the complete Wythenshawe had grown from 90,000 to ninety-five thousand. It piously repeated the hope that Britain's economic situation would improve rapidly so that Wythenshavians could be allowed their community buildings. The slip included some 'Facts and Figures':

Number of Municipal houses at present 20,449; ultimately 21,350. Number of Private Houses on land leased by Corporation: at present 3,034: ultimately 4,350. Applicants for Municipal Houses: now on the books 21,000, representing approximately 73,000 people.

Rents of Municipal Houses:

Aged Person's Bungalow (living room with bed recess or bedroom, kitchen, bathroom, etc.)	12s.	5d.	-	15s. 10d.
Single Women's Flat (similar), A1, One bedroom	15s.	4d.	-	17s. 7d.
A2, Two bedroom house	19s.	11d.	-	21s. 1d.
	22s.	1d.	-	24s.
A3, Three-bedroom non-parlour house (living room & kitchen)	21s.	8d.	-	23s. 7d.
	25s.	4d.	-	26s. 10d.
A4, Parlour, four-bedroom house	25s.	7d.	-	26s. 4d.
	32s.			

(12s. = 60p,   16s. = 80p,   20s. = £1,   32s. = £1.60p)

The reality expressed in *Plan and Reality* differed somewhat from the reality experienced by the new settlers. The problems of the time were not stressed in the leaflet. The concrete houses, some of which at Northern Moor were dubbed giant cubes by the local papers, were seen by many as poor substitutes for brick houses. Shortages were not the only problem. Reports of hooligans regularly delaying building in the Baguley area were made in 1948. In 1953 a vast store of window frames went up in a huge bonfire and raids on materials were common. Strikes, particularly in 1947, often held up work, and when the houses were completed squatters were sometimes the first tenants. Even land cleared for building might be lost for a while when gypsies took over, as in Northenden in 1953 and Greenwood Road in 1955.

Building went ahead in Baguley Hall and in the Crossacres regions and spread south and east to embrace the areas of Woodhouse Park, Moss Nook, Northern Moor and Brooklands. In 1946 about nineteen hundred houses and flats were commenced, and over the next twenty years this rate was maintained. Pockets of land, especially around the proposed civic centre, were left vacant, apparently because the city was unsure of how to use them. Conversely, pockets of virgin land in the Rackhouse, Sale Road, Benchill, Newall Green and Royal Oak area were filled. In 1957 the first post-war council houses to be built in Northenden appeared in the Royle Green area, which was called 'Little Hulme', although quite a few of the new families there came from Woodhouse Park after the Viscount air crash. From the outset flats in Wythenshawe were kept to two or three storeys, but the walk-up areas were increasingly vandalised. By the 1960s Woodhouse Park could boast Manchester's first nine-storey flats, the Kingsgate, costing a basic £135,000. High-rise problems there would be, but for a while the sky-flats were still a novelty.

Private houses, it may be noted, were included in the leaflet's statistics. An ideal of Barry Parker's was that housing should be balanced in social classes. Thus it hoped that Wythenshawe's industry, needing both a management and a labour force, would be matched by the manpower available in Wythenshawe with little commuting in or out. The committee aimed at a proportion of council to private houses of six to one and a survey in the 1960s shows that the ratio was just above this. In practice many workers had to commute out and some management in.

To the few private pre-1931 houses scattered over Wythenshawe (including Brooklands and Styal Roads), pockets of private houses were added in eight main groups. Started before the Second World War were: Altrincham Road in the Sharston Area; Altrincham Road in the Spinney and Baguley area; Wythenshawe Road with the Cherry Tree Road area; Hollyhedge Road and Baxter Park. Started after the Second World War were: Newall Green — Firbank Roads and roads off; Peel Hall, Cherrington Close and Yew Tree Lane area; Brooklands and Shady Lane areas.

Occasionally, disputes revealed pockets of mistrust between council house tenants and private house owners. Late in 1956 the complaints of owner-occupiers in Styal Road that 'children from the Estate invade and strip the private gardens', coupled with a demand for a barrier, brought the reaction from Harry Lloyd of 'snobs of Gatley', an epithet that was given wide publicity. There was similar trouble in the Brooklands area a few years later.

Lesser headlines occasionally appeared after incidents arising from the landlord-tenant relationships of the city and council house occupiers. The problem of car parking caused friction until 1961, when the council at last allowed cars to be parked in gardens. The restrictions on the decoration of council houses sometimes brought gestures of defiance and retaliation.

The Brooklands estate, commenced in 1952 at Ferndown Road, was built on land given in 1926 by Ernest Simon, and housed a population of 4,800 in an area of 330 acres. An early householder, Les Sutton, recalled in 1973 that something of the rural atmosphere remained. In the Baguley stream 'fair sized specimen of catfish are said to bask there still in the truce of school hours. Along the banks there were voles and in the fields crows, gulls and even herons'.

Of the services provided by the local and national government, education drew the most publicity in the early post-war period. 'A lead to the rest of the country', was the claim made for Crossacres' Primary School when it was planned in 1946. Designed with prefabricated parts, the Acting City Architect, Mr. L. C. Howitt, maintained that 'the roof will be on as soon as the walls are up'. It was 1950 before Crossacres was in fact opened by

Alderman Jackson, by now the grandfather of Wythenshawe, but from 1950 to 1954, reflecting the growth of housing, 13 Wythenshawe primary schools were opened:

1950 Crossacres	1953 Poundswick
1950 Baguley Hall	1954 Sandilands (Brooklands)
1951 Newall Green	1954 Peel Hall
1951 Sacred Heart R.C.	1954 St Peter's R.C., Newall Green
1952 Oldwood	1954 St Anthony's R.C., Woodhouse Park
1952 Greenbow (Infants)	1961 Royle Green (Infants), Northenden
1953 Woodhouse Park	1961 St Wilfrid's C. of E., Northenden
1953 Button Lane	1964 St Elizabeth's R.C., Peel Hall

All but Peel Hall and St Wilfrid's were single-storey buildings of brick, glass and aluminium. Generally designed to hold 320 children, many opened with half this number but were soon swamped by pupils. Woodhouse Park had over nine hundred children by 1958 and many were taken in bus fleets to Peel Hall and Royal Oak until huts were available. In 1957 Sharston Primary became an extension to Sharston Secondary School.

In this fluid situation vandalism was rife, but in spite of everything each school had character. Ex-navy man Jim Myatt ran Oldwood in service style and with naval discipline 'to settle in the problem families'. Baguley Hall was designed by the future City Architect, Besant Roberts, as 'the most expensive primary school of the era'. Poundswick was noted for its country dancing. Woodhouse Park felt the blast and the anxiety of the 1957 Viscount air crash.

Secondary schools under the 1944 Act were categorised as county secondary modern, technical or grammar. The pre-war schools of Yew Tree, Sharston and Brownley Green became modern schools and were joined in 1951 by Baguley Hall. The dates are thus:

1951 Baguley Hall	1955 Oldwood
1953 Newall Green	1956 Poundswick Grammar
1954 St Columbia's R.C., Northenden	1957 All Hallows R.C., Peel Hall
1955 Brookway Technical — boys/girls	1961 Yew Tree Comprehensive

Poundswick was the area's only grammar school. Under Mr. Gilpin it was known for its academic work and its 'cracking reviews'. Yew Tree became a modern school in 1947 when the municipal and central schools merged. In 1961, with an added five-storey block opened by Sir Hugh Gaitskill, it became Manchester's first comprehensive school, though Councillor Morris protested that 'with the continued existence of selection Yew Tree is comprehensive in name only'. Dr. Davies, the headmaster, was known for his liberal views.

In the 'educational area' of the Parker and Nicholas Plans, Brookway schools were joined by West Wythenshawe College of Further Education, gorging on sandwich-course apprentices and police cadets, and Park School, for children needing extra help. For children needing further help Piper Hill School, on Yew Tree Lane, opened. The wartime nurseries closed early in this period and one new nursery school, Gresty, built in 1957, was used as an overflow for Peel Hall.

In Further Education the local authority extended its control. The Northwerthen Guild, Dr. Hall noted sadly, 'was reluctantly merged with Yew Tree Evening Centre and as such ceased to exist ... it had provided cultural interest for the people of Wythenshawe, particularly in the war years'. New evening centres were set up at Brownley Green and Oldwood in 1956, and at Broadoak, Moss Nook and Newall Green in 1957. Courses ranged from shorthand to coastal navigation. An Area Principal was appointed in 1959, but students were lost to the new West Wythenshawe College. When the Civic Centre shopping complex opened in March 1964 the area office moved in, with borrowed furniture, to become the nucleus of the Birtles Adult Education Centre.

Neighbourhood shopping parades, it had been intended, should be built to keep pace

39. Palatine Road, *c*.1955. Many Wythenshavians continued to use Northenden as their shopping centre into the 1970s; a new parade was built and more houses were converted into shops and business premises.

with the erection of houses. In practice the need to agree tenancies and the policy of delaying openings until all the shops in a parade were taken, brought long delays. Newly-arrived housewives often had to exist for months by journeying for bread and butter items to established parades, to Northenden or by catching the unco-ordinated visits of the vans, and fish and meat carts; 'when you heard the horn or the bell, or sometimes they just shouted, you had to drop everything and run down to queue'. Some shops were 'ramshackle wooden ones they put us off with for years'.

Parades usually consisted of a butcher, a baker, a general grocer, a greengrocer, a clothier/ haberdasher, a hardware dealer, a stationer or newsagent/post-office, a chemist and, often at the end of the row, a fish and chip shop. Added to the pre-war shops at Sale Circle and Sharston, and the prefabricated ones at Crossacres, were new parades built at Baguley Precinct, Blackcarr Road, Bowland Road, Button Lane, Cornishway, Gladesdale Road, Greenbrow Road, Hall Lane, Haveley Circle, Lomond Road, Ministerley Parade, Newall Green, Portway and Wendover Road.

With Northenden's larger shops three dusty miles north of Woodhouse Park, there were demands for civic-centre shopping. But it was not until 1962 that building began. Woolworth, Boots, Coop, Tesco and local chain stores took leases. In spite of its austere bleak early form and the spate of plate-glass window breakages, trade flourished. But by 1964 the *Wythenshawe Express* asked, 'Are there too many shops in Wythenshawe?'.

The police, after twenty years of making-do in temporary accommodation — first in a hutted garage shared with the Fire Service, in police boxes and later in council houses adapted as sub-section stations, as for example at Solway Road and on Cornishway, at last moved into a purpose-built police station. Hall Lane Police Station, controlling Wythenshawe west of the Parkway, came under E Division of the Manchester Police at

Platt Lane, and was built in 1953. Brownley Road, coming under D Division at Longsight, was built in 1959 to control the east side of the Parkway. These were two of the largest stations in Manchester. Each had a staff of about a hundred, but due to lack of space some C.I.D. officers had to work from Didsbury. The old Moor End station in Northenden remained, with its staff of three, until 1969 and would not be replaced until the 1980s. Vandalism and burglary were the most frequent crimes in the area, but one problem, exceptionally prevalent in Wythenshawe, was that of stolen cars. Narrow roads and lack of parking spaces near houses were factors arising from plans drawn up in an age when the idea of car ownership by many council house tenants seemed unlikely.

From 1941 the Fire Station had been the Coach House at Sharston Hall. By 1956 it had become the third busiest city station, with 429 calls, compared with 78 in 1949. In April 1957 the *Wythenshawe Recorder* was able to record as a feature news item that Wythenshawe would have, at last, its own fire station. It was an opportunity for the paper to look nostalgically back to the hutted station on Altrincham Road and the days in the coach house at Sharston Hall, though the emphasis was on what was new.

> A permanent Fire Station to serve Wythenshawe will be officially opened. On Wednesday, May 1st, the Lord Mayor of Manchester, Councillor Harry Sharp, opens a new fire station — the first to be built in the city since the war — at Crossacres.
>
> That event will be of two-fold importance in Wythenshawe. The new station, though on the fringe, is the first building to go up on the Civic Centre site. There will be a guard of honour consisting of senior officers and men from the South division and on the forecourt the Brigade Silver Band will play. A commemorative plaque will be dedicated by Rev. Eric Saxon, the Brigade Chaplain. One of the most modern stations in the country it still has the traditional slide-down poles but it has, too, a 55 foot high tower for fire practice, a far cry from 1934 . . .

The account described the first major outbreak that the first station had to cope with: a haystack fire at Sharston Mount.

The first home for two ambulances was the garage left by the fire and police services on Altrincham Road. Following exile at Withington Hospital, the ambulance service received a new depot at Leestone Road on the Sharston Industrial Estate in 1959. In time this became the depot for the whole of the southern area of Manchester, with fifty vehicles.

At the beginning of this period servicemen were still in a hutted hospital at Baguley; by the end a new Maternity Hospital would be open and plans for the main hospital ready. The huts had been used for military casualties and in November 1946 a military wing was opened, with a plastic surgery team installed and 126 beds. Under the National Health Act Baguley Sanatorium came under South Manchester Hospital Management Committee, at Withington. The military left in 1948 and the hutted area became Wythenshawe Hospital on 1 January 1951. Short of staff, it began to take part in the group-training of both State Registered Nurses at Baguley and Assistant (State Enrolled) Nurses at Wythenshawe.

The Baguley Sanatorium did not wish to see its baby leave home, but the Manchester Regional Board planned a general hospital, with Baguley remaining a chest hospital. On 1 January 1952 an independent Wythenshawe Hospital was born, with its own House Committee, Administrative Officer, G. C. Chadwick, and matron, Miss Morgan (later Mrs. Doolan). Its own problems included derelict huts, unkempt grounds, shortage of cash and staff, and 200 patients, including 75 from Christie's cancer hospital. The hospital was to serve the new township of Wythenshawe and there would be 375 beds in all, for 115 males, 165 females, and 95 children.

Aware of Wythenshawe's need for a completely new hospital, in July 1955 the Ministry of Health included Wythenshawe in its list of the first few new hospitals to be built under the National Health Service. It was originally planned to build on the site of the Emergency Military Sanatorium hospital and the Maternity Hospital would be built first. J. L. Pugh was appointed the first full-time administrator. Temporarily the hutted hospital had to serve and the main corridor was covered in.

A scale model was made, but the Ministry of Health, to avoid Manchester's clean air rules, contorted the plans to fit its own land north of Baguley Hospital. A new approach road from Southmoor Road was included on the north side. The Maternity entrance was on the south. 1963 saw more open heart surgery at Baguley and the start, six years late, of the building of the Maternity Hospital.

Consultant Gynaecologist R. Martin battled for the highest standards in the Maternity Hospital. The architects, Powell and Moya, for instance, had been the designers of the Skylon at the Festival of Britain. Plans for the Main Hospital and Training School were agreed. On 18 October 1965, with a marquee on the old Baguley Bowling Green, the new Wythenshawe Maternity Hospital, at £500,000, was opened by the then Minister of Health, Mr. Kenneth Robinson.

Changes were beginning to take place in transport and industry, too. The Cheshire lines were not nationalised until six months after the rest of Britain's railways. By an oversight, the 1947 Rail Act overlooked Joint Committees, but Bessie Braddock, M.P. for Liverpool, reminded the government just in time.

Dr. Beeching's plans for efficiency in 1964 caused Northenden and Baguley stations to be axed in 1965, though not the line itself. Ironically, it was just as the Wythenshawe Liberal Party were demanding more railways for the area. 'Despite howls of protest, Wythenshawe and Northenden possibly got the railway service they deserved.' In the 1960s only a hundred people used the stations daily. One resident commented to the *Wythenshawe Express* in 1961, 'I didn't realise they were still running. I've noticed a lot of goods trains using the line, but I thought they'd stopped passenger traffic years ago'. On the other hand, British Railways did little to advertise the passenger facilities of the Cheshire Lines.

By 1946 Wythenshawe people were getting restive about their bus services. Parker's low housing density meant unfilled and uneconomic buses, but the Traffic Commisioners had forced Manchester City Transport to give up subsidising the Wythenshawe services from other areas and raise the return fare from 8d. to 10d. As compensation, Wythenshawe was given through buses during the day. The trams were left with only the Princess Road traffic.

The *Wythenshawe Recorder* of 1 November 1946 noted local resentment under the headline 'No possibility of a full bus service — lack of vehicles'. The M.C.T. explained that no area in Manchester could have a full service. Two hundred thousand passengers (double the 1939 total) were chasing 85,000 seats in the rush hours.

> The department has the same number of vehicles in use as in 1939, some so old that they are due for scrapping as replacements come in. Since July the Traffic Commissioners have resumed their annual inspection [so] . . . even more buses may be condemned as not road-worthy.

A bus strike in November aggravated the complaints about services and fare increases.

In October 1947 the *Wythenshawe Recorder* objected to the proposal for Parkway trolley buses. 'But our real reason for deprecating trolley wires down Princess Parkway is that we regard this highway as too beautiful to be so marred.'

In December 1949 another increase in the return fare to Manchester, from 10d. to 1s., roused Harry Lloyd, Chairman of the Federal Council, to write to the Transport Minister, who refused to meet a delegation: 'There is a lot of bitter feeling about the increase. Wythenshawe is different from other parts of the city because buses have to be used far more to get people from their homes to places of entertainment'.

Meanwhile A. V. Roe Aviation vacated the Northenden Bus Garage on 14 January 1946. In September 1948 an M.C.T. booklet declared that the garage would shortly be opened with all manner of wonderful additions — offices (built by A. V. Roe, under the Ministry of Aircraft Production), a recreation room, snack bar and a canteen for employees as well as the clubhouse, Cringlewood, on Yew Tree Lane. But, despite hopes, the garage was not ready until the 1950s. It closed in 1986, a casualty of the need for economy in the wake of bus deregulation.

In 1948 services to Wythenshawe were:

Benchill to Barton Dock	23x	Ringway	64
(later to Poundswick Lane)		Sale Moor	99
Lawton Moor	43	Woodhouse Lane to East	
Benchill to Piccadilly	45	Didsbury via Ringway	56x
(later to Poundwick Green)		Newall Green (limited stop)	101
Crossacres	46	Baguley Hall Estate	102
Brooklands	50	Brookland to Piccadilly via	
Styal	64x	Northern Moor (new service)	111

70 and 71 were work buses to Trafford Park. In all 161 buses were to be operated from the Northenden garage.

To people from Manchester, Baguley and Wythenshawe were still the countryside as this excerpt from the M.C.T. booklet *See Manchester by Bus*, dated 1948, implies:

> Baguley. Service 99 to Baguley Station. Walk along Shady Lane to Floats Road, thence via Floats Road, past the Sanatorium to Clay Lane, turn right into White Carr Lane, left into Roaring Gate Lane, to Davenport Green, thence into Thorley Lane and to Bailey Lane. Along Bailey Lane to Poundswick Lane and Crossacres bus terminus. Return to the City.

A new spirit of revival was engendered elsewhere in Wythenshawe by *The City of Manchester Plan* (1945), but bus services did not match housing expansion and complaints persisted. To be fair, M.C.T. increased its bus services from 15 to 30 (including five works services). Routes 103, 106, 107 and 116/117 were introduced, and 1951, 1953, 1956 and 1957 seem to have been the great years for this extension. Complaints continued, however. Some were answered. In 1961 the Peel Hall residents, calling themselves the 'Forgotten Estate', demanded their own circular-route service instead of a rush hour 106, or a single-decker connecting 128, to Benchill. After two years the 128 (in time the 148) was extended to the town centre and seven years later it divided into the 117/118/119 — the Circular Route. Others complaints failed. Sharston factories demanded better links than the 64 and a few works buses into Wythenshawe, where their workers lived, but this evoked no response. In December 1962, however, route 103 was honoured with the first 77-seater fleetline buses.

The main traffic roads in Wythenshawe were completed. By and large they followed the Parker Plan, as revised by Nicholas, to Simonsway, the east-west road south of the Civic Centre. Princess Parkway wended south (on paper only for the moment), increasingly thought of as an adjunct to the motorway network, but the Western Parkway bit the dust.

At Ringway on 1 January 1946 civil flying resumed, though there was still much R.A.F. activity. The airport was closed for two weeks at the start of June for repairs to runways and taxiways before the aviation companies' schedules began for the summer season. The runways were in poor condition after intense wartime usage and work continued for some time afterwards without affecting air traffic.

When Air France opened its Paris service on 16 June it was the first post-war scheduled service from Ringway. On 1 February 1947 British European Airways (B.E.A.) was formed and took over most of the scheduled services within the British Isles. By 1 August 1947 civil air movements predominated. On 3 August an R.A.F. Dakota crashed on take-off, fortunately with no casualties. In September 1947 there was the first helicopter visit to Ringway, a Westland Demonstrator Sikorsky S-51, G-AJHW. The Amsterdam-Manchester route was reintroduced by K.L.M. in May 1947. On 24 September at 8 p.m. a Loxham's Anson crashed through a boundary hedge on landing, but the crew and seven passengers were unhurt.

The major events in 1948 were two air displays, the City of Manchester 613 Squadron Air Display on 24 April, and the September air display. The former was the first to be held since May 1939 and by an amazing piece of planning was on Cup Final Day (Manchester United 4, Blackpool 2). The latter was the last to be held at Ringway. Later displays took place at Woodford because of the increase in air traffic. Sivewright Airways quickly took up the Isle of Man route, dropped by B.E.A. that year. Well remembered are the Dragon Rapides, the staple aircraft on that route. Swissair began a Zurich service on 15 December 1948.

In 1949 the battle Manchester City Council had waged with the Labour government since the end of the war for control of Ringway reached its zenith (the council finally won in the mid-1950s). It was, therefore, highly embarrassing for the then Aviation Minister, Lord Pakenham (later Lord Longford), to open in February the new passenger-handling facilities behind B.E.A.'s hangar. All scheduled airlines used the new tarmac in front of this hangar, no more to be seen in front of the control tower. Lord Pakenham promised the airport a much-needed runway extension; in his book *Early Ringway* R. J. Webb says: 'The possibility of cash for this extension was used to coerce Manchester into handing over control, without success, and permission to extend the runway was continually delayed for over two years'.

On 19 August a B.E.A. Dakota, G-AHCY, returning from Belfast, crashed on Saddleworth Moor in bad weather whilst approaching Ringway — the first fatal crash involving Manchester passengers. Only eight of the 32 people on the plane survived.

In those days air-traffic control opened at various times of the day during the year. In February 1950 it opened from 8 a.m. to 8.45 p.m., though in the case of special or late flights it stayed open to accommodate them.

1951 was a year of change. 'The hopes and initiative of the first post-war years had given way to the grim realities of austerity and shortages and a Labour Government bent on wholesale nationalisation', writes R. J. Webb. Many charter companies succumbed through lack of work. The main runway was closed to traffic in August 1950 to allow a 600-yard extension to be laid at the eastern end. The threshold of the original runway 24 was at the highest point on the airport and extending from this point created the infamous hump. The first 200 yards of extension opened on 21 January 1951, the remainder finally being finished during the summer without the need for further runway closure.

At 12.30 a.m. on 27 March 1951 an Air Transport Charter Dakota, G-AJVZ, took off on a newspaper flight in freezing conditions with cross-winds. It lost power due to carburettor icing and failure to select carburettor heat. 'The aircraft knocked some slates off the roof of Fullalove's Off-licence on the corner of Woodhouse Lane and crashed into the market gardens beyond, killing both the crew.'

In April 1952 Ringway opened 24 hours a day. Many new services began in the summer, for example B.E.A. to Zurich, Amsterdam/Dusseldorf. This year the airport handled 163,000 passengers, one-and-a-half times more than Liverpool, though in 1947 Speke handled more than Ringway. On 3 November the new Conservative Minister of Aviation, Mr. Lennox Boyd, ended the strife between the government and Manchester. He agreed that Ringway would be an international airport. Manchester would retain ownership, but the government would pay 75 per cent of the costs towards a new terminal and further runway extensions.

Sabena Belgian World Airlines began operating their Ostend service on 13 June 1953. Ringway became an intercontinental airport when Sabena introduced their transatlantic service, the 'Manchester Premier', for New York, with a scheduled refuelling stop at Gander.

By 1954 passenger numbers had reached 265,000 — too many for the 1949 terminal to handle. It was modified, therefore, No. 5 hangar demolished, the runway/threshold lighting upgraded and the tarmac extended. The airlines introduced new services, such as the B.O.A.C. London-Manchester-Prestwick-New York flights, and turbine-powered airliners appeared in April 1954 with B.E.A. and Aer Lingus. October 1953 saw a report submitted to the Airport Committee, which envisaged passengers increasing to 525,000 by 1963 and recommended the building of a new terminal. Fortunately, the design allowed for further expansion later, which was just as well because in 1963 the numbers exceeded one million, two hundred thousand. A Canada service was introduced by Lufthansa on 23 April 1956, Hamburg-Dusseldorf-Manchester-Shannon-Montreal-Chicago.

In 1957 came Ringway's second fatal crash since the war. On 14 March a B.E.A. Viscount from Amsterdam fractured a wing-flap on its final approach. It plunged into some council houses on Shadow Moss near the primary school, killing 20 passengers and two people on the ground (the tenth house on Shadow Moss Road still shows the scars). Both dead and injured were taken to Shadow Moss School. Captain Breheny and his co-pilot, Douglas Palin, were killed. The captain had been with B.E.A. since its beginnings.

Work on the terminal began in October with clearance and piling. On 23 April 1958 the main runway was extended from 5,900 to 7,000 feet. The A538 Altrincham-Hale-Wilmslow Road had to be diverted around the new threshold. 1958 also saw the tragic Munich air crash on 6 February, which almost annihilated the Manchester United Football Team. Six months later there was the first visit by a jetliner, a V.I.P. trip by a French Caravelle demonstrator. On 16 April 1959 B.O.A.C. introduced the short-lived Bristol Britannia on its New York schedules, the last of the propeller aircraft to be produced. Jet airliners had come and though the Caravelle was a short-haul aircraft, the next jet to appear at Ringway was not. Sabena began its first scheduled jet service to New York, using a Boeing 707, on 20 April 1960. Inclusive tours were on the increase from Ringway, using Skymaster, Convair 400, Hermes, etc.

Towards the end of October 1962 the new terminal was officially opened by the Duke of Edinburgh, and it was in use by December. In April 1963 B.O.A.C. started its New York schedule at Ringway with Boeing 707s. At the end of March 1964 Sabena withdrew its New York service after 10 years of pioneering. The British government would not allow them to operate more than two services a week, a retrograde step.

The vacant industrial sites at Sharston began to fill as soon as the war ended, and by 1953 two thirds of its 110 acres were taken. The Wythenshawe Committee made outline plans for the western and southern estates at Roundthorn and Moss Nook, but their development was held up by the difficulty of getting government sanction. As firms turned from wartime to peacetime products, there was a resurgence of enterprise and companies competed for labour, materials and sales: Johnson's 'model factory', Wearlee's 'spacious new premises' and numerous 'ideal work places' jostled for publicity in the press.

The war had brought unity among firms, with the Industrial Fire Fighters Association becoming the Wythenshawe Industrial Association in 1948. This had more power and was able to lobby the city council successfully. Local employment was urgently needed by 1947 and a report in that year showed that 68 per cent of workers in Wythenshawe had to find employment elsewhere.

Wythenshawe: Plan and Reality recorded in 1953 'The first site was let out only in 1933 and more than twenty firms are now in full production . . .'

Bennett Motor Spares	Leyton Studies
Birkbys Plastics	Manchester & Salford Co-op Dairy
Bond Motor Spares	Pioneer Telephones
Brooks Biscuits	Thornton Electrics

40. Manchester Airport's famous chandeliers. The new terminal was opened in 1962 but this view of the main concourse is after further expansion.

Crampton (Paxo)
Eva Cartons
French's Tapes
G.P.A. Tools
Holden & Brooks Pumps
Iddon Electrics
Isola Insulation
Johnson's Wire

Foods Walmer Clothing
Wearlee Clothing
Wilcox Fuses
William Morris Press
Wylex Electrics
   and . . . a bus depot
   post and sporting offices
   a school meals depot.

There was rapid industrial growth in the three years between 1953 and 1956, and the addition of the following firms left few vacant sites:

Adjello Pianos
Alder & Mackay Gas-Meters
Allied Dairies
Anderson Weaving Cards
Barrel Builder
Benrath Machine Tools
British Fondants
Callon Confectionery
Clydol Oils
Davies & Timmin Nuts & Bolts
Dawson & Rodgers Soft Furnishings
Disincrustant Marseillaise

Hyde Braiding & Insulation
Kaumograph Transfers
Loder Switch Gear
Lucy & Sunderland Timber
May Hosiery
Nettle Electrical Accessories
Pipeweld
Rolinx Plastics
Rushworth Knitwear
Thor Engineering
Tie Weaving
Trojan Electrical Engineering

Fielden Electronics   Walls Ice Cream
Fram Concrete   Wild Casement Cloths

The only firms listed at Roundthorn in 1956 were Brookside Clothing and Geigy (U.K.) Pharmaceutical — the firm that discovered D.D.T., the new insecticide of the time. The Moss Nook Industrial Area was by that year established, however, and firms there included: Bates Ventilation; British Rayon Research; Milnes Boxes; Ministry of Supply Engineering; Reynold Chain. No mention was made of Ferranti's 'colossal project', begun in 1950.

On the Floats Road area of the Roundthorn Estate Metro-Vickers was taking shape, to give employment to 1,300 by 1957. Nearby in Southmoor Road A.E.I.'s factory was opened by the Duke of Edinburgh in the same year. They painted the stones along the railway track white where he was going to walk and put up a canopy for him — 'ordinary folk couldn't get on a train for miles around here', complained a resident to the press. A.E.I. announced their 'revolutionary new generator' in 1962 and Griffin and George's Scientific Instrument Centre was hailed as the most modern in Europe. Wythenshawe did not suit all firms, however. After 14 years, Birkby's Plastics Factory moved back to Yorkshire in 1962 with a loss of 200 jobs. More problems were to come.

Voices of the People

The press, residents and the spokesmen and women of official and other organisations now sometimes disagreed about the transformation of Wythenshawe. Clearly, with a variety of houses and a greater variety of residents, there would be conflicting ideas of the ideal home. Family standards were varied. While one Benchill man had a Rolls Royce outside his door, another used his floorboards as firewood. Some parents would not or could not control their children to the level expected by others. Some condoned the vandalism of their children. Rents, bus fares, low-flying jets, the fire-hazards of certain pre-fabs, lack of garden gates were all subjects for complaints in varying degrees at different times.

Flats were regarded by some as Utopia. 'We wouldn't live anywhere else. You can see the City Lights, the hills and the planes', one delighted couple was reported as saying. Another resident, in the third of four identical three-storey blocks of flats in Baguley in 1948, was less sure.

We were bussed to Brownley Green School which was so packed you had to move all the desks forward to get out . . . For shopping we used a van . . . he'd pip his horn and people came out to queue . . .

Then they were putting up Tin-town in Newall Green, steel upstairs and concrete down. Royal Oak still had pre-fabs — ten years expected but they lasted twenty. In Baguley, in Woodhouse Park and in Newall Green there are two main roads and everything else is off them.

The flats were very good, very warm with a coal fire. Everything off one long hall — two bedrooms, a wash-house and a gas boiler for washing. But noisy. You could hear everything, especially above. And the rubbish chutes — stuff got stuck in the pipe. And the coal men wouldn't deliver very often. You had to sweep your front by 10 o'clock, no ball games, but nobody paid any attention. Many who came had been bombed out and they built thousands of homes — and no amenities, no pub, nor a petrol station. There was no vandalism at first, but then people started exchanging and everything went downhill.

The mother who, after losing her Didsbury home to a building society in 1933, had been a satisfied council tenant (as we saw on page 67) had since been in Altrincham Road then in Benchill, and she was to move once more.

. . . the war came and our family grew to ten . . . and Grandpa too . . . they started building some houses on Greenwood Road, some of them four bedrooms. I at once applied . . . One day I was waiting for a bus and got talking to Walter Frost (a Councillor) . . . I went back to the Housing Department and stated our case. We moved in August 1946 . . . been here ever since.

At the Town Hall in Manchester, in March 1946 while a civic film of the city councillors in debate was being made, the chamber was invaded by a placard-waving deputation with a ten-thousand signature petition for better amenities for Wythenshawe. One poster read 'End Monopoly', and another respectfully asserted 'Sir, Wythenshawe Needs a Post-Office'. At the core of the invasion was the Wythenshawe Community Council (W.C.C.) and its vociferous chairman, Harry Lloyd. The W.C.C. had grown out of the Rackhouse, Royal Oak and Benchill Community Associations, which dated back to 1934. The first meeting of the W.C.C., in 1943 after national affiliation, had been addressed by Alderman W. T. Jackson, two years before his death. From time to time the W.C.C. confronted the Wythen-shawe Committee, which listened politely.

Jackson's fellow conspirator, Ernest Simon, was made a peer in 1947 when he joined the Labour Party. As Baron Simon of Wythenshawe and Didsbury, he received the Freedom of the City in 1959, dying a year later. Barry Parker left his Wythenshawe task, 'my greatest achievement', in 1941 and died in 1947.

Six of the Wythenshawe Committee lived in Wythenshawe, two in council houses. Elected from the Wythenshawe wards were Elizabeth Yarwood, Walter Frost and Councillor Cave. The chairman, Councillor Bentley, lived in Northenden. Petitions, deputations, protests, demands for home rule and for a civic centre to provide a heart for the new area punctuated their routine.

The first M.P. for Wythenshawe, for 14 years from 1950, was Eveline Hill, a Conservative. As Wythenshawe grew the Labour vote increased and in 1964 the first M.P. of the completed venture was Alf Morris, who was Minister for the Disabled until 1979.

The *Wythenshawe Recorder*, started in 1937, reappeared in 1946. 'A voice for the people of Manchester's glamour satellite city' was the *Recorder*'s claim at the time. Harold Geldar took over from the Chamber of Commerce and added '*and Express*' in 1958. It became the *Wythenshawe Express* when Lancashire and County Papers became owners in 1964. The word that appeared most frequently in the paper's headlines was 'vandalism'. It frequently ran 'War on Vandalism' campaigns, but while the damage was there for all to see, other towns had far worse vandalism and parts of Wythenshawe never seemed less than a garden city.

'Autonomy for Wythenshawe' was the cry of Harry Lloyd, chairman of the Wythenshawe Federal Council from the mid-1950s. The *Wythenshaw Recorder* echoed his cry. It began by referring to Wythenshawe as 'Our New Town', but in time it was less confident and asked 'Only a Suburb?'. Comparisons were frequently made with much smaller towns that had their own councils and often a mayor. The civic centre remained a mirage and the City of Manchester made it clear that an independent council was out of the question.

When Wythenshawe Garden City was not being set up against the City of Manchester, Northenden was presented as its adversary. In September 1958 a feature article was headlined 'A Letter Revives an Old Old Topic — Northenden v Wythenshawe'. George Griggs, the new chairman of the Federal Council, accused the *Recorder* of creating a barrier by referring to 'Northenden and Wythenshawe'. He accused Northenden and Brooklands of being isolationist. A letter in reply complained that the garden city got all the attention, while Northenden lacked basic amenities.

> Northenden was a little community before Wythenshawe was thought of. You cannot expect the people here to suddenly forget about their village life, forget the very name of their village and say: 'Now we are Wythenshawe'. It's too much to ask.

The paper itself drew attention to Wythenshawe's own isolationism and to the fact that the football league for the area is called 'The South Manchester and Wythenshawe League'.

In the article from which the above extracts are taken Arthur Royle wrote his urbane comment, 'Northenden and Wythenshawe were enemies for a short period!'.

Chapter Nine

Festivals, Fun and Commitment

During the war years those societies and associations which had managed to survive were generally manned by the young and the elderly. The churches, which had been established in Wythenshawe in the late 1930s, continued to be the centre of social activities, partly for the practical reason that, as there were limitations on building, the parish halls provided ready-made meeting places. The community associations, some of which had started in the 1930s, notably Royal Oak, continued to flourish and shortly after the war others were formed. There had been restrictions on travelling during the war, caused partly by shortage of fuel and partly because the blackout discouraged movement far out of the home area. Thus a situation was created in which local groups became very important. Later, as restrictions were gradually lifted, the emphasis shifted to some extent away from the churches and localised events in the direction of larger festivals, Civic Weeks and grander celebrations. The community associations contributed enthusiastically.

A Wythenshawe Civic Week in 1948 was the first large, joint venture of this kind to be held after the war. It did not get off the ground without some discussion, disagreement and heartache. An interesting article by Harold Lloyd of the Community Council appeared in the *Wythenshawe Recorder* of August 1946. It shows the earnest attempt by some people to inculcate a sense of belonging and identity in Wythenshawe residents.

> Wythenshawe lacks many things to make life easier, but it also lacks tradition which of course will develop in time, but what kind of tradition will it acquire? A Civic week for Wythenshawe should have as its main role the instilling of civic pride in each of us to make us feel proud that we belong to Wythenshawe and Wythenshawe belongs to us and that it is our responsibility . . .

A large operation such as a civic week needed financial backing and there was opposition to this in the following year, for as plans were made and discussed many problems were raised, such as the siting of fairs, routes for the procession, and dignitaries to be invited. In 1948 the event finally got off the ground, but the Lord Mayor of Manchester refused to perform the opening ceremony and it was opened by a local M.P., Mr. Shepherd. Despite the teething troubles, the first Civic Week celebrations got off to a great start with a splendid pageant, said to be one and a half miles long. For the next few years the Civic Weeks continued to flourish. The pageant and processions involved all the community associations. One of the continuing problems was a suitable venue. Some of the places suggested and used were Greenwood Fields, St Columba's and the grounds of The Cedars. The first Grand Parade culminated, appropriately enough, in Wythenshawe Park. Oak from an old beam removed during the restoration of the Hall was used to make the casket to contain an illuminated scroll. This was given to the reigning Miss Wythenshawe as a token of her office. However, one of the difficulties in holding the affair in the park was that at first the authorities would not allow a fun-fair to be erected or charge to be made for entry into the grounds. The fun-fair was essential to the celebrations and the entrance money to the finances. We have the opinion of one lady involved at the time:

> If we had it in Wythenshawe Park then it was a beautiful setting, and all the glamour but we couldn't charge for the people to come in and sit down and yet we were putting on a terrific show and no one was paying for it. It was better to put it on in Greenwood Fields and put palings round and charge people to go in. This is how the fair came to be in Wythenshawe Park because we used to get Ingham's Fair and at the beginning they used to pay us £70 for the week so all this went into

the funds, but the troubles with Wythenshawe Park was that they wouldn't let us have the fair. They eventually did and then the fair went into the park every time. It was a terrific week and every association used to put on a full week of activities, say a table tennis competition on one night, a big dance on another and a darts competition on another night, and Miss Wythenshawe and her retinue used to go round them all . . .

Until the authorities allowed the fair to take place in the park, various other sites were used. Even when permission had been granted the Federal Council sometimes chose other sites for the culmination of the procession and the performing of events. In 1959 the venue was Greenwood Fields.

There is an interesting account of one of the Civic Weeks through the eyes of the eighth Miss Wythenshawe, Miss Ruth Bell. She describes a visit to the hospitals, where the children cheered her as if she really was a queen. The same evening she attended an 'impressive' service at St Martin's church and on Monday paid a visit to the Sharston Community Art Section, where she saw 'wonderful' work. Tuesday was spent opening the second half of a football match on Brownley Green Playing Fields, where a large crowd of spectators gave her a warm welcome. On Wednesday she attended a baby show at William Temple Church and in the evening there was a Civic Week dance at the *Mersey Hotel*. A visit to the Royal Oak Drama Group and two other dances concluded her week, with the highlight of the procession on Saturday, followed by a visit to the fair and a party-supper provided by the ladies of the Sharston Community Association.

For almost ten years there were mixed accounts of the Civic Week happenings and popularity. Occasionally it was hit by rain. In 1955 the stand was wrecked by vandals, and in 1958 the pageant was reported as a 'Blaze of Glory', although the month before there had been an article in the local paper entitled, 'Who cares about Civic Week?'. By the beginning of the 1960s support from the community associations had fallen to its lowest level and that year only two community associations took part. The Civic Week Committee was short of money and, when tackled, many of the residents said that they were fed up with the pageantry.

It ended because many of the associations folded up. Newall Green dropped out, just disintegrated through lack of interest . . . apathy. There was a lot of T.V. and people started to stay at home and watch, and lots of pubs opened on the estates, lots of working men's clubs. People would rather go out to those sort of things where there was adult activities and drinking than give their time to the youngsters. Woodhouse Park C.A. had developed communist leanings . . . but they were very good workers. The delegates on the Wythenshawe council that came from Woodhouse Park were always biased. Once they were talking about the catering and someone said, 'We'll have a Coca Cola stall' but the man from Woodhouse Park said, 'No, no Coca Cola. It's an American-based firm . . .'. The rot seemed to set in straight away after that. People started to stay away as they didn't want to hear political views and whenever Woodhouse Park put on a parade the Wythenshawe Communist Party used to put a big piece in it and a lot of people didn't like walking in a Parade that had a Red Flag in it. They didn't want their children walking behind a section that was concerned with the burning issue of the day and carrying banners with the hammer and sickle on them . . .

In 1962 there was a short revival and a profit of £100 was made. A combination of factors social, political and financial brought the Civic Weeks to a halt in the mid-1960s.

Community associations by the 1960s had become fairly powerful within their own localities. This has been shown by the fact that it was in part the withdrawal of their support that helped cause the collapse of the Civic Weeks. They had various functions within the society some social, some political. Northenden Community Association, which was started after the war, launched mainly by Mr. Arthur Hooley, was not primarily a social body as were some of those on the estates. A member of this association in the 1950s remembers:

Community Associations were being set up all over the estate and it seemed right that Northenden should have one too. We had put the pressure on for a community centre but at that time there was

41. The Riverside Café and the Brunt family. For over sixty years the café and adjoining stadium were popular for eating, skating, boxing, wrestling and boating. It became a residential caravan park after a fire in 1962.

no money. We did however act rather as civic societies do today, but of course there were no members. There were simply people appointed from various organisations. As I recollect we arranged for Orchard Road to be labelled East and West to avoid confusion and we provided a pillar box on the corner of Kenworthy Lane and Parkfield Road. We were the sponsors of the Festival of Northenden which was held in the Church Rooms and in which a lot of Northenden organisations took part.

The interest in this particular association does not seem to have been great, for more than once there was a report in the local paper to the effect that at their recent meeting the association was unable to form a quorum and so the meeting had to be cancelled.

The Wythenshawe community associations, on the other hand, during the 1950s and 1960s had good followings. The Rackhouse Community Association, the oldest established, had its centre at Daine Avenue and 300 members in the late 1950s. Activities included billiards, table-tennis, handicrafts, morris and folk dancing and ballroom dancing. Outside the centre they sponsored a bowling team for both ladies and gents. The Benchill Community Association also catered for a vast range of interests, similar to Rackhouse, and they sponsored a Silver Band which they declared 'was among the best in the city'. Successful football and athletic clubs were in existence.

The Royal Oak and Baguley's Residents' Association achieved successes in sport spheres, but it was especially well-known for its varied cultural activities, particularly its dramatic and musical productions. Royal Oak Community Association continued to be housed in the Royal Oak Centre, the complete social hub of the district, and from where the association pioneered many notable activities. One of these activities was morris dancing. The first group to be started in Wythenshawe was sponsored by the Royal Oak Community Association and trained by Miss Joan Lawrence, whose parents had been founder members of the association. To quote from Miss Lawrence:

> I started the first morris troupe in Wythenshawe, probably the first in Manchester after the war. I did it for 20 odd years. We went everywhere. One week we used to go to Wythenshawe Conservative Club, the next week we went to the Labour Club — politics didn't come into it. Wherever there was a fête we went. We had three morris troupes, the first in Royal Oak. Then Newall Green said they would like one so I started one there and then Sharston C.A. said they'd like one and then when most of the C.A.s had got morris troupes we had big morris dancing competitions. The *Wythenshawe Recorder* gave them a cup and I gave them a cup, but some of the troupes started to travel further afield, but the Royal Oak Troupe preferred to go to the smallest garden party in Wythenshawe than into competitions where you could get a lot of money . . .

The principle of supporting events in Wythenshawe seems to have been very much a part of the Royal Oak Community Association philosophy, and one that paid off. While over the years the most of the other associations dwindled or disappeared altogether, the Royal Oak Community Association continued to flourish. Each year they produced a pantomime which 'was a sell-out every time and almost embarrassing the profit that was made'. By the 1950s and 1960s many of the people taking leading parts in these dramatic productions had their own children starring with them, so long-term was the support given by many to this association.

Sharston Community Association was one of those founded after the war in 1948, when it was given part of Sharston Hall as a community centre. In 1950 the whole of the premises were occupied and in 1957 the association took over the old coach house, which the fire brigade had converted. The membership in this year was high, well over five hundred, and there were 23 affiliated organisations. There was a section that catered for the needs of the neighbourhood and a large youth section. Their aim was 'to serve the community, to further education and to encourage personal service and good fellowship'.

The newest community association in this period, the Woodhouse Park and Moss Nook Community Association, did not have a centre of its own in the late '50s. Nevertheless, it managed to accommodate in various school premises a chess club, a horticultural society and a women's section. It also ran a morris troupe and a youth club.

The post-war period was a time of affluence and success for the community associations. They were filling a social and, in many cases, an educational need. Television had not yet become readily available and people had to create their own entertainment in Wythenshawe, as neither a cinema nor a theatre had been provided on the highly-populated new estates. As well as the one concerted effort of the Civic Week Committees, there were many small pageants and carnivals taking place in Wythenshawe. Royal Oak had its annual Harvest Queen, a nostalgic title, perhaps reflecting the fact that a few nursery gardens survived around the outskirts of the area. Other places had their Rose Queens, May Queens and Rosebuds, but there could only be one Miss Wythenshawe — the Civic Queen.

As noted in the previous chapter, Northenden held its own festival in 1951, a three-week affair involving all sections of the community. It was opened by Dr. Mabel Tylecote, Chairman of the Manchester Federation of Community Associations, and Alderman F. E. Tylecote, Alderman for the Northenden Ward. For the young there was a children's field-day at Yew Tree School, organised by the Parent Associations of St Wilfrid's School and Northenden County Primary School. For the older inhabitants there was an evening outing and a trip round North Cheshire, and for all ages there were dramatic and musical performances.

An exhibition was mounted in the Church Rooms on Kenworthy Lane that showed the wealth of talent and diversity of interest to be found in Northenden. Amongst the contributors were the Northenden Chess Club, the Rosemary Fund, the Northenden Dramatic Society, the Northenden Players, the National Savings Movement, the Northenden Women's Conservative Association, St Wilfrid's Y.P.U., Northenden Allotment and Garden Society and Northenden Methodist Church. Northenden had a tradition of musical and dramatic work, as can be seen from the programme of the Northenden Festival, but drama by the well-known and award-winning N.A.D.S. dominated the village for many years.

There were many groups of amateurs throughout Wythenshawe during this period wishing to entertain or arranging for people to be entertained, as the following list of a week's events offered in the 1950s shows: the Benchill C.A. presented *An Inspector Calls*; Northenden Dramatic Society presented *The Two Mrs. Carols*; The 1st Wythenshawe Girl Guides and Brownies presented *Cinderella*; the Brownley Green Methodists presented *The Comet Concert Party*. For those who desired something more physically taxing, the Wythenshawe Irish Society offered 'A Grand Irish Night'; Benchill and District Conservative Association, a 'Grand Social and Dance'; the Wythenshawe Ward Conservative Association, 'A Crazy Nite Victory Dance' (presumably it was about election time); R.A.F. Ringway, 'A Dance'; Wythenshawe Communist Party, a 'Social and Dance', and the Northenden Stadium declared it was open for roller skating.

Many clubs and associations catered for the needs of the young and the old, the energetic and the sedentary. For the young the Y.H.A. offered a talk on hypnotism and the 18 Plus Group one on marriage guidance. The Royal Oak gardeners held a Brains Trust, the Northenden Chess Club welcomed new members, and the Irish Society gave children dancing lessons. These were just a few of the happenings in Wythenshawe in the 1950s and 1960s.

Apart from the self-made entertainment of the community associations, which was so enjoyable but hard work for the organisers, there were the commercial funfairs that for years before the war had visited Northenden and delighted the villagers with their colourful, exciting action. When they returned after the war the attitude of some people in the locality towards them had changed. They were looked on as noisy, dirty and trouble provoking, not at all suitable for siting in residential areas. In 1948 objections were raised to the fair on the site of the old Pavilion near the river. Shortly after this the fairs ceased to come to Northenden at holiday times and became established in Wythenshawe Park.

Another branch of commercial entertainment available to the people of Wythenshawe was the two cinemas, which were operating in Northenden within sight of each other. Sometimes on a cold Saturday night the film being shown was irrelevant. The length of the queue was the criteria used for deciding which to patronise. This could be judged from a point halfway between the two on Longley Lane, outside Mrs. Sherratt's nursery garden.

The Coronation cinema was the smaller of the two, seating approximately four hundred, but warm and cosy with plenty of double seats down the aisles and along the back row. There one was under the constant surveillance of the owner/manager/projectionist, Mr. Wilf Leigh, who would frequently descend from the back, and if any slight insurrection was thought to be imminent would proceed down the aisle as a precautionary measure. On a summer evening the whirring of wheels and the hollow voices of film stars would be heard flowing through the open door of the same projection box, which let directly on to Longley Lane. Despite its humble origins, the Coronation, or 'Peter's' as it was known by the local people, was believed to be the first cinema of its size in the country to have Cinemascope, the lenses having been flown in specially from Italy in 1955. Unfortunately, this attraction was not enough and it finally closed as a cinema in 1964, opening a few months later as a bingo hall.

The Forum, a larger, more plush edifice, seated approximately eighteen hundred and ran to three queues on a busy evening at the front of the building, a small one for the circle, a longer one for the back stalls, and down the side the longest of all for the front seats. Not

42. The Coronation and A.B.C. Forum Cinemas, Northenden. With the building of the Hollyhedge Cinema abandoned in 1939, the two Northenden picture houses were much in demand as Wythenshawe's only cinemas.

43. The Forum Cinema, now carefully restored by the Jehovah's Witnesses as their 'cathedral of the north'.

that the price paid for the tickets necessarily matched the seat taken up in the dark of the cinema. The A.B.C. group owned the Forum and in 1947 they started a club for children called the A.B.C. Minors. This was held on a Saturday morning and, as well as showing films, the company offered competitions for the young. On one memorable occasion the car park was entirely covered with small children clutching biffbats, a wooden bat with a small ball attached to it by elastic. The object was to keep the ball hitting the bat for as long as possible — the prize a two-wheeler bike. The sponsor of this competition was a chocolate firm, and when a ball sagged away from the bat a marshal would rush up to the faltering child, put a cross on his bat with a copy-ink pencil, so that he could not re-enter the competition, and thrust a block of chocolate into his hand. This was only one of the many activities that took place in and around the Forum. Each year during the Christmas season a pantomime was staged there, the last being *Red Riding Hood* in December 1951. In 1956 the Didsbury Amateur Dramatics and Operatic Society staged the world première of *The Gypsy Baron* there, and the next year Frankie Vaughan starred in a midnight matinee in aid of boys' clubs. During the late '40s and early '50s, the Rosemary Fund hired the Forum as the venue for the annual treat for hundreds of local old people. Another annual event was the 'Miss Wythenshawe' competition, for which the well-lit stage provided a good setting. Thus the Forum, probably the largest secular building in the area, was the meeting place for people of all ages, well justifying its Roman name.

Throughout the war the young actors and actresses of The Younger Generation continued to entertain the people of Northenden. They were well supported, for with the blackout and the very limited bus services operating during this time, people were unable to move far out of the district. As all were similarly constrained, young people were glad to join a local society where they could express themselves dramatically and meet people of like minds, so the casting committee was never short of applicants. The war ended and slowly people started to drift back into the jobs and hobbies they had left in 1939. Young people in the local dramatic scene had had almost five years of playing leading roles, choosing plays and organising productions, and with time competence and confidence had been gained in all these fields. It was difficult for these young players immediately to take back seats to people whose ideas in the drama field had stood still since 1939. At first some compromise was tried and it was agreed that the home-comers and the 'new' players should act in performances together. This they did for four productions, and a legal amalgamation was mooted in the spring of 1946, but arguments and problems were constantly being aired and antagonism seems to have reached its highest point by the A.G.M. in June 1947. At this meeting a member spoke angrily of how the trustees of the N.A.D.S. had been approached at the beginning of the war by Bill Roper with a request to borrow the equipment and properties of the society, so that plays could continue to be performed and that the youth of the village could have a healthy outlet for their energies at a very difficult time. The speaker went on to say that this request had been willingly complied with but advantage had been taken and a new society named The Younger Generation had been formed. It had never been the intention of the N.A.D.S. for a new society to be formed, the speaker declared angrily. In this heated atmosphere a proposal was made that there should be no amalgamation.

> I am making no specific charges but I am aware of the reason that a number of their society are anxious for an amalgamation of the two societies, and I feel sure that members of the N.A.D.S. would suffer much in the process for in spite of every effort to appease we have been met in certain quarters with bitterness and unfriendliness. I cannot recommend that an amalgamation with this society be completed.

A vote was taken and out of the 40 people present there were only three dissenters. In the

same issue of the *Wythenshawe Recorder* from which the above quote was taken there appeared
the following announcement:

NORTHENDEN DRAMATIC SOCIETY
The above society is resuming its activities and will consider applications for membership in:
Acting — Scenery Construction — Production etc.

This set the seal on the schism. Both societies continued to function for a time after this,
their performances being reported locally. In 1951 each group produced a one-act play for
the church's Old English Fayre and in 1953 there is an account of how the Northenden
Players floodlit the church for a special occasion 'loaning their valuable equipment entirely
free', indicating that the newer society had built up a stock of its own and was now a thriving
company. The name had been changed from The Younger Generation to the Northenden
Players. The pioneers, adolescents at the time of its inception, were now mature and felt
the old name inappropriate. The N.A.D.S. disbanded in the fifties.

Sport throughout the area also had its up and downs. With the increase of families came
an increase in the number of potential sportsmen and sportswomen looking for places in
leagues of a variety of indoor and outdoor sports. Weekly the local paper carried fixture
lists for snooker, dominoes, cribbage, darts and billiards, amongst others.

A boxing club was started in the early 1950s as an offshoot of the Sharston Civic Youth
Club. A ring was rigged up in the loft over the stables of Sharston Hall, and a punch ball,
a punch bag and other boxers' requirements were acquired for the room. Here the lads were
coached with enthusiasm which had its rewards. An 11-year-old schoolboy, a member of
Sharston Boxing Club, was chosen to fight for England against Wales. In 1960 two boys
from Benchill Community Association's Lads Club scored well in the Manchester Schools
Boxing Amateur Association Championships, when they had nine finalists, including three
who won inside the distance. They were all aged between 11 and 15 years. The previous
year the area had raised five Manchester Champions, three Lancashire Champions, one
English Schools Finalist and two National Boy's Club Champions.

After the war the popularity of football grew rapidly. Many boys' clubs, community
associations, local works, schools and churches had their own teams. One or two places
around the district were used for matches, such as Brundritts Park, Raymond Road and
Peel Hall Fields, but, generally, teams leased pitches in Wythenshawe Park. By 1960 there
were 12 football pitches and two hockey pitches being used by 250 players each weekend,
but the players had very spartan conditions with which to contend. Their changing room
was an old cattle shed, as one player recalled: 'The shippon changing room had neither
lighting nor heating and the nearest water was 200 yards away. Space was so limited that
there was less than a square yard of space for each of the players on a busy afternoon'. In
1960 the shippon was condemned as unsafe by the Director of Parks, Mr. McMillan, and
scheduled for demolition, and the footballers looked with envy at the bowling and tennis
pavilion being built in the park. Eventually, a £23,000 open-quadrangle-type soccer pavilion
was opened. The charges to the footballers were increased but the facilities were deemed
to be the best in Manchester.

The Wythenshawe Cricket and Lacrosse Club continued to play both their games with
success. In the early 1960s a match drew great crowds to Northenden. It was the benefit
match of Michael Hilton and Roy Tattersall. One official of the club reported to the
newspaper, 'This will be the first time that professionals have played at the Wythenshawe
Cricket Club'. G. Fullar, the Lancashire and England opening batsman, played in the
match and the Wythenshawe team included Ken Grieves. Brian Statham played for the
Roy Tattersall Eleven. The Wythenshawe innings finished at 165 runs, the Tattersall
Eleven winning by 12 runs, and a very good game was enjoyed by all. In contrast, a slight
tragedy occurred in this year when some of the lady viewers were marked as they sat

watching a game on newly-painted, bright-yellow forms. Fortunately, one of the members came to the rescue with a tin of paint remover.

In 1964 Brian Statham opened a new £7,000 cricket pavilion at the Wythenshawe Cricket Club on Longley Lane. Roy Whittaker, a Northenden newsagent, was a schoolboy lacrosse champion and in 1948 an Olympic team member.

Golf was another sport which flourished after the war, and the Northenden Golf Club continued to grow, making alterations to the clubhouse and the greens. The social life was a great feature of the club, and in 1953 a week of events social and sporting was held to celebrate the Coronation. On the Day itself it was thought members 'would be more interested in watching the Coronation ceremony on television than playing golf', so only one competition was arranged. In keeping with their tradition for helping charities, an exhibition match was held in 1961 to which important names in the golfing world, such as Ken Nagle, Ken Bousfield and Max Faulkner, were invited. The proceeds went to the National Society for Cancer Relief.

The long awaited Sharston Baths was opened in 1961 by Lord Derby. They had come to fruition through many disputes and delays, and by the time they were available they were already heavily booked up by swimming clubs and schools.

Bowling was both a very popular pastime and a keenly competitive sport in Northenden and Wythenshawe. Most public houses had their own teams, and the Parks Department ran a full list of bowling events. Interestingly, the league was entitled the 'Wythenshawe and Northenden Bowling League', although Northenden had a much longer tradition of competitive bowling.

Horticultural Societies also blossomed at this time. During the summer and early autumn it was always possible to find a schoolroom or church hall ablaze with colour and heavy with the mingled scents of freshly-cut vegetables and prize blooms, for Wythenshawe abounded with horticultural societies, and garden and allotment associations. Some were founded before the war, such as the Royal Oak Horticultural Society, but many came into being in the 1950s. Among these were the Woodhouse Park and Moss Nook H.S., who won the Wythenshawe County Express Silver Cup at their fourth show, and the Newall Green and District H.S., the A.E.I., Wythenshawe H.S., the Brownley Green and District H.S. and the Hey Head and District Chrysanthemum Society, who started showing their prize blooms in 1950.

There was a competition organised by the council for the best kept garden and nicest window box. This was open to two Manchester estates, Wythenshawe and Langley, in the early 1960s. Another cup was offered for the best allotment. The Northenden Garden and Allotment Society was the oldest of these societies, having its origins back in the early part of the century when the annual show was more than an exhibition of home-grown produce. It was a gala day-out with music and entertainment, too.

The Wythenshawe Caged Bird Society annually held a show of many different breeds of bird. This took place in the Church School and was always well attended, the bright colours of the exotic birds on show being fascinating to children and adults alike.

There were a few well-established public houses in Wythenshawe by the end of the war. In Benchill and Sharston there were large hotels which took their names from the district. In the Lawton Moor area there was another large building, the *Yew Tree Hotel*, and across the park was the new *Royal Oak*. In the extreme south of Wythenshawe there was an old pub, the *Tatton Arms*, Moss Nook. Outside this small inn there were forms so that travellers returning to Northenden after a walk across the fields could sit, perhaps take refreshment, and wait for the 64 bus, which had its terminus there. With the growth of the airport and the consequent development of the road system, this area was by-passed by a straighter, wider route, and the *Tatton Arms* was relegated to a quiet inn in a cul-de-sac.

The *Airport Hotel* close by had been a mecca of entertainment and dancing during the war, being in such close proximity to the airmen's living quarters and the aircraft factories, but its popularity declined as new pubs were built on the estate. The erection of some of these public houses caused much concern amongst residents. The questions were constantly being asked, 'Are the pubs badly sited?' and 'Who wants more pubs?'. One projected public house evoked a great deal of emotion. It was to be built on the corner of Wythenshawe Road and Rackhouse Road, opposite the park gates. One of the correspondents in this dispute was Dr. Muriel Edwards, a much-loved local G.P. and resident in the area. She wrote: 'Let us as residents show the council we care and that we do not want Wythenshawe spoilt by more and more public houses and all that follows in their wake'. A mammoth petition was sent from the area, containing 3,000 names. These protests were effective, for a public house was not built on that site.

In other parts of Wythenshawe three large establishments were erected, namely the *Cock of the North*, reputed to be the largest in the area. *The Greenwood Tree* and *The Black Boy*, the latter named after a racehorse, winner of the Ascot Gold Cup. This was not a very large pub but it had a huge car park, and on this point the minister of one of the local churches condemned it, land being a valuable commodity. In order to placate the public, the landlord offered free parking to anyone who required it.

For years little change had taken place in the public houses of Northenden until, in the mid-1960s, the new *Spread Eagle* on Royle Green Road was built. The old terraced house, which had served customers well for many years, was replaced by a modern building with living quarters above.

After the war the Rosemary Fund no longer promoted the colourful processions and fêtes of the 1930s, but its work of caring continued. Childcare had developed nationally since the war and in the 1950s and 1960s was reaching its zenith, so the Rosemary Fund had to widen its horizons and it took under its wings 'the blind, the cripple, the aged and the sick'. In 1948 they gave a party for 1,200 veterans and this pattern continued throughout the following years.

There were other charitable organisations at work in Wythenshawe. A branch of the W.V.S. met at Sharston Hall and had a clothing depot there from which it served the needy. The Rotary Club did good works and the 'Wythenshawe Inner Wheel' received its inaugural charter in the late 1950s. At Christmas time the British Legion ran a children's treat taking hundreds of children to the circus. A branch of the Toc H started locally in 1945 and stated that its aims were, in their simplest terms, 'fellowship and service'.

The Churches — Wythenshawe

Whit Week Walks, Trinity Sunday Walks and other walks of witness figured largely in the lives of the people of Wythenshawe during the month of June. Each year the local newspaper had pages of photographs of children, carrying banners, coming from every area and of every faith. By the end of the 1950s these processions had become ecumenical in character. In 1960 Northenden held a United Church procession, and after a short service at St Wilfrid's it was led through the village by St Wilfrid's Church Choir. An account of the same afternoon tells what was happening in Wythenshawe:

> In the blazing afternoon sunshine six Benchill churches and nearly 2,000 walkers set off in a splendour of colour pageantry on the annual Whit Walks on Sunday. Once again thousands lined the route to watch the United procession of witness.

Churches included this day were the Salvation Army and the Haveley Mission.

On Trinity Sunday people from another area of Wythenshawe walked together, St Martin's, Baguley, Baguley Congregational, Woodhouse Park Methodist Church, William

44. Rev. Hancock, St Michael and the Angels, Lawton Moor. The church could teach community associations a great deal about pageantry. St Michael's church had an unusual star-shaped design and the parish was the first to be carved out of Northenden parish in the 1930s.

45. St Luke's, Benchill, 1934.

46. The opening of St Francis' church in 1961, with Basil Spence, the architect.

Temple Church of England and others. Later in June the Roman Catholics observed the Feast of Corpus Christi with walks in their parishes. After short services most of the Roman Catholic churches held Benediction services before open-air altars. Also at this time St Michael and All Angels held united processions with the Lawton Moor Methodist Church, and the Philadelphian Tabernacle 'also entered a colourful procession of witness'. During the last week of June Newall Green Baptists and Brooklands Evangelists made their witness.

The post-war period was a prolific time for the building of new churches. Although during the war all building operations had been suspended, the people of Wythenshawe had continued to worship undaunted. Many places were used, schoolrooms, wooden huts, old halls, works canteens, a Nissen hut and private houses, and when the time came for building to begin it was the Nonconformists who were the first to erect their churches. In 1949 the Philadelphia Tabernacle was built by the worshippers themselves on Crossacres Road, and in that year Baguley Hall Methodist Church was built on Bowland Road. In the next two years a Baptist church appeared on Simonsway, a Congregational church on Floatshall Road and the Hebrew Jewish Reform Synagogue went into operation in Sharston Hall. Throughout the late 1950s and early 1960s churches of various denominations continued to spring up around the Wythenshawe estate. In 1957 Brownwood Undenominational Christian Brethren came into being and in 1962 the Church of the Nazarene Evangelical started. Also in that year a house on Moor End, Northenden, was converted into a Kingdom Hall for the Jehovah's Witnesses. One building, attractive in design and imposing in size, was the Church of Jesus Christ of the Latter Day Saints, built on Altrincham Road in 1964. The architect engaged to design this church was Sir T. Bennett who was also the architect for Crawley New Town. The building, set in a spacious car park, flanked by a wooded copse and private dwellings, seated 500 people and was surmounted by a 40-foot fibreglass steeple costing £2,000. This was more than just a place of worship, it was a cultural centre costing £100,000.

The Roman Catholics were active in church building at this time. Although some years elapsed after the end of the war before any Roman Catholic churches were dedicated, this did not mean that there was not work going on, but only that the Roman Catholics did not dedicate their churches until they were finished and paid for, unlike the Anglicans who consecrated them at the outset of the work. In 1953 St Peter's on Firbank Road was dedicated and two years later the people of Northern Moor, who had for years been celebrating mass in their schoolroom, also opened their own church in Wythenshawe Road — St Aidan's. The people of Woodhouse Park had been using a green Nissen hut in which to say mass since 1951, and in 1960 this was replaced by the church of St Anthony, on Portway. This parish had become one of the largest Roman Catholic parishes in Manchester, having a total of 6,000 parishioners. The building cost £115,000 and was the biggest church in Wythenshawe when it was completed. Built of Portland stone, it was designed on classical lines with a 100-foot tower, surmounted with a 10-foot illuminated cross, nick-named the threepenny bit tower as the children of the parish collected bags of threepenny bits to pay for it. The interior was spacious and the altar constructed of Roman stone and Italian marble.

The Methodists built the first non-municipal building on the Civic Centre site, St Andrew's Methodist Church. It was opened by Lord Derby, the Lord Lieutenant of the county. The church was built along 'simple but dignified lines' and was the only one of its kind in the country — including a coffee bar as part of its 'revolutionary' design.

Anglican churches generally took longer to build than those of Nonconformists, as they were usually larger and had more elaborate and expensive furnishings. The new Church of St Martin, Wythenshawe, was the first church to be consecrated and built in a post-war new housing area. The parish it served was also the first to be created in a new area after the war, partly out of the parish of Northenden and partly out of the parish of St Michael's and All Angels, Lawton Moor. The dedication of the site for the new church and the cutting of the first sod took place on 15 November 1958, by which time the Christian community was well established, the people already worshipping at the Mission Hall on Altrincham Road. A large site at the top of Hall Road was obtained for the new church, which was designed by Harry S. Fairhurst in the 'idiom of traditional ecclesiasticism' and was kept within the cost limits. Its style is Romanesque and the use of tile arches over the windows, main doors and aisles emphasises the link with tradition. The inside of the church was lined with brick and the east wall panelled on either side with mahogany. Immediately above and behind the altar is a hanging, Byzantine in style, depicting the Ascended Christ. In total the church seated about four hundred and twenty people. In 1961 another Anglican church was built on Greenbrow Road, dedicated to St Francis of Assisi. The architect for this church was Sir Basil Spence, who designed the new Coventry Cathedral. It was described as a building 'seeking to speak to its own age in a new language' designed to work side by side with the rewritten Bible. The church had four foundation stones, each taken from a place important in the history of Christianity — Greece, Assisi, Canterbury and Iona.

Church life continued relatively unchanged in Northenden. The general resurgence of church-going which followed the war was apparent in the area. The Roman Catholics continued to worship in 'the pretty half-timbered building, set back in leafy surroundings' on Kenworthy Lane. The size of the building was no indication of the strength of its support for the church was often packed to overflowing. The social activities of the church were numerous and a branch of the brothers of St Vincent de Paul flourished and did many good works. It had been obvious for many years that the building was inadequate for the needs of the people of Northenden, so in the 1960s plans were evolved for the building of a new, larger building.

The other well-established church, apart from the parish church, was the Methodist Church, and this continued to draw large congregations. The societies of this church flourished and among these were the Bright Hour, the Men's Circle and notably the Methodist Little Theatre. The constitutional aim of the drama enthusiasts was 'to contribute to the cultural life of the community by presenting the best in drama to the best of our ability', and this they did very adequately. This church was also the home of uniformed organisations and after the war a commemorative shield was awarded annually to the best all-round scout of the year. This was named the Whittaker Shield and was given in honour of two scouts who were killed in the Second World War, George Whittaker and Fred Hughes. In 1953 a new church hall was added. St Wilfrid's church, too, offered its memorial to those of the parish who died serving in the Second World War. On 23 July 1949 the church bells were again put into commission and a mural tablet unveiled. The cost was defrayed by contributions from the whole parish. The ceremony seems to have been a colourful one, led by the Bishop of Middleton, the rector and the churchwardens, as one eye witness reports:

> The day was sunny and warm and sound of the bells after a silence of a couple of months, was as cheerful as meeting an old friend who had been long bedfast. The procession conducted the Bishop to the South West corner by the font, which he consecrated to the 'Lambs of God'.
>
> The Tablet which is placed above the warden's seat to the left of the belfry door was then unveiled, the Bishop reading aloud the inscription 'To the Glory of God the Bells of this Church were rehung in grateful remembrance of those of this Church and parish who gave their best towards Victory in the Second World War, 1939-1945. Silent during the War they were to have been rung as a warning of invasion'. The belfry was next visited and the bells rededicated. The Prayer of Dedication expressed

the hope that 'these bells would continually call together God's faithful people for prayer and worship'.

There were other additions or improvements to the fabric of the church. In 1961 a font cover was given in memory of Mrs. Margaret Chignell, the wife of a previous rector, and in 1962 after almost ten years of doubt, indecision and financial crises, a new organ was dedicated by the Archdeacon of Manchester. The old organ had been removed from the north side of the church in 1954 and it had 'gone with much dust and dirt', but, on the advice of the architect, the new one built by Harrison and Harrison, the builders of the new Coventry Cathedral organ, was placed at the west end.

The societies and organisations continued to flourish: there was the Young People's Union, St Wilfrid's Fellowship, and a St Wilfrid's Scottish Dance Group was formed in 1958. The choir boys formed their own football and cricket team and a group from the Mothers' Union went to Oberammergau. The 3rd Northenden Scout Group was formed in 1953, and in 1956 St Wilfrid's Guides won the shield for the best group in Wythenshawe. In 1963, amidst all the reports and statements of these societies, we read the following:

> May I draw your attention to the service of Inter-communion on 11th April at 8.00 p.m. in which we are to join with the local Methodist Church. Arrangements for this service had been made by the Rector and Mr. Page, before their death, and it was their hope that this service would be well attended. I feel that this is one way in which we can all pay tribute to both men and to their work for Christian unity, by attending this service in large numbers.

Both the Anglican minister and the Methodist minister of Northenden died suddenly within days of each other, leaving two thriving churches. 'In the midst of life we are in death.'

The smallest religious group in Northenden still held its services at the Gospel Hall on Mill Lane, and the devotees under the leadership of the Missionary in Charge, Mr. Black, contributed to the life of the village by helping to care for the young and the old and by joining in the Whit Week Walks 'in colourful witness with other churches'. The small building was well attended and the strains of joyful music were very pleasant to hear when passing by on Sunday evenings.

Chapter Ten

Complete with a Complex: 1964-89

With the population of Wythenshawe in 1964 close to 100,000 people, the rate of house building became progressively slower. At last attention was given to a Civic Centre to provide the larger communal amenities and at the same time act as a focal point, so helping Wythenshawe find an identity.

The analogy of a heart transplant to describe the shift of emphasis from Northenden to the new Civic Centre was often used at the time. As Northenden became totally enclosed by motorways it became less of a mecca for shoppers. The emergence of a civic society symbolised a return of the pride that existed when it had been a village. As Wythenshawe neared completion Northenden became less important as a centre. Transferring the name 'Forum' from the Northenden cinema to the Wythenshawe civic complex symbolised the change.

Respect and self-respect for Wythenshawe, its garden setting and its historical legacies grew as the catchment area for the new Forum complex, theatre and library widened. The control of the garden city remained firmly with the parent city but the earlier agitation for Home Rule lessened after the Federal Council had disbanded. This may have been due to a sense of resignation or because as leisure activities became more available the responsibility for them was seen to be accepted by the Council's Recreational Services. Whatever the reason, the call for independence diminished, though the cry 'Fair Shares for Wythenshawe' was still heard.

A Northenden Civic Society was formed in 1969 from the Owner-Occupiers Association and the Community Association. It was created to stop the duo-rail through Northenden (*see* Transport, *below*) and 'to preserve and relish its past history and develop the present amenities'. It then fought the changes to the Parkway and the dangerous siting of bus stops there. Later targets were the office blocks that district status had brought, and Race's scrapyard, that increasingly blighted the village centre; it survived a public enquiry but eventually moved to grace the shores of Ancoats in 1988. 'For those who care about Northenden Village' became its call as it worked for the older part of Northenden to be made a conservation area. Some natural rural beauty was retained. After the extensive works to tame the Mersey the river area became part of the Mersey Valley Park scheme.

In Palatine Road, as the Wythenshawe centre drew customers south, chain stores such as Timothy Whites, Boots and MacFisheries closed, though Woolworth's had a reprieve when its Civic Centre hypermarket failed. Near the Mersey the last true cobbler's shop closed, but two garages and Hunter's Handicrafts attracted wide custom. Nearby the remains of the old mill were cleared and replaced by Camperlands, whose huge orange awning was a landmark till it flew away in a gale.

Television, carpet and paint traders came and went, but, in the shops in converted houses and in the new parades, there was still some counter and delivery service, while the Post Office remained, without 'crown' status, at the back of a sweet-shop.

The few houses to be built in Northenden at this time were balanced by those lost by demolition. High-rise flats in Royle Green for pensioners and flats with wardens in Lee Court, Longley Lane, flats opposite the old Forum and 10 expensive houses off Ford Lane were put up, but old houses came down in Church Street, Govan Street and Moor End.

47. Ravenswood House, the home of Joseph Johnson, arch instigator of Peterloo. The house was converted to shops in the 1890s. The picture shows one of the shops in about 1900; they were demolished early in the 1970s. 'So passes glory.'

Increased house dealings allowed local estate agent Harold Tucker, one-time Lord Mayor of Manchester, to build Hatro House on the site of a former post office on the south-west corner of Palatine Road and Church Road, opposite Tesco's supermarket. Further down Church Road, on the same side and on the site of the last magpie cottage, the library's old caravan was at last replaced by a new building which was opened by Alf Morris, M.P., in 1982. Next to this an impressive clutch of Redwood retirement homes was laid in 1988.

Barrows' Garage, nearby on Palatine Road, was extended early in the 1970s to Church Road by demolishing Ravenswood House (former home of Joseph Johnson of Peterloo fame but by then derelict shops). In 1987, now owned by the Co-op, Barrows extended its frontage by demolishing the Co-op stores of the 1920s and, unintentionally, the end wall of the adjacent row of cottages.

Moor End Police Station, demolished in 1969, was replaced by offices. In 1965 it had to deal with a savage affray in Church Road that resulted in serious injuries and four Northern Moor youths each being given four years' gaol. In the same year 70 hymn books stolen from

St Wilfrid's church were being sold from door to door and, in 1980, £1,000 was snatched from the Burnley Building Society on Palatine Road. At last, in Ford Lane, sited between the *Spread Eagle*, the *Church Inn* and the *Crown Inn*, a new Northenden police station was erected, its opening graced by the presence of Chief Constable James Anderton.

Mugging and graffiti arrived when the new subways spread under the rebuilt Parkway, and in 1979 a double-decker bus landed across one path after collision with a fire-engine. After years of complaining by locals, in 1988 the expensive warren was eventually filled in. Early in the decade the 30-year-old Princess Mansions flats, at this same junction with Wythenshawe Road and the Parkway, had been replaced by the *Post House Hotel*.

Northenden doctors' group practice moved into a smart new medical centre in 1984 on the site of the old Mormon church opposite the *Post House*. The new Mormon church moved to Altrincham Road and opposite that, on a triangle next to the Royal Thorn, was built an adult training centre for the physically handicapped. Between there and the Sharston Baths, Altrincham Road now straddled the gorge of the Sharston By-pass, the M56 to Stockport.

The Church Rooms in Kenworthy Lane, Northenden Village Hall for half a century, were demolished in 1965 after much public wrangling. The church school next to it, as we have seen, had been replaced by St Wilfrid's School in Patterdale Road, and the new Church

48. *Post House*, subways and athletic bus. *Guardian* photographer Denis Thorpe caught this mishap; the graffiti was edited out before publication. The *Post House* and the expanded parkway were completed in the early 1970s. The subways were included at enormous cost, despite huge protests. In 1988 they were filled in at even greater cost.

Rooms, with flat roofs, were in Ford Lane next to the proposed village green. At this time the Dramatic Society decided to convert the old Armoury behind the *Tatton Inn* into its own 40-seat theatre. Tesco's Supermarket was built on the Kenworthy Lane site.

In the new Church Rooms an impressive mural of the Mersey at Northenden was painted by Harry Hollins, head for a time at St Wilfrid's School. A huge painting, once in the old Church Rooms, *The Icebergs* by the American artist Frederick Edwin Church, came to light in 1979. It had been given to the Church Rooms 'for the People of Northenden' in 1915 by Mr. Parkyn when he sold Rose Hill, but was returned in 1921 when it interfered with Rev. Herald's pantomimes. The matron of Rose Hill Remand Home, after a tip from America, contacted Sotheby's and the painting sold in 1980 for a record near £2,000,000 — a fortune to be fought over in the courts.

As the new Wythenshawe matured some of its earlier architectural works of the 1930s, in particular the churches of St Michael and of St Luke, swelled the number of historical or architecturally worthy buildings 'listed' by the Department of the Environment. The list comprises:

Baguley Hall, off Hall Lane	Rose Cottage, Hasty Lane
Chamber Hall, off Styal Road	St John's church, Brooklands
Haletop Farm, Thorley Lane	St Luke's church, Benchill
Moss House, Bailey Lane	St Michael's church, Lawton Moor
Newall Green Hall farm	St Wilfrid's church, Ford Lane
Northen House, Ford Lane	Sharston Mount, Altrincham Road
The Old Rectory, Ford Lane,	Wythenshawe Hall, Mount and Lodge
Old Thatch, Ringway Road	Yew Tree House, Sunbank Lane
Ridgeway Farmhouse, Hasty Lane	(Peel Hall bridge is an 'Ancient Monument')

Peel Hall Farm had been listed, but hours after the Shenton family left in 1966, as with Hollyhedge Farm in 1938, vandals attacked. The sale of the farm for £3,000 fell through, and despite a local campaign it was 'put into storage' in the late 1970s so that then only the ancient bridge remained. Kenworthy Hall was lost when Princess Parkway was enlarged in 1974 and other farms to go included Royal Thorn, Floats Hall, Haveley Hey, Knob Hall and Stone Pale Hall. The cottages which faced the *Spread Eagle* in Royle Green must 'hold the record as Listed Buildings with the shortest survival time. Found to have been of unique construction, they were listed for preservation early in 1982 and demolished the following morning'.

New buildings are not immune from decay. The flat roof of the rectory of St Michael's church, built 1935, began to leak badly and the rectory was evacuated; at the time of writing the city and Church authorities are debating three options — repair, adding a pitched roof, or demolition — how best to deal with the problem.

Baguley Hall was nearly lost, in spite of being the only building listed as of outstanding importance. At the eleventh hour petitions and deputations prodded the Department of the Environment into taking it over from Manchester in 1967. In the war its windows were sent for safe-keeping to Baxendale's vaults in the city — and received a direct hit! Restoration work proceeded under a huge corrugated-iron cover from 1972 to 1983. In a report Mr. and Mrs. Warner summed up the work being done:

> Drawings and details precede work in a section at a time. A special resin is used to fill gaps in old timbers; replacement is of 'oak for oak'. The ceiling lathes had been covered with plaster made of ox dung, straw, clay and a little ox fat. Stonework supporting the interior is being reinforced.
>
> The rafters and their complex structure of joists are in the main original but rot has set in at the birds' mouth joints where the eaves join the wall plate. Damp, rot and beetle in this area allowed the rafters to slide down and push out the walls. Of the Victorian repairs it has been noted 'One can see the rough adze marks and note the greater skill of the original craftsmen'.
>
> Mr. Latham, who knew the hall as a young man, and with Councillor Paley campaigned to keep the hall, is now custodian.

In the early stages of the new Wythenshawe, Sharston was a frontier outpost, giving temporary refuge to the police, fire, ambulance, social, employment and welfare services. North of Altrincham Road were Sharston Hall and Manor (the original hall), and on the south side are Sharston Farm and Sharston Mount, where from 1913 Miss Southern has lived, Wythenshawe's earliest and longest-serving council tenant. In reviewing changes since the 1920s, she remembered Nield's Sharston Tea Rooms, the new *Sharston Hotel*, now brewery offices, and the Shentons farming the land. Sharston Hall, before the Henriques were killed in a motor accident,

> . . . could be called a small Stately Home with beautiful and well-kept grounds. The Hall became flats and then housed the police, fire services and the Home Guard. Some of its buildings are used by the Highways Department.
>
>   Mr. and Mrs. Goodfellow were the last family to reside in Sharston Manor: a beam in the cellar is marked H.W. [Worthington] — 1661. They left about 1934 and in the war the A.R.P. and the Territorial Army moved in. It is now derelict and badly vandalised. Sharston Mount, once part of the farm, is Georgian in appearance but the staircase is said to be 17th century and shippon beam is dated 1646. Mrs. B. Shenton still lives at the farm.

Sharston Hall was demolished in 1986 and replaced by an office block with 18th-century features.

There are two active farms in Wythenshawe. Newall Green, an early brick building, dates back to 1596. Still in the hands of Shentons, a name synonymous with much of Wythenshawe, mixed farming takes place on the remaining 60 acres. Chamber Hall Farm absorbed Peel Hall and still has 200 fragmented acres. The present tenants, Mr. and Mrs. Sam Bayley, are related to the Shentons. In 1979 the city council spent £400,000 restoring the 17th-century (or earlier) building. Submissive Friesians thrive as no human could under the flight paths.

In an exercise in correlating the Old and New in Wythenshawe, in 1982 Anthony Appleyard was able to trace the routes of over twenty pre-Parker lanes and a similar number of farm sites. He noted that Wythenshawe Hall home farm is 'mostly just a park maintenance depot but a few cattle are kept in the park still, also a shire horse (which works, not just show!)'. In 1988 a Community Farm was established in Sharston.

Rose Hill, once the home of 'Railway' Watkins, became a hospital and an orphanage. It was in the house's final role as remand home that Edwin Church's *Icebergs* painting was, as noted earlier in this chapter, rediscovered in 1980.

Sixteenth-century Wythenshawe Hall, after coming through the Civil War and transportation from Cheshire to Manchester in 1926, only just survived fires, woodworms, architects, visitors and weddings post-1945. Oliver Cromwell's statue was brought from the Cathedral area to face Wythenshawe Hall in 1968. Fittingly, in Wythenshawe he is with the kindred radical spirits of Jackson, Parker and the Simons, and he looks contented enough in spite of losing his sword for a while and occasionally being daubed with paint.

In the unfinished garden city of Wythenshawe, however, there were more practical problems to concern the corporation. Housing was still the government's priority at the start of the 1960s. Throughout Wythenshawe small numbers of houses continued to be built to infill vacant plots. Building included 103 council houses in Woodhouse Park in 1962 and over a thousand private and council houses in 1966 near the Civic Centre, but the most notable feature of the time was the acceptance of the high-rise flats. Against the Barry Parker tradition, the first nine-storey flats of Manchester mushroomed in Woodhouse Park in 1960, and more grew in Benchill, Royal Thorn and on the site once earmarked for a cinema and baths at the Hollyhedge-Brownley Road roundabout.

Some tenants enjoyed the seclusion and outlook of the ivory towers. Pensioners at Royal Green and Park Court publicly praised their wardens and the effective security screens. For young parents with children and those with irresponsible neighbours, the flats seemed like prisons. By 1962 the Woodhouse Park flats were being labelled modern slums though more were built at Newall Green in 1964 and at the Civic Centre in 1966. With vandalism, heating, lift troubles and condensation getting publicity, exactly 10 years after the first went up, in July 1970 it was announced that there would be no more high-rise flats in Wythenshawe.

Rent was an ever-present problem for some, and the arrears in Wythenshawe reached £400,000 in the 1960s. The Child Poverty Action Group claimed 5,000 children were living below the poverty line; half Wythenshawe was declared to be a social priority area — on free meals returns. Within Manchester, Wythenshawe also has the highest percentage of supplementary benefits paid (16.5 per cent) and highest proportion of one-parent families (19.3 per cent).

Modernisation of poorer council homes began in 1972 and converted the early gas-lit, outside-loo Bucklow council-built houses into desirable homes. Prefabs at Newall Green that had become fire risks were also renewed. The projected sale of council houses by the Conservatives to sitting tenants in 1967 became a political football that was still there even after a Northern Moor tenant's case went to the House of Lords.

Old people's homes were erected by private and sheltered housing. The Social Services Department ran homes at the Coppice on Wythenshawe Road (on the site of the first municipal airport), High Grove in Peel Hall, Holly View in Benchill, Newall View, Templemead in Woodhouse Park and Weylands in Baguley.

A number of pockets of new owner-occupied homes included houses in Brooklands, Shady Lane, Lorna Grove and Peel Hall. The proportion of private to council houses nevertheless remained high in Wythenshawe. A survey in 1969 showed 13 per cent private homes in the new town and two-thirds of these were in Northenden. One reason suggested for this was that of the 30,000 jobs planned for the area, only 20,000 had materialised and 40 per cent of these were for women. Aircraft noise and sound-proofing grants were subjects over which private owners in south Wythenshawe fought. In Northern Moor a blocked culvert flooded the private houses on Cherry Tree Road in 1972. Unlike the veterans of the lower reaches of Northenden, the occupants were taken completely by surprise.

The census of 1971 confirmed the owner-occupier figures and told us that the Northenden ward matched the Manchester average of 33 per cent, while in Benchill and Baguley the proportion was 16 per cent and in Woodhouse Park only five per cent. The proportion of working or unskilled classes was only just over the Manchester average in the Benchill and Woodhouse Park wards — the wards with some over-crowding.

Wythenshawe had a greater than average percentage of children, especially in Benchill and Woodhouse Park, but a below average proportion of pensioners except in Northenden. One-parent families were over-represented in Benchill and Woodhouse Park, but car ownership was above average everywhere. In Northenden the number of people travelling to work by car was also above average. All areas of Wythenshawe were shown to have better than average homes and the Medical Officer of Health consistently proved that the air in Wythenshawe, one of the first smoke-controlled areas in the country, was exceptionally clean.

While the air was fine, plentiful and free, public facilities and services were still poor and meagre. Nearly forty years after its inception the new Wythenshawe had no civic centre and it was not till the late 1960s that conditions were at last favourable for this to be remedied. Government restrictions were easing and the new town was overflowing with homes. Plans for the centre went back to the 1945 plan by Nicholas, who had enlarged Barry Parker's location for a town square and moved it south. On 72 acres a council hall, chamber, public hall, health centre, fire station, hotel, church, cinema and theatre were to be built next to 130 shop units, 'a unifying element in the huge Wythenshawe community', wrote Michael Moss.

Plans evolved in the 1950s. It was quite clear that the neighbourhood shopping parades were insufficient and the City Librarian decided that neighbourhood branch libraries (only Hollyhedge had been built) would be better sacrificed for one large library combined with a theatre, as at Manchester Central Library. In 1958 the Libraries Committee and the Town Hall Committee proposed a composite scheme which was then prepared by the City Architect in 1960. The Libraries Committee approved a library and theatre project costing £397,000, but meanwhile work had started on the £514,850 plan for shops, market, offices and flats on the civic centre site. Priorities for the two remaining schemes had then to be decided.

At joint conferences in and after 1960, the Estates, Finance, Libraries, Town Hall and Baths and Laundries Committees, with the back-up work of the Architect's Department, thrashed out the composite scheme of library, theatre, public hall and baths. Huge savings would be made by sharing heating and car-parking facilities.

In the years of waiting for cash every opportunity was taken to make refinements to the plan. Delays were due to the need for money for Sharston Baths, opened by Lord Derby in 1961, and for the Civic Centre shops. Boots, Tesco, Woolworth and the Co-op battled for sites in 1960, and the second phase began in 1961. A fire at the baths and a toppling crane at the Civic Centre meant further set-backs. An assembly hall gained at this time was the £38,000 Civil Defence Building of 1965 on Brownley Road. Of 4,000 recruits expected, only 100 arrived.

At last the £1,203,241 needed for the augmented complex was available. The foundation stone was laid in September 1969 and the opening was in 1971. Michael Moss wrote, 'Wythenshawe could be said to be substantially complete'.

49. Wythenshawe Forum, opening, 1971. From the left are Lady Anne Rhodes; Sir George Ogden, town clerk; Lord Rhodes of Saddleworth; Lord Mayor Douglas Edwards; Sir William Downward; Alf Morris, M.P.

On the other hand, many of Wythenshawe's schools built in the 1930s were, by this time, beginning to look mature. The only new schools to be completed in the period were St Elizabeth's R.C. Primary School at Peel Hall, built to an open-plan design, and St Augustine's R.C. grammar school on Altrincham Road, opened in 1965. As the fall in the birthrate continued some new schools died in infancy.

At the secondary level, the period would see a succession of reorganisations, re-namings and closures. The Manchester change in 1967 to comprehensive schools, covering all abilities, saw the new high schools emerge (from the ashes of grammar, technical and modern schools) at Brookway, Brownley Green, Newall Green (which took in Baguley Hall Secondary School) Poundswick, Sharston, South Wythenshawe (previously Moss Nook Secondary) and Yew Tree. The linking of high schools to local primary schools was introduced in 1977, but four years later the formation of sixth form colleges caused Yew Tree to become Arden College. This left Northenden having to link with Newall Green and Poundswick, with the result that new pupils attended elsewhere. The Poundswick staff were involved in a lengthy dispute that hit the national headlines over graffiti and the exclusion of four alleged pupil-artists in the mid-1980s. Falling rolls reduced the high schools to Brookway, Newall Green, Poundswick and South Manchester in the 1980s, while the names of All Hallows, St Columba, St John Plessington and Cardinal Newman vanished from the Catholic sphere to leave only St John's high school.

One benefit of more space, however, was that the Wythenshawe Music Centre, now putting on regular concerts and festivals at the Forum, was able to find a home. The Spring Festival, when local schools exhibited work at the Forum, was a feature of the 1970s with attendances of over four thousand each year.

The majority of further education classes moved in 1968 to the 'Birtles' — part of the first floor of the Civic Centre shopping complex — though evening centres continued at Baguley Hall, Brownley Green, Newall Green, Oldwood, the Park school, Yew Tree and Moss Nook. Under the Area Principal, Deryck Moore, there was integration with the W.E.A. (the Workers Educational Association) and expansion from about four hundred to a peak of four thousand adult students in the mid-1970s. About a hundred and fifty courses covered topics from crotchet, speech therapy, machine knitting and television repair to keep fit for businessmen and pre-retirement and office skills. Vocational, City and Guilds and Open University degree courses were popular. 'It was surprising how many Wythenshawe people wanted to improve themselves', commented one centre head. Under the new title of 'Community Education', evening centres, such as the Social Centre at Brownley Green and centres at Newall Green, Oldwood and Yew Tree, together with the Youth Clubs and Evening Play Centres, continued as affiliated groups.

By the late 1970s the emphasis was shifting from adult education to bridging the gap for young people who had left school. More day-release courses were being offered, too, many of them in conjunction with the Manpower Services Commission, and others were aimed to give help to the mentally and physically handicapped.

The long-awaited Civic Centre shops appeared in stages between 1960 and 1962. Officially renamed the Town Centre in 1966, the patois 'going to the Civic' remained in use. Trade slowly picked up, in spite of vandalism and the Siberian wind across Leningrad Square. The market and food hall added in 1974 brought wider custom. Regional rather than national chain stores flourished. Woolco's Hypermarket failed in 1978 and a Co-op Shopping Giant moved in. Above the shops were the quarters of Further Education and Welfare Services and, while it lasted, the *Wythenshawe Express*. The Social Services and Job Centre were set up in the office blocks east of Rowlandsway.

Elsewhere in Wythenshawe from the 22 parades the cries of 'too many shops' increased. The Roundthorn Estate's only retailer, Arnold's Cars, was succeeded by Habitat after only three years, but the real problem seemed in 1975 to be at Sharston, when the new shops found themselves cut off by the motorway that had caused them to be re-sited. The harsh building styles of the 1950s and competition from the Civic Centre were blamed for a slump in business at the Minsterley Parade, but arguments about the necessary action here dragged on into 1989.

Reorganisation affected the police, too, in this period, but to the customers of Wythenshawe police stations the merger of Manchester and Salford Police in April 1968 and the further expansion in 1974 into Greater Manchester Police might have seemed only of academic interest. The completion of the Princess Parkway as a motorway extension, the M56, emphasised the divide between the two areas of control: Hall Lane, in E Division, patrolling the west; and Brownley Road, in D Division, extended in 1975, in charge of the east. From 1976 the local police became responsible for the airport because of the increase in terrorism. With a change in tactics Northenden had a new police station, and by 1989 plans were on hand to replace the divided control by a new police headquarters for all Wythenshawe.

As the population of children from Wythenshawe grew, so too did one of the main problems of the police, vandalism. Yet a police spokesman at Hall Lane could report, 'We have a great number of municipal houses but we don't get any more trouble from them, than you would expect'. Available targets grew, too. The new plate-glass windows in the Civic Centre, unattended at night, contractors' huts, vehicles and their gear boxes, motorways and their signs were most inviting targets for bricks, sand and paint sprays. Bridges crossing the motorways created a new sport — bombing the cars. Schools, churches, glasshouses, trees in parks, curtains at the baths, marquees, scout huts and Christmas trees continued to be the occasional victims of petty vandalism, whilst thousands of pounds' worth of damage were reported after vandals had run amok in factories. As the child population decreased in the late 1970s, so too did vandalism.

The Wythenshawe Fire Service suffered, too, from vandalism in the direct form of small fires and also from malicious calls, of which the division had the highest rates in Manchester. In 1972 the brigade had to attend the ignominious end of its old quarters at Sharston when they were burnt down by vandals.

It was a fire that brought increased status to Wythenshawe's ambulance depot in Leestone Road. When the ambulance depot at Withington Hospital was burnt down in the early 1970s the Sharston depot was enlarged to take 20 vehicles, to cover all South Manchester, and it was further upgraded in 1978.

The new Wythenshawe Hospital was the second major structure, partnering the Forum complex, to be completed very late in the new town's story. The hospital was officially opened on 11 July 1973 by Princess Margaret, 21 years after the wartime huts had been first dubbed Wythenshawe Hospital. The Maternity Unit had been opened in 1965 and the same year saw continued limited development at Baguley, particularly in open-heart surgery. Preparations for the main hospital brought many varied problems and solutions. Arguments at Baguley Sanatorium about lifts in the towers to the wards and whether they could take beds as well as stretchers dragged on till the Board ruled stretchers only. Wythenshawe was approved for the complete training of midwives and the Salmon Report of 1968 took a new look at the work and training of nurses and doctors. The plastic surgeons reluctantly moved out and geriatric medicine moved in.

Baguley Hospital was able to think itself back in pre-1931 Cheshire for six years when the new 'Wythenshawe and North Cheshire' Group was formed in 1968. Tenders from J. Gerrard and Son for the building of the main hospital at £3,730,736, excluding furniture and fittings, were accepted, and following this £12,000 was spent in adapting hostels to accommodate the Group Headquarters, which moved from Altrincham.

The next two years saw improvements at Baguley with the construction of a cardiology unit. Changes in plans to meet new ideas, such as plate meals, meant expensive equipment, including conveyor belts and new food trolleys. Contact with North Cheshire was now important and to this end Dobinnetts Lane and parts of Floats Road were improved. Extra staff were taken on to match new equipment and in 1971 a Chief Nursing Officer, Miss Goldrick, was appointed.

Slowly the piecemeal handing over of the new hospital took place, leading up to the official opening in 1974. The following year Wythenshawe Hospital's six years reunion with North Cheshire ended when it was returned to the South District of the Manchester Area Health Authority, at Withington. These frequent changes caused fragmented administration, but improvements went on. Some of those veteran huts were again upgraded and more covered ways were built. To the visiting public the children's wards, with free visiting times and a sunny classroom, were on the credit side. Less acceptable to the public was the retention, in spite of frequent complaints and an article in the *Parish Magazine*, 'of the blanket appointment system for out-patients and the consequent wasted hours of waiting'.

A comparison of the bed complement of the hospitals between 1952, when a New Wythenshawe Hospital was conceived, and what finally resulted follows below.

1952			**New State**		
Wythenshawe Hospital	—	375	New areas, F & B	—	583
Baguley Sanatorium	—	420	Old area, A	—	200
			Maternity	—	98
Total		**795**			**881**

Transport, too, saw many interesting developments at this time. Northenden Railway Station, then a request stop, was closed to passengers in 1965 though the line was still used by through freight and passenger traffic. The track at Northenden became the largest cement depot in the region. Baguley Station, 'a neat stucco rendered building', almost became a craft shop in 1968 and allotments in 1977, but in the end it became a house.

Tube trains for Manchester had been proposed in 1902 and in 1936, and rejected in 1914 and 1945. By 1965 the duo-rail, a train-like short tube locomotive and coach unit that can be inset into the road, was recommended. One route would have linked Manchester and the airport and sliced through Northenden and Wythenshawe Civic Centre. In January 1979 a feasibility study for a rail link on the same route was again made.

In the mid-1980s the possibility of a rail link between the centre of Manchester and Manchester International Airport was put forward and seriously discussed. Work was planned to begin some time in 1987.

Although there were well-grounded fears that the new M6 would put pressure on roads in the Altrincham area, the city council, in 1960, wanted to defer the extension of Princess Parkway to the south until 1971. It was in fact started in 1969 and cost £1,000,000 a mile. Only four years earlier 'a monstrosity of a footbridge' had been thrown across the Parkway near the Wythenshawe Road Junction.

Of the proposed motorway treatment of the Parkway Harry Lloyd commented, 'Apart from being a delight to the eye for visitors it would also be a sacrilege to destroy the Parkway. It is a picture by an artist and craftsman combined'. Protests rained down from all quarters and questions were raised in the House of Commons on the 'unnecessary bends in the road'. But work started and 50,000 trees and shrubs were torn up. There remained vestiges of the original greenery in the end, augmented by considerable replanting. Even so the Parkway has not returned to 'its landscaped beauty that was the pride of Wythenshawe and the envy of many other cities'. To some 'the road planned by Barry Parker and Mr. Meek, and encouraged by Lady Simon, is now just another urban motorway'; to others the spirit of Mr. Parker still shines through. Problems arose because the Parkway was also a major bus route. The Greater Manchester Transport Action Group was led by Rita Oughton, a stalwart executive of the Civic Society. She wrote, 'A local all-purpose road is for the benefit of all people [including] kids going to school and grandma out for an airing . . .'. Eventually new bus lanes were added and the speed restricted to 40 m.p.h.

The Western Parkway Bypass, sketched in by Barry Parker and by Nicholas in his plan on the fringe of Wythenshawe, was never built, being overtaken by the urban motorways M62, M63, M66 and M67.

Motorways predicted in the 1945 Plan included the M56 linking Manchester and the airport and continuing as the North Cheshire Motorway. One branch, Princess Parkway, in going north crossed the M63, while the M56 itself branched east to meet the M63 west of Stockport, so trapping Northenden in a neat triangle. Built by the MacAlpine/Fairclough Consortium, the network was opened between 1974 and 1975.

Amendments to many bus routes were instituted in 1967.

45 renumbered 105, extended to the Civic Centre and linked to 101.
45 new service from the city to the Wythenshawe Forum (Town Centre) via Palatine Road and Sharston.
100 diverted from Parkway through Longley Lane and on to Portway.
101 extended along Greenbow Road and Tuffley Road to the Forum, linked 105.
103 diverted to the Forum and Portway terminus and linked to 106 service to Ringway on Saturday and Sunday as 104.
106 all day service extended from Peel Hall to Portway — linked to 103.
110 extended from Benchill to the Forum.
148 extended to the Forum; Saturdays to Peel Hall, as 128 to Benchill.

Other services included 104 to Moss Nook, 50 which became 41, 99 Sale, Baguley and Piccadilly, 11 express Woodhouse Park to Exchange, 107 express Woodhouse Park to Piccadilly, 11 limited-stop Baguley to Piccadilly — the first one-man-operated double deckers in M.C.T., becoming 109 in 1968, and 63 and 64 to Styal. But economy cuts in 1968 included the 116 and 134 works bus to Trafford Park.

In 1969 South East Lancashire and North East Cheshire (Selnec) was formed and took over from Oldham to Altrincham, including the North Western Road Car Company routes, by then part of the National Bus Company. The 115 and 63 were withdrawn, while the 120 became part of the 144 route. Still only the 109 and the 143 served the expanded Wythenshawe Hospital, though in 1973 the 117/118/119 services joined them.

The Greater Manchester Passenger Transport Executive (G.M.T.) took over in 1974 and brought in the 114 Sale to Wythenshawe via the hospital, 294 Altrincham to Wythenshawe Hospital, 310 Stockport to the hospital, and the 500 Saturday Express Bolton to the airport via the Forum. A new bus station, using steel and dark tough glass, was commenced on the market car park at the Town Centre in 1980, and was in operation by the end of 1984.

On 26 October 1986 the Bus Privatisation Act came into force and all the bus routes in Greater Manchester were deregulated. G.M.T. became the Greater Manchester Bus Company (G.M.B.C.). Most of the G.M.T. routes were continued, although with some curtailment of services. Just about a year before its demise, G.M.T. introduced the Localine buses in Wythenshawe, single-decker buses, mostly run for the convenience of the elderly. These were retained after deregulation and in February 1987 the Manchester Bus Company began its Beeline services, a private bus company running minibuses between Sale, Altrincham, Northenden, Wythenshawe, Didsbury and Manchester with a frequency of one bus every five minutes.

At Ringway Airport Aer Lingus introduced B.A.C. 1-11s on their Frankfurt service on 7 June 1965. About a month before, on 6 May, the *Excelsior Hotel*, with 264 beds, was opened by the Lord Mayor of Manchester. Over a year later, in July 1965, B.E.A. began to use jet Tridents on their Paris service.

On 15 March 1967 runway 24 was extended 1,100 feet to accommodate the new jets. It had to extend across the A538 on a bridge that needed four tunnels, two for pedestrians, two for road traffic. On 6 October 1967 Ringway had its heaviest passenger load to date, 261 people in a DC-8 of Trans International.

The last scheduled Douglas-Dakota service — Cambrian Airways — from Ringway was in September 1968. So far the Dakota is the longest serving civil aircraft, in use from 1939 to 1968 — 29 years. On 7 January 1969 the main runway, extended from 7,900 to 9,000 feet, was opened officially. The first scheduled non-stop flight to New York began on 29 April 1969 with B.O.A.C.'s Super V.C. 10s. The first Boeing 747 Jumbo jet landed at Ringway on 17 August 1970, to familiarise airport staff with wide-bodied aircraft. A year later a Court Line Lockheed Tri-star paid its first visit to Ringway. On 2 April 1975 Laker Airways operated the first transatlantic service A.B.C. flight on any route. It was a D.C. 10 to Toronto. Both the D.C. 10 and Tri-star were quiet aircraft, despite their size. At the end of May nose-in parking was introduced at the International Pier 'B'.

In the same year Runway 24 presented more problems. It had been originally laid in wartime conditions. There were no proper foundations or drainage, and the runway was cracking and flexing under the weight of modern aircraft. Engineers were called in. They said the runway would need major repairs by the early 1980s. The work was estimated to involve the total closure of the airport for eight to 12 months. The Airport Committee drew up plans for a second runway, 10,500 feet long and 1,500 feet to the south-east of the existing Runway 24 (a possibility first aired in the 1945 *City of Manchester Plan*). It was later withdrawn after pressure from the Greater Manchester Transport Action Group, who objected to the second runway as being unnecessary for many years, and by the people of Styal, whose houses and peace it threatened. A new plan was put to the planning authorities in May 1976. It still maintained the need for a second runway. That would have meant not only a second tunnel for the A538 but the runway would have crossed the Bollin Valley, designated by Cheshire County Council as a country park. That idea was shelved. But Runway 24 had to be rebuilt and recontoured. Greater Manchester Transport Action Group, in their first objections to the second runway, had pointed out that, working round the clock, and much more intensively through the night, it would be possible to complete this in two months. But the Airport Committee maintained that it could not close down the airport even for that short length of time without losing money and putting people's jobs in jeopardy. So a compromise was reached. The work was begun in March 1979 and finished by the end of October.

On 29 October a *Guardian* newspaper article on Ringway's runway described the strange way in which the runway was being built.

> The massive engineering job on the runway would be carried out at night, between the hours of 11.00 p.m. and 7.00 a.m., when take-offs and landings are already limited in the interests of local residents. Ringway would be able to operate normally for the remaining 16 hours of every day, and 5,000 people whose jobs are in some way dependent on the airport would be spared the hardship of a three-month lay-off. No other airport in the world had ever tried to stay in business while rebuilding and recontouring its only runway. Hundreds of dumpers, diggers, mixers and lighting towers would be expected to converge on the airfield as the roar of the day's last departing flight faded away, and roll off again, leaving a serviceable runway, as the first flight of the new day positioned itself on the glidepath. The operation would call for military precision by an efficient and disciplined workforce if the gamble was to succeed.
>
> Instead of flattening the hump, which could not be contemplated in the short nightly working spells of six hours, a labour force of more than 200 has built up the rest of the runway to meet it, laying no less than 222,000 tons of asphalt during the past six months.
>
> But few now question that the region's main 'gateway to the world' will eventually have to be wider. The second runway, though no longer necessary to meet present demand, is by no means

abandoned. The airport is already linked by way of M56 with the M6, the M62 and the rest of motorway network, and there are plans to provide it, in the not too distant future with a direct rail link too.

On 25 March 1974 the Intercontinental Pier 'C', the multi-storey car park and Terminal Extensions were officially opened. Pier 'C' was first used by a Jordanian Airlines Boeing 707 with King Hussein on board. It had been diverted from Heathrow because of bad weather. In June the same year Wardair's Boeing 747s began their first regular operation from Ringway. Six months later Ringway had its first and only hijack from the airport, a B.E.A. Super 1-11 to Heathrow. The hijacker was overpowered at Heathrow. In late July 1975 Manchester Airport Joint Committee was renamed Manchester International Airport Authority. Ringway was now officially Manchester International Airport.

One of the great events in Ringway's history was the first visit by a British Airways Concorde. Fog at Heathrow diverted it to Ringway on a Washington flight. Watched by thousands of people (the A538 was blocked) it took off, much to everyone's surprise registering a lower noise than the Boeing 747 which had taken off five minutes before.

Ringway, as the largest provincial airport in the country, handled five million passengers in 1983, the year a new two-million-pound taxiway was opened and a six-million-pound cargo terminal planned. Early in 1984 it became the first airport with automatic docking and the G.M.C.C., approved a further twelve-million-pound expansion on a fifty-fifty basis to cope with an expected nine million passengers by 1987.

Sadly, on 22 August 1985, the largest aircraft disaster in Ringway's history happened. A British Airtours 737, G-BGJL, full of holiday-makers bound for Tenerife, was forced to abort its take-off because of an engine fire. As the fire swept through the fuselage 58 people, including many locals, died.

On 1 April 1986 Greater Manchester County Council was abolished and its half of Manchester International Airport was handed over to a consortium of the borough councils of the County of Greater Manchester. In 1986, M.I.A. was the fastest growing airport in Britain in terms of passenger numbers. .

Industry, too, was changing in Wythenshawe. Good communications along with homes, shops, amenities, a forum and recreational facilities are important elements in any community, but for the complete garden city as planned by Barry Parker there must be local work for the inhabitants. On the industrial estates, as at Wythenshawe, this must mean constant change, expansion and progression. In the highly-competitive industrial field things never stand still.

Although industry in Wythenshawe had troubles enough, the successes of the mid-1960s were many and notable. At Sharston, between the long established Brook's Bakery (now the Manor Bakery of Mr. Kipling Cakes) and the Post Office, the Petrocarbon factory was established in 1965 at a cost of £70,000 and was soon to double in size. During the building another crane toppled onto temporary offices, missing clerks by a few centimetres. Before being taken over Petrocarbon's exports included a 125-million-pound plastics plant to Poland. Rolinx Plastics' exports included TV safety screens to Russia, and Fielden Electronic alarms circled the world in the liner Q.E.2.

Timpson's 1968 building housing the new factory of the shoe firm of the early Royal Oak Community Association benefactor, Noel Timpson, was visited by the Duke of Edinburgh. Just 20 years later Timpson's factory was demolished to make way for a hypermarket. Wylex and Kipling Cakes each enjoyed bigger and better, and in the second case, refreshingly aromatic, extensions. Kiplings and Mother's Pride Bread, on the Roundthorne estate, were both major factories in the Rank Hovis McDougall Group.

Amongst other new names in Wythenshawe were Portland Cement, with its reputed output of 200 tons per hour, Burmah Oil at Sharston, and Vimto and Kodak at Roundthorne.

The computer centres and headquarters of major banks and firms, such as Barclays, Shell and Smiths, booksellers, opened in the Civic Centre, though the dominant building there for a decade was an empty office block.

Among the firms that came and went were Granada Television Rentals, and Sperry and Hutchinson's Pink Trading Stamps. Great Universal Stores projected a seven-million-pound depot, but it was never built. Difficulties assailing Wythenshawe firms included serious fires at Brookside Clothing and Peter Williams Advertising (both started by 11-year-olds), and one at Express Dairies. Fram Concrete survived complaints about noise from householders on the Roundwood Estate, but Pipeweld in Baguley decided that if they could not work at night they would have to move and serenade householders elsewhere.

Financial take-overs were a feature of this period and were always serious threats to jobs. G.E.C. took over A.E.I. and two years later closed down with a loss of 1,250 jobs, only half of which were available again when Ingersoll Rand took the factory over two years later. Ferranti, on the other hand, after coming through a lock-out 'over £4' in 1972, was able to take on more labour after the government bought a 50 per cent stake in the firm in 1975 and it entered the micro-chip era. Employees of Fielden Electronics were not so lucky, for after a take-over by a Swiss firm 250 lost their jobs.

The following firms were operating in Wythenshawe in the mid-1970s:

Sharston

Anderson Pattern Books	Kaumagraph Transfers
Atlas Air Freight	Kilbride Print Engineers
Barrell Builders	Kno-Waste Bias Binding
Beatties Biscuits	Locomotors Coaches
Cement Marketing	Lucy Sunderland Timber
Clydol Oils	Lyons Maid Ices
Crampton Stuffing	Mr. Kipling Cakes
Crompton Lamps	Nettle Wiring
Davis & Timins Screws	Nu-pax Adhesive Tape
Dawson Rodgers Soft Furnishing	Petrocarbon Plant
Disincrustant Marseillaise	R.H.M. Foods
Dynachem Printed Circuits	R.T.R. Radio Services
Dynaflex Lubrication	Remploy Printers
Express Dairy	Rubber Latex
Fielden Electronics	Scott Electric Alloys
Flexibox Engineers	Smith Thompson Buildings
French's Tapes	Spinks Confectioners
Fram Concrete	Thiokol Photochemicals
Gatewood Vending Machines	Thornton Instruments
Hellerman Electrical	V.G. Garments
Hilson Wire	Walker James Gaskets
Hirst Jigs	Walmer Clothing
Holden Brook Pumps	Websons Appliances
Insuloid Wiring	William Morris Press
Isola Insulation	Wilmslow Asphalt
Johnson Wire Mesh	Wylex Electrical Products

Roundthorne

Almond Bakery (Mothers Pride)	Griffin George Labs
Arnold Car Sales	Henderson Textile Linings
B.S.P. Designs	Hilton Tuck Grinding
Barnes Printers	Hughes Textiles
Barry Wilkinson Tyres	Kodak Photographs
Baxter Hoare Shipping	Rolinx Plastics

Braddock Underwear
Brookside Clothing
Ciba Geigy Pharmaceuticals
Cartwrights Engineers
Danish Bacon
Easicut Grinding
Electrical Power Storage
Endress Hauser Electronics
Ennis Civil Engineers

Spafax Motor Trade
S. & H. Stamps
Stewson Plant
Telephone Rentals
Thornton Labs
Timpson Shoes
Vendops Supplies
Wright Ofland Glass

South, Civic Centre and Airport

Airviews
Atlas Air Express
Barclaycard 'back-up'
Barton Moss Engineers
Decca Navigation
Elliott Dynamos
Everard Flours

Ferranti Automation
Males Tractor Service
Northern Executive Services
Reynold Chain
Shellmex Computers
W.H. Smith Office

There were many changes on the industrial scene in the 1980s. The most notable was the engulfing of Petrocarbon by Costain International, of world repute, to form Wythenshawe's largest concern. Costain's projects include the London orbital motorway and the Channel Tunnel — the latter with a hint of historic justice as the first serious plan was made a century earlier in Wythenshawe by Edward Watkin of Rose Hill (*see* Chapter One). In 1988 ambitious plans for a thirty-million-pound business park by Manchester International Airport were announced.

*   *   *

With Wythenshawe's industry in hearty shape and housing and social facilities 'substantially complete', the question, 'Is Wythenshawe a success?' often surfaces. The answer depends on the dimension considered, of course, but it seems self evident that overall it compares very well with other similar developments.

Physically Barry Parker's garden city, with the dogged perseverance of the Parks' Department, has materialised. 'The first full-scale municipal garden city — certainly in Britain', is not such an easily-recognised concept as the concrete cows of Milton Keynes, but it may be just as much a reality. Reflecting this is the fact that the epithet Wythenshawe Garden City, after fading from use in the its middle years, is now being heard more frequently. Whether looking over Wythenshawe from the motorway, where the prospect is almost entirely green, or walking at street level, the abiding impression is of a city set in a vast woody garden.

There are barren patches, of course. One particular grey spot is the concrete of the Civic Centre. More shelter and mature trees might soften the chilly wind that blows across Leningrad Square. More well-designed bins, a discreet face-lift and some wardens might lessen the litter and graffiti of the shopping area — at present so different from the classical concept of both Parker and Nicholas.

The preservation of open spaces has been a concern from the 1930s, when A. P. Simon (*see* Chapter Four) complained of their erosion between neighbourhood units. Walter Creese in 1966 was laying the blame for environmental desecration on 'expedient adjustments' due to the creation of Wythenshawe lying 'between two world wars and athwart a great depression'. But in 1989 we still find the city council wanting to use the Sharston Green fields as an industrial business park, arguing that this would bring employment and income. We also find Gatley and Northenden residents arguing that the development of the adjoining

John Plessington School site as an 'organised recreational space' would not compensate for the loss of ancient common and natural open land.

Since the 1930s, when Simon insisted that Wythenshawe needed its own council, the lack of self-government and over-dependence on Albert Square, eight miles away, has been blamed for any lack of civic pride. Many towns with their own council and mayor, from Wem to Winchester, are a fraction of the size of Wythenshawe. This is an anomaly common to many suburbs, as is the issue of under-representation: Wythenshawe constituency has almost eighty thousand voters, twice and, on occasions, three times the figure of more privileged areas.

The debate on home rule rumbled on through the 1970s, especially in the *Wythenshawe Express*, the Federal Council and the Chamber of Trade where Mr. Fred Robinson wanted an autonomous Wythenshawe within the framework of Manchester. Fred Hoyle, rector of St Martin's Church, claimed that 'the creation of an independent township for Wythenshawe is inevitable'. But as the house-full sign went up the pioneering spirit faded. The Federal Council disbanded. The Civic Weeks, as such, were abandoned though they were reincarnated as Art Festivals in the 1970s with a little finance and not a little direction from the city. The nearest Wythenshawe has come to autonomy is with the Wythenshawe Consultative Committee, which embodies the local councillors. Relevant planning applications and the like are considered and recommendations passed to the city council. If it has few teeth of its own, at least it has a sensitive ear responsive to civic societies and the public in general, who are invited to attend and air their views.

Northenden had its own concerns, though with the emigration of Race's car-breakers' yard, which had long debased the village, there was a resurgence of spirit — and property prices. The siren atop of the many-storeyed *Post House* hotel continued to lure travellers from Princess Parkway, and joining it on the Palatine Road's west-end came, in the late 1980s, prestigious high-tech-high-sec offices. Into one of these, County House, came with great secrecy the most important British provincial branch of Reuters News Agency — 'we don't like people to know we are here . . .'! Less bashful were the domestic electrical shops of Comet and Currys at the other end of Palatine Road and the many restaurants and take-aways that mushroomed throughout the village. Surrounded by a triangle of motorways and with a Civic Society proud of its history, Northenden's sense of identity has been less of a problem.

The question of community spirit in Wythenshawe has been more enigmatic. But banks of trees and ranks of houses do not a garden city make — necessarily. Claire MacGlennon in a sociological study in 1971 blamed any lack of identity on its unnatural growth to such a huge size and the consequent remoteness of authorities, church leaders and '. . . voluntary services in the main staffed by people who did not live in Wythenshawe'. A lack of cohesion was emphasised in 1988 in a Church of England Urban Aid pamphlet circulated nationally that included the assertion by the rector of Benchill, Oliver Forshaw, that Wythenshawe is 'the opposite of a community'.

Yet the hundreds of secular and religious clubs and societies, meetings, classes, sports and other activities listed in the area, or a visit to the Forum concourse and the entrance to the library there, would seem to testify to the existence of a community with a very wide and lively variety of interests. Nor must we forget that Barry Parker did not intend there to be one, but 10 communities. A closer look in the last chapter at a few of these interests might give us an impression of the nature of these communities, and of the community spirit generally, in Wythenshawe.

Chapter Eleven

A New Spirit
'Growing every Year in Size, Quality and Enthusiasm'

Early in the 1960s the Civic Weeks festivities petered out, as support from all quarters became less and less. This was due to a combination of factors which affected people at the grass roots, and as the decade progressed it was from outside the Wythenshawe area that some of the organisation of leisure pursuits came. The Parks Department, which previously had been merely guardians of the parks, planting them, caring for them and patrolling them, became more active in its efforts of attracting people to use them, and one of the ways it did this was to hold 'Open Days'. On 30 May 1964 the first Open Day and Exhibition was held in Wythenshawe Park. The emphasis was on Nature, so there were organised tours of the glasshouses and the gardens. There were demonstrations of modern bee-keeping, with live bees in the garden adjoining the hall, and of floral-arranging in the art gallery. An exhibition of dolls of all nations was held in the courtyard and an exhibition of painting and handicrafts in the hall itself.

Alongside this there were other events taking place throughout the day. One year there were demonstrations of archery by the Bowmen of Bruntwood, sword, lance and revolver displays by the Mounted Section of the Manchester Police, and obedience and agility testing by the Police Dog Section. The Road Safety Section offered their 'reaction tests' and, just for fun, there was a children's entertainer and pony rides. Adults were entertained by the expertise of the Fianna Phadraig Pipe Band and Dancers. The Ministry of Labour had a marquee on the grounds, where they offered to help 'solve your work problems', and a Careers Advisory Officer was on hand at the Youth Employment Bureau Stand. Attempts were made to cater for all with hobbies, employment and items just for pleasure.

In 1969 there was added excitement:

> A massive gamble paid off on Saturday when the sun shone hot and bright for Wythenshawe Park's annual open day . . . Top showjumpers had flocked from as far afield as Worcestershire to compete at Wythenshawe's horse show.

Ten years later the Open Day was not so well supported, although interesting events had been arranged. The Royal Green Jackets Free Fall Parachute team dropped from the skies onto their appointed target with great accuracy, but for the first time the horse show, which by now had become a tradition and was such a great draw with the crowds, was cancelled. Financial reasons were given, yet a few years earlier a Parks Department spokesman had said of the gymkhana, 'This event proves more popular each year'.

Wythenshawe Park, as the largest public park in the area, is well-used at holiday times when the large fairs arrive. Its popularity can be seen in the following report:

> . . . the rare Easter sunshine brought thousands of children and adults to the annual fair at Wythenshawe Park. People came from all over South Manchester to the park resulting in traffic jams on Altrincham Road. As with everything else the price to have fun on the fair had gone up!

As has already been recorded, Wythenshawe Park has had its own large open day since 1964, but the hall, which, between deathwatch beetle scares, has for many years been used as a museum, is also made available to the public for wedding receptions, anniversaries and other functions in the three rooms at the east end of the building. In some ways it is unfortunate that this large and beautiful park is near the northern outskirts of the housing estates, for it is not easily accessible to many Wythenshawe people. Although the Parker Plan provided gardens for all its dwellings, children and adolescents still require larger open spaces in which to play.

In the 1960s people petitioned for neighbourhood parks and adventure playgrounds, particularly in the Peel Hall area, with little success, but one of those that eventually came

50. Old Post Office Corner, Northenden, c.1887. Pidgeon's shop (with a private school above) was replaced by a 1920s Co-op and is now a garage forecourt. The corner premises to the right lasted a little longer. The terrace to the left remains in spite of the collapse of the end wall during alterations and so do the distant terrace and church behind.

into being was Painswick Park. One of the last official duties of Mr. McMillan, the head of Recreational Services, was to perform the opening ceremony. He spoke of it as 'the most memorable experience, for Painswick Park, which was once just a field, now had a boating pool, a pavilion and playground'. Unfortunately this park had to be closed in 1975 'following incidents'. Adventure playgrounds were also situated at certain points but were misused, the equipment badly damaged and fires started within the grounds. The adventure playground close to the town centre had to be boarded up.

The River Mersey Valley Scheme began to take shape towards the end of the 1960s. It was an ambitious scheme, incorporating 12 miles of river, part of which passed through Northenden. The idea was for a longitudinal park, one end being in Carrington and the other in Stockport. One press report hailed the park with the headlines 'Twelve mile rubbish dump will become giant playground'. Despite the motorway, which runs for a short stretch over and along the river, the Northenden/Didsbury section is thought to be most attractive.

Apart from the professional gardeners and planners of the parks, Wythenshawe had many amateur enthusiasts. Local gardening societies continued to flourish and hold their shows annually, except the Brownley Green Horticultural Society, which got into financial trouble because of the expense caused by their annual show and lack of interest generally. It disbanded and gave its remaining funds to local charities, and the Northenden Allotment Association bought its hut. This latter society was outspoken when the plot rents were raised and, although it was decided to boycott Platt Fields Annual Flower Show, many of the societies did not comply with the boycott and the increased rents had to be accepted. Again in 1975 the Northenden Allotment Association spoke out about a further increase in rents, saying that the increase had been 380 per cent in three years.

Allotments still continued to be in great demand and one humble plot of land in Sharston became nationally famous when it was chosen as the setting for BBC 2's television series, *Mr. Smith's Garden*, first televised in 1974. The Sharston Allotment Society had started during the war, taking part in the 'Dig for Victory' campaign. Over the years this particular society had become so successful that one year it was banned from entering for the Councillor Rodgers Cup. This success was despite the fact that their site was twice moved, once on the building of the Sharston Swimming Baths and later for the shopping precinct.

In 1970 the Cage Bird Society held its twentieth Nest Feather Show in the Royal Oak Centre and had more entrants than ever, as did the Royal Oak Chrysanthemum Show, when all the exhibitors were competing for the Noel Timpson Cup.

Sport in Wythenshawe continues to be varied and prolific, and football is top of the list in popularity. Many of the soccer teams are sponsored by local firms and public houses. The Ferranti team fought their way into the last four of the Wythenshawe League Cup in 1970. The same year Newall Green came top of the first division of Wythenshawe Sunday League and scored a double by becoming league champions, too. In the 1970s there were so many teams in Wythenshawe that Manchester Parks had difficulty in sorting out the pitches. One year this was complicated by very wet weather, and when the fixture list reached crisis level Manchester Parks extended the season at three Wythenshawe parks, Hollyhedge, Painswick and Firbank. Attempts were made at various times to get permission for more school pitches to be opened and a survey was made by the Education Department, but the idea was not found to be practicable. Seven new pitches were opened in Wythenshawe Park, but this was still not enough and 10 teams had to resign.

There was another difficulty, which was peculiar to Wythenshawe, and that was the problem of allegiance. The clubs had for some time been trying to get into the Manchester Premier League and it was reported in the *Wythenshawe Express* that 'According to the Football Association, Wythenshawe is not a part of Manchester and that is causing confusion'. There was a meeting between Manchester and Cheshire representatives and the outcome was a letter from the Football Association in which the secretary, Dennis Fellows, ruled that there would be no change in the football boundaries and that the clubs in Wythenshawe would continue to remain under Cheshire jurisdiction. It appears that after the Manchester Extension Act the Football Association issued a directive saying 'the city boundaries remained the same' and forty years later this situation still remained unchanged.

South Manchester and Wythenshawe Cricket Club held an annual Charity Match in which for many years they competed against a West Indian team. This was always well-supported and in the evening, weather permitting, the entertainment was extended when a West Indian steel band played for dancing. The ground on Longley Lane continues to be well used by local firms during the week and club members at weekends. In the 1960s the club faced a fierce challenge but finally walked off with the Cheshire Cricket Association title. In 1983, in order to increase the annual income, it was agreed that a local football team should be allowed to use the ground.

One of the tributaries of the River Mersey is the River Tame and it comes down through the north-western industrial areas of Saddleworth, Ashton and Hyde, collecting effluent on the way, until it reaches the River Mersey at Stockport. In 1968 steps were taken to purify certain stretches of the river including that which runs through Northenden, mainly at the instigation of the South Manchester Anglers. In the early 1970s fish were put into the river. The River Mersey was also used by canoeing clubs to 'shoot the rapids' at Northenden weir.

Because of the interest in boxing that there had been for many years in the Wythenshawe area it was decided to invite the Amateur Boxing Association to start a course for aspiring pugilists and referees at the Woodhouse Park Youth Centre. The South Manchester and Wythenshawe lacrosse teams remained fierce challengers in that sport and in 1970 five players were chosen to represent Lancashire. This has been only one of their many successes. Bowling remains a popular game in the parks and behind the pubs of the area. The Wythenshawe Park team 'battled its way through Siberian-type weather to win the *Wythenshawe Express* Trophy for the second time' one August. For the less hardy the fixture lists of indoor games includes snooker, darts, cribbage, dominoes and Nine Card Don. The teams taking part are drawn from the hospitals, local firms, pubs and local associations.

The Sharston Swimming Pool was opened in 1961 and was the first municipal bath to be opened after the war, except for the Empire Pool, Cardiff. There were many complaints about its size, it not being up to Olympic standard, but the Director of Public Baths and Wash-houses spoke out, informing the public that the Bath was of national championship size. Such major events are not generally held there, however, because there is not the hotel accommodation locally for competitors. To have been 'Olympic' size it would have had to be 50 feet longer and wider. The bath is well used by schools, swimming clubs, the general public and local organisations. For example, the Scouting Movement hold their annual galas there.

The bath has also been used for other, not quite so conventional, events. In 1970 the Florida Dolphin Show arrived with Flipper, two sea-lions called Bonny and Clyde, 'Two 300lb dolphins, two sea-lions and a penguin named Percy and Sharston Baths is their new home for the next 8 weeks and they are settling nicely'. Many local people visited the exotic aquatic show that was presented. Another show or event held there was not for such public viewing, in fact council workers blocked out 'almost 300 feet of glass at a Manchester Swimming Pool . . . to keep prying eyes away from the nudist swimming group . . . with soap and soda ash'. This session was booked by the Central Council of British Naturists.

Wythenshawe swimmers are fortunate in having more facilities at the Civic Centre sports complex, where there is a pool of national championship size, a small teaching pool and facilities for a variety of sports in the Sports Hall. There is netball, basketball, tennis, five-a-side-football and volleyball, but as there is only one court only a limited number of people can play at any one time. The hall attendants have to stand around waiting to change over equipment. There are four cricket nets, archery bays, eight golf lanes and four badminton nets.

Commercial entertainment can be found in Northenden and Wythenshawe operating at all levels. An attempt was made to open an amusement arcade in one of the shops on Palatine Road, but a great dispute raged over this and the fruit machines never appeared. There was less success, however, for the people who fought to keep the A.B.C. Forum as a cinema, for this was not to be. The other Northenden cinema, the Coronation, had closed in February 1964 and re-opened as a bingo hall in June 1964. It rapidly became the major centre for bingo in Wythenshawe and was renamed the Wythenshawe Casino. The addiction to this game was great, mainly among the ladies. One regular player gave birth to a baby shortly after one of the games, and another was back in her seat a couple of days after her baby had been delivered. Large queues at the bus stop close by the bingo hall showed that many of the participants came from the Wythenshawe area. The drinkers at the *Farmers Arms* next door were alerted when a voice over a loud-speaker in the bar told them that the interval was over and the game was re-starting. In July 1971 the gaming laws were changed and 'prize bingo' became legal. Alas, in 1987 all games ceased when the old cinema was demolished and the ground turned into a car park for the *Farmer's Arms*.

When the Forum Cinema was closed and another bingo hall mooted, the residents of the area were determined that they would not have a second such establishment in close proximity to the other, the Wythenshawe Casino. They were disturbed by the amount of litter and noise that occurred when the players burst from the building onto Longley Lane. A petition was raised in 1971 and 3,000 people signed against this change of usage. This was successful and bingo was banned from the A.B.C. The great increase in colour television meant that the Forum was no longer a viable commercial proposition as a cinema, so the building was sold to the Jehovah's Witnesses, and the mighty Wurlitzer organ dismantled and sent to do service at the Town Hall, Burton-on-Trent.

Outside Northenden the promised cinema in the vicinity of Hollyhedge Circle was not built, nor did the planners at the Town Hall think that this type of entertainment was necessary. Instead a large building was erected at the town centre in 1966, which was to be become the Wythenshawe Bowl, bowling alleys being in vogue in the 1960s. The bowling alley did not survive long, for there were some incidents of trouble and fighting around it. Mothers complained that at one time there were 17 dogs running around outside, presumably after waste food, but this was denied by the manager. The police had to be called frequently, so it was sold. In 1968 it was adapted to become the nightspot of the north.

Re-opened under the name of the Golden Garter, the interior of the old bowling alley was redecorated in lavish style. A 50-foot bar was installed and a retractable stage. An atmosphere of pleasure was created. The soft lights, the curtaining, the plush decor and even the drapes on the stage were designed to relax the customer. That may have been the intention, but in the beginning the amplification of the music turned the nightspot into 'a throbbing bowl of sound'. Shortly after it was opened the Chief Constable objected to the supper licence, unsuccessfully. .

The club was patronised by people from all walks of life. Local works held their Christmas outings there and it was a popular venue for retirement and other celebrations. The Cavendish Boxing Club held a boxing tournament there in 1977 to raise funds and in 1974 the current Miss World, American Marjorie Wallace, visited the nightspot.

The Golden Garter soon became known as a place for a good night out, and in the mid-1970s a new manager decided to make 'a more intimate atmosphere of soft lights and smooth sounds, with the stars nearer the audience'. The stars engaged were those in great demand and had to be booked at least a year ahead. Some of the well-known ones were Ronnie Corbett, Val Doonican, Ken Dodd, Harry Secombe, Cleo Laine and Johnny Dankworth, Frankie Vaughan and many more. In 1976 Princess Margaret visited the club. She came to support a charity show in aid of the Invalid Children's Association and the Dockland Settlement Adventure School for Boys and Girls. The Golden Garter closed as a nightclub in the mid-1980s and became a bingo hall.

The Forum Theatre, across the town centre from the Golden Garter, was another building that attracted people to a different kind of live entertainment. It was opened in 1971 with David Scase as the first director. The opening production was *Lorna and Ted* by John Hale. The seats cost 40p, 50p and 70p. As there was no tradition of theatre-going in the area fears about its success were rife and were expressed by Mike Pratt, who played the male title role in the first production. He said that he was 'more nervous than usual as I am terrified that if we flop the theatre has had it for the rest of the season'. It did not flop, although two old ladies walked out in disgust during the second act as it was a rather 'rude' play. On the opening night the audience was over-weighted with theatrical people, who had come along to give the theatre a boost as a formal opening was not planned.

This theatre is municipally owned and 'sister' to the Library Theatre in St Peter's Square. Between them they have the largest repertory company in the country. Types of play performed are varied: drama, tragedy, comedy, musicals off-beat and conventional, and at Christmas time a pantomime. The Northern Dance Theatre dances classical and modern ballet and occasionally a group of local amateurs, such as the Royal Oak Residents' Association, puts on a show. Many of the performances have been very well supported; often it has not been possible to gain a seat unless booked well in advance. There were some plays that were not so well attended, noticeably *Waiting for Godot*. In 1980 a new director came to the Forum Theatre, Howard Lloyd Lewis.

To foster children's interest in the theatre a group of people from the theatre, with the help of Didsbury College students, started a club with a permanent base in the Forum small hall. This is named SMASH, or Saturday Morning Activities Start Here and its aim is 'to provide release for youthful energies in a creative and constructive way with a bias towards the theatre'. Mime and music play an integral part in these Saturday morning activities, which are for children aged six to sixteen. A similar group has been formed for the five- to eight-year-olds, called 'Adventure Playhouse'.

Amateur entertainment

Originally commercial entertainment was so sparse that amateur productions were well-supported, and over the years there have been many good amateur groups. The Sharston Youth Drama Group was perhaps the most outstanding in Wythenshawe, having a trophy-studded history, gaining 82 awards in their first 10 years. They were instituted in 1965 by playwright/director Andrew Winton, who wrote many of the scripts they performed. One of his plays, *A Sleep of Death*, was particularly successful. With it they were the first Manchester team to win the Stanley Arnold Trophy at Sheffield (they were only the second group in the North-west to walk off with this prize). They won coveted honours in many places, including Denton, Buxton and Birmingham, and two years running they won the top award in the County Arts Festival.

A less fortunate group was the Alpha Players. They lost their original premises and so brought the company to perform at St Wilfrid's School, Northenden, in 1971. Their first play, *Mrs. Gibbon's Boys*, was a great success and they played to packed houses, but this triumph was not repeated. Bad publicity and lack of interest from the people of Northenden was thought to be the cause, and they decided to make a fresh start in Rusholme.

The Celesta Players, who came from Didsbury when the church hall in which they performed was closed, had more success. St Luke's, Benchill, took them in and they played there and at other church halls in the area.

The Northenden Players produce six plays a year in their cosy, compact theatre on Boat Lane, usually to full houses. Their membership was 425 in 1978. They seemed to have a penchant for mystery plays with a strong story line, but farce, tragedy and comedy they also execute competently.

There were many other groups performing in Wythenshawe with varying amounts of success, such as the William Temple Players, the Russell Players and the Portway Amateur Society, but all getting a great deal of pleasure from their Thespian activities.

The Royal Oak Residents' Association continued to put on pantomimes annually at the Royal Oak Centre, under the direction of Miss Joan Lawrence, and they also performed on the Forum Theatre stage. As the years go by the young dancers become the leads, often following in mother's footsteps.

In Northenden in the early 1970s a group calling themselves the 'Omega Players' arose, affiliated to St Wilfrid's church. Each year they produced a pantomime, in association with the Pearl Yarwood Dancers, the first being *Dick Whittington*. One year a member wrote his own version of *Jack and the Beanstalk* and this was very well received by the Northenden audience. After a few years the audiences became less in number and in 1977, the centenary of the building of the church, Rev. Gordon Jones, the then incumbent, wrote a play in celebration of the event called *Snort, or Dragon Down Ford Lane*. This was scheduled to take place in the summer, but on the weekend of the performance there was a heat wave, which meant that the company again played to small audiences. Disheartened by this and the small Christmas-time audiences, the society decided not to produce any more pantomimes for a while. In 1988, in response to the need to raise money for repairs of the school roof the group went into action and *Jack and the Beanstalk* played once more to packed houses.

Musicals, often Gilbert and Sullivan, were performed by the Yew Tree Operatic Society, later the West Wythenshawe Operatic Society, at the Further Education Centre on Moor Road. At one time they were dogged with problems, difficulty in finding a producer, then a pianist, but they overcame these troubles and the shows they put on were very successful and well supported.

In the 1970s the Forum Music Society was formed in Wythenshawe and attracted many people, but the Northenden Operatic Society found it hard to get recruits. They complained that although they had advertised in Wythenshawe the people on the estates were not interested. Yet there were some local musical groups in Wythenshawe, the Wythenshawe Youth Concert Wind Band and the South Manchester Swing Band. Older, more well-established bands, such as the Northenden Silver Prize Band and St Wilfrid's Pipe Band, later the Phoenix Pipe Band, still grace garden parties with their music.

Dancing schools are numerous, but two of the oldest, catering mainly for children, are the Joan Lawrence School of Dancing and the Pearl Yarwood School of Dancing. Both of these schools train children for shows locally, in Manchester and, occasionally, for television. The Meeta Thomas School of Ballet in Northenden was another well-attended school. The Wythenshawe Navalettes and Corvettes Dancing Troupes won medals and shields, as do the many Morris Troupes in the area. At the town centre there was the Harry Flood Dancing School, which had its premises in the Melody Ballroom. Ballroom and Latin American dancing were taught there, amongst other things, and, similarly, at the Redfern School of Dancing, which operates in the Cricket Club on Longley Lane.

Public houses and hotels proliferated in Wythenshawe. It seems that almost every time a new pub was mooted for the estate it was hailed with a storm of protests and petitions, but usually to no avail. At the present time there are approximately forty-one licensed houses in the Northenden and Wythenshawe areas, and this does not include clubs and associations, such as the British Legion, Labour Clubs or Conservative Clubs. Although many opened, only one closed — the *Sharston Hotel*. It had been opened in 1935 when the first houses were going up in Benchill, and in 1972 it received a much needed £50,000 face-lift, which included the installation of the 'Bird's Nest' discotheque. The restoration was celebrated with 400 pints of free beer. Unfortunately, the discotheque caused a disturbance on more than one occasion. When teenagers were refused admission because they were considered unsuitably dressed by the management they made 'Spider-man' ascents up the drain pipes and fighting broke out when they were discovered. This and other incidents caused the local inhabitants to remark 'At one time it was a decent hotel but now it's just a dive which serves no useful purpose in the area' and in December 1977 the pub was closed, a large office-block now being erected on the site.

51. Baguley Hall — back from the past. One of the finest old buildings in Manchester, the Department of the Environment spent 10 years repairing it, for much of which time it was shrouded in scaffolding.

Other pubs had more success, even though they caused a stir as did the opening of *The Red Beret* in 1967 when 'five men plunged from a tiny plane over Woodhouse Park and dropped in at the local for a pint'. The *Yew Tree Hotel*, one of the first pubs to be built in the Northenden area of the estate, has become one of the largest establishment pubs in the North-west, with its concert room, which holds 400 people. Top cabaret stars are booked and often there is not even standing room for the customers.

The Moss Nook Rest, originally the Skyways Café, which had been in such trouble when the Hell's Angels gathered there, was voted one of the top restaurants of the year, its Georgian-type interior being much admired.

Two of the most lavish hotels were owned by Fortes, the *Excelsior* at Ringway and the *Post House* at Northenden. The *Excelsior*, built within 300 yards of the terminal building, had 154 bedrooms, excellent dining facilities and all the accoutrements of a luxury hotel built, not to serve locals, but the travelling public. Similarly, the *Post House* is situated at the intersection of two motorways and was designed to accommodate travellers, as its name might suggest, but, being in close proximity to the village of Northenden, it is used by the local people for functions, such as the Civic Society's 'Northenden Ball'. Lord Robens performed the opening ceremony of the hotel, saying it was good to be back in Northenden, a place where he had once lived and where as a boy he had spent many hours cycling around the area. The reigning Miss World was the first guest at the *Post House*, a few days before the official opening. Two other Northenden pubs changed dramatically, modern buildings replacing the old cottage-type edifices, the *Spread Eagle* in 1965 and the *Jolly Carter* in 1977.

Charities and Community Groups

Most people in Wythenshawe support charities in one way or another. Many of the public houses and clubs organise events and activities, the profit from which goes to buy such things as guide dogs and kidney machines, and to other worthy causes. A branch of one of the world's largest and most active voluntary community organisations, the Lions International, was formed in Wythenshawe. It was called the Northenden and District's Lions' Club and was presented with its charter in 1979. The club takes part in many local fund-raising activities, noticeably at Christmas when they charm the busy shoppers with the sight of Father Christmas sitting on his sleigh outside Tesco's, shaking his collection box to the sounds of piped Christmas carols. In 1979 they organised a Village Fair in Wythenshawe Park as part of the Fun Day during Festival Week. They encouraged all local organisations to take part and run stalls. The Lions took 50 per cent of all the profits for charity.

Another group of hard-working philanthropists are the Rotarians. They have for a long time been helping people in various ways, sometimes by giving them a much-needed holiday in Wales or, as in the case of one Wythenshawe pensioner, paying for her trip to Canada to see her relations.

The League of Friends of Wythenshawe Hospital raise money by holding garden parties and sales of work to provide extra comforts for the patients. The W.V.S., as well as performing their many other activities, opened an office in a disused shop in Northenden from where until recently they supplied clothing and bedding to the needy. The many churches in the area, as might be expected, make their contributions to charity.

Uniformed groups abound in Wythenshawe. There are Scouts, Guides, Cubs, Brownies, Air Training Corps Cadets and the Sea Scouts. The Wythenshawe A.T.C. did particularly well one year, gaining five Duke of Edinburgh Awards.

Some of the community associations were still operating in the 1960s (the Royal Oak successes have been noted). The Woodhouse Park and Moss Nook Community Association was active in encouraging people to clear away the rubbish from around the houses and streets. They spoke out, through the local newspaper, urging the local residents 'to prevent Wythenshawe from becoming a suburban slum'. Benchill Community Association was in trouble in 1966. It lost its own premises and looked certain to close, but fortunately it was offered alternative premises at the Civil Defence Headquarters on Brownley Road. Later, when Sharston and Benchill Community Associations joined forces at the Civil Defence headquarters, they boasted the title of the Wythenshawe Community Association. It was said by some that these groups only fulfilled a primitive need and that if they were to survive they should merge. Even so their hey-day in the 1940s and 1950s was not to be equalled again.

Wythenshawe Arts Festival

In 1970 there began a tradition of Arts Festivals in Wythenshawe, which have expanded and developed so much that at the present time they are financially successful and give great pleasure to both participants and onlookers. They fill a social and cultural need in the area, highlighting skills and allowing for much self-expression in diverse fields. The concept behind 'Impact '70', the name given to the first great event, was similar to that voiced by Harry Lloyd, Chairman of the Federal Council, back in the 1940s when, at the inception of the first Civic Week, he spoke of Wythenshawe's need for an identity and feeling of responsibility towards its environment and activities. The Civic Weeks, as large combined efforts, had faded away, although microcosms of them survived in small pockets of Wythenshawe, where local community associations still organised special events. Royal Oak chose its Harvest Queen and Woodhouse Park held celebrations and its own Civic Week. There are other Rose Queens and Rosebuds about Wythenshawe, enjoying their own very special day.

The man who appears to have inspired the revival of interest in civic pride and activity on a large scale was Rev. David Hirst, the curate of William Temple Church in 1970. He was chairman of the organising committee and a man full of vitality and infectious enthusiasm. He led a team of keen workers from all parts of Wythenshawe, acting as a catalyst, bringing people together in a common cause. The lack of help from central services was underlined by him in a few sentences printed in the local paper, just prior to the opening of the Festival.

> The support from the Town Hall, from the people concerned with youth work, who ought to be caring for and involved with 100,000 people, doesn't come. True the Lord Mayor wrote a letter for the brochure but the people who run the youth services and so on should have been aware of what Wythenshawe was trying to say. They should have been encouraging people who wanted to improve things. I think Manchester does things a bit on the cheap, they want voluntary organisations to do things for them.

Fortunately, Wythenshawe was not short of voluntary organisations and in January Impact '70 got off the ground with the resultant headlines 'Who'd have thought Wythenshawe had so much talent?'. More important was a letter received by the vicar of William Temple Church from Jenny Lee, the Minister of State for Sport and Entertainment with Special Responsibility for the Arts, in which she thanked the organisers '. . . for providing such a valuable focus on local groups and organisations'. Wythenshawe was on the cultural map.

The focus of the Festival was the newly refurbished Wythenshawe Centre on Brownley Road, where the exhibitions were mounted, brightly-coloured paintings, pencil sketches, exquisite embroidery, sculptures, songs and poems decorating the walls. There was a dressmaking section and a carpentry section, a display of puppets of all shapes and sizes and of model aircraft and many more things. The room was full with colours and ideas, and 'above all the quality of the exhibition was staggering'.

The week before Impact opened, local bands played rousing music at various points in Wythenshawe, while pretty placard-carrying girls announced the impending Festival, and on the following Saturday the Franciscan Folk Group sang and played Gospel songs in the Wythenshawe Town Centre as part of the entertainment. Throughout the week of the Festival there were displays and musical concerts, held mainly in the Wythenshawe Centre. But sometimes, because of lack of space, community halls were used. It is difficult to include all that could be seen or happened, but the success and independence of this first Wythenshawe Festival is summed up in the leader of the *Wythenshawe Express*:

> Don't get the idea that the Town Hall is behind Impact '70, the Town Hall is uninterested in the whole affair, indeed it took a fight by certain pressure groups to make the Education Department at Crown Square agree to stick to what they had promised and let the Festival be staged at the centre on Brownley Road . . . Don't go away with the impression that the whole exhibition is nice and pretty. The whole event has been an eye opener as to the quality of art in Wythenshawe and to the interest in life that people round here have.

This interest did not peter out when Impact '70 closed. Almost immediately another organising committee was formed for the '71 Festival, but this time without Rev. Hirst, who left Wythenshawe to work in another parish. In December 1971 the Forum complex was opened and became the new home of the Festival. The accommodation was greater. Performances and events could take place in the large and small halls and the theatre simultaneously, and a large concourse and library were available for exhibitions. In his welcome speech in the 1972 programme, Alderman Downward referred to the change of venue and so reflected the change in attitude that had taken place. 'In its new surroundings we expect Impact to grow year by year, in size, in quality and in enthusiasm, until it becomes a major event not just in Wythenshawe but in the life of the new Metropolitan Manchester.'

Another change took place in 1975, in the timing of this occasion. Wythenshawe's M.P., Alf Morris, wrote:

> The change this year from January to July will add much to the interest of many events during Festival Week. Then secondly there are open air events for the first time. These also should give added interest to the programme and attract new participants.

The new programmes included an ox roast and an 'It's a Knockout Competition'. So big had the Festival grown that four events venues were listed in the programme, the Forum, Wythenshawe Park, Wythenshawe College and William Temple Church.

Churches

The spiritual side of Wythenshawe also continued to grow and diversify. New churches were built and others refurbished. Two new Anglican, one Roman Catholic and two Nonconformist churches arose in Northenden and Wythenshawe.

The Anglican Church of William Temple was opened in 1965 on the corner of Robinswood Road and Simonsway as the church of the Civic Centre. The mission was already well-established, having begun many years previously in Shadow Moss School Room, latterly operating in a dual-purpose building on Simonsway. The architect, George Pace, agreed with the proviso that he should not design a 'pseudo' building, but that it should be modern in concept. This he did and particular attention was paid to the acoustics with a view to music and drama being performed there. One of Pace's stipulations was that, as with all the churches he designed, there must be no plaques attached to the walls commemorating the dedication of the church or in memory of anyone, for he said he built his churches to the Glory of God. The only lettered stone is on the back wall of the church and it has on it the date of the consecration and a symbol, which is Pace's original sign for William Temple Church.

The internal supports of the church are black-painted steel girders, not romantically symbolising the industry of the area, as it is sometimes said, but because when it was discovered that the church had been built on swampy ground an extra £2,000 was needed for foundations; the wooden beams of the original design had to be changed for cheaper steel ones. There is symbolism, however, in the placing of the font between and beneath the three main weight-bearing supports of the church.

The pews have an interesting history, having been brought from derelict churches in and around Manchester. The present lady churchwarden said:

> whenever we heard of a church being demolished we borrowed Mr. Owen's coal cart and went off to see if we could buy any of the pews. Many times I've sat on the back of the waggon, in the pouring rain, with the pews, bringing them back to Wythenshawe to be stored until our church building was completed!

Some time after the building was opened a fire damaged some of the pews. With the insurance money all the pews were stripped and bleached, giving an element of uniformity and a bright welcoming atmosphere in the church generally. An interesting thought was voiced that as many people living in Wythenshawe now had their origins near to the centre of Manchester they may be sitting in the same pews in which their ancestors once sat.

The church dedicated to St Richard on Peel Hall Road was consecrated in 1969 and developed from a prayer cell. It was originally the Church of All Saints. Worship there was sacramentally based, centred around prayer and parish communion. The building is constructed of large greyish stone blocks, easily confused with breeze blocks. Set into the inside walls are stones from York, Canterbury and Chichester cathedrals, and one ancient

52. Into the future — the new health centre, 1988. A *Wythenshawe World* photograph of the Under Secretary of State for the Environment, David Trippier *(left)*, at the unveiling of the commemorative stone, with two of the workmen, Des Edwards and Neil Rainford.

stone from Manchester Cathedral. The building was designed by Gordon Thorne and seats two hundred. The silver and wood cross, which hangs in the sanctuary, was donated by St Aidan's College, Birkenhead, as was the bell, which has now been electrified. Flanking the altar are four stone amboses set at varying heights, which give a pleasant balance to the whole. Some of the furnishings of the church were made by the congregation, the men constructing the wooden pews and the ladies embroidering the vestments.

Although the parish has been said to be somewhat like a 'transit' camp, there is a nucleus of people who carry forward the work of the church and perform many of the practical tasks which other churches have done professionally. One example is the *Church Magazine*, which is written and printed by the clergy and parishioners, thus showing a profit.

An even more do-it-yourself church was the Full Gospel Church, which was opened in Crossacres. It was built in 1970, at a cost of £6,000, by the worshippers themselves on the site of the old building. Later the church was insured for £40,000. Resources both of labour and materials from around the area were used. The rubble from the old 1949 building was used as 'fill' and the members of the church were the labourers. Even the girls helped with the digging. Non-members helped too, for some of the local residents, admiring the keenness of the workers, supplied them with hot soup on the cold days. As each expense or difficulty arose a solution was quickly forthcoming. For example, when the time came for the electrical system to be installed money was not available, but an Altrincham businessman, newly converted to the faith, came to the rescue by allowing his electricians to do the work free of charge, and also by loaning the cost of the equipment. A pattern of good luck and goodwill obtained throughout the building of the church.

In 1970 the Roman Catholic church in Kenworthy Lane was also opened. The new church of St Hilda was built alongside the picturesque half-timbered building, which for a long time had been too small for its rapidly-growing congregation and has now been demolished to make way for flats. The new, brick-built, wigwam-style church is just as attractive as its predecessor was. The unusual design incorporates an octagonal, open-plan nave with baptistry, sanctuary, chapel, narthex and choir with an organ. The church seats 350, and has two confessionals and a literature store. Behind the baptistry is a parish room. An interesting feature of the church is the off-set apex, which supports a six foot cross. This presents an unusual view between the houses to the shoppers on Palatine Road. The building cost about £60,000, some of which was raised by 'National Fireside Bingo'. Although the church was opened at Easter the first sung mass was celebrated on 19 June in remembrance of the first mass said in the old building, on 19 June 1904.

Members of the Jehovah's Witness faith bought the A.B.C. Forum Cinema in Northenden after attempts to turn it into a bingo hall had failed. Since its purchase, often at weekends many people can be seen with ladders and paint brushes enthusiastically decorating the outside of the building. The inside, too, has been refurbished by the worshippers. They quickly turned the old cinema into the northern 'Cathedral' of their faith, and on Saturdays and Sundays the two large car parks are full and overflowing onto the side roads with vehicles that have brought members to the services.

The ecumenical movement is quite strong in the Wythenshawe area. In some parishes at Easter time open-air services are held instead of the annual Whitsun Walks, but in others the traditional type of witness continues. When William Temple, Woodhouse Park, St Anthony's Roman Catholic, St Mark's and the Salvation Army joined together the *Wythenshawe Express* reported:

> Two and a half thousand children, adults, band members and clergy took part in this year's combined Procession of Witness and found the idea of one meeting place for all five denominations a much better arrangement, but the longer route was not so popular.

In Benchill, Brownley Green Methodists, St Luke's Church of England and Brownley Green Baptists walked together in the Whit Walks. Although in general the Roman Catholics joined with the other churches in making their witness, they also hold their own ceremonies. Pictures in the *Wythenshawe Express* during the 1970s show St Aidan's, Northern Moor, holding its annual 'Crowning of Our Lady' and children performing, in mime, aspects of Mary's life.

The four or five new churches which were built in Wythenshawe during this period had come into being because of the local people's Christian beliefs and generosity of spirit, as well as their Christian stewardship. From the mid-1930s onwards, when the first houses were erected, the people of Wythenshawe have shown how important corporate worship was, and still is to many of them, by the building of churches of all denominations, often requiring considerable self-sacrifice. Some of the churches were paid for completely by the contributions of the parishioners and local residents, and others were physically built by the worshippers. Wythenshawe is regarded by many as a cultural and spiritual wilderness and yet here, in the influence of the churches, can be found a commitment rarely seen elsewhere.

*   *   *

Sixty years ago Wythenshawe was merely a plan on paper. For a true assessment of how convincingly it can be thought of as a garden city one would need a crystal ball of the finest quality.

There has been much to frustrate the dreams of Jackson, Simon and Parker: the battles with Cheshire; the slump; the war and the post-war turbulence, only now subsiding. The pride of being the inheritors of both the charm of Cheshire and the might of Manchester may be tempered by a feeling of isolation. Suburbs anywhere tend to be under-represented, but by any standards Wythenshawe's population of 102,000 lacks the autonomy of towns a tenth its size. 'Wythenshawe — The Forgotten Community' was a very active group in 1980. Yet there is much to suggest that Wythenshawe is a thriving community. The details set out in this chapter give an idea of its vitality but an even more convincing picture of the life in the area can be drawn from a fleeting mental tour.

Five o'clock, machines cease as the roads of the industrial estates become thronged with white-hatted bakery workers, blue-coated machine operators and the cars of the managerial staff hastening on their way home. An orange-coated group of people, a canoeing team, take to the river at Northenden after consuming hot snacks from the riverside café — their route from the old footbridge, recently elevated on concrete blocks, to the newly-painted Palatine Road bridge. The people of the district fill the school field behind Royle Green Road with the colour, life and music of the Annual Ram Roast. Around St Luke's, women and children home-in onto a Bring and Buy Sale. At the Civic Centre people bustle around the market stalls looking for a bargain until, satisfied they have seen all, they wander into the large stores in the shopping precinct. In the precinct the 'Cheshires' are advertising themselves with music and displays. It is only a few steps up to Leningrad Square, where the Forum Complex holds its treasures. In the large library people gaze at the handpainted trinket boxes, paperweights and pictures by a local artist. Those seeking refreshment and a few minutes quiet respite from 'Sweet Charity' at the theatre find they have left the violent music of 'Rhythm of Life' for the reggae and rock of 'Journey into Life', an evangelical mission being promoted in the large hall.

A mile away people enter the park-like grounds of the ultra-modern Wythenshawe Hospital to visit their friends. Wythenshawe Park itself, for the most part a haven of peace with a few strollers, harbours in one corner football pitches where lusty young footballers are at work. Overhead a jetplane thunders away from Ringway's international airport. From the air the passengers catch a glimpse of Wythenshawe — our garden city.

References

Material is listed against the chapter where it was first used.

1. Shercliff, W. H., ed., *Wythenshawe: a History of the Townships of Northenden, Northen Etchells and Baguley* (1974); Garner, Winifred A., *Call Back Yesterday* (1986); Dore, R. N., ed., *The Letter Books of Sir William Brereton of Handforth, Vol. 1*, Record Society of Lancashire and Cheshire, Vol. 123 (1984); Dore, R. N., ed., *A History of Hale: Domesday to Dormitory*, (John Sherratt & Sons Ltd. 1972); Hodson, J. H., *Cheshire 1660-1780: Restoration to Industrial Revolution*, Vol. 9 in the History of Cheshire series (Cheshire Community Council, 1978); Million, Ivor, *History of Didsbury* (Morten 1969); Tatton Family Papers, John Rylands Library, Manchester; Northenden and Etchells probate inventories in Cheshire County Record Office.
2. Redford, A., *The History of Local Government in Manchester*; Frangopulo, N., *Tradition in Action* (1972); Potter, S., *Transport and the New Towns* (1976); Howard, E., *Garden Cities of Tomorrow* (1902); Mumford, L., *The Fate of Garden Cities* (1927); Burton, A., *Remains of a Revolution* (1970); Acts of Parliament, Addison, 1919, Wheatley, 1924; Abercrombie Report (1920); *Manchester Guardian, The Times.*
3. Creese, W. L., 'The Garden City Before and After — Wythenshawe', in *The Search* (1966); Conway, E., *History of Wythenshawe 1919 -1934* (1971); Wythenshawe Estates Special Committee Minutes; House of Commons Papers, Manchester Extension Bill, 1930; Reiss, R., 1922, Chambers, T., and Purdom, C., 1926, Reports; Parker, B., Report on Wythenshawe, 1928; Joyce, J., *Roads and Rails of Manchester, 1900-1950*; *Evening Chronicle; The Advertiser*; St Wilfrid's *Parish Magazine.*
4. Simon, E., and Inman, J., *The Rebuilding of Manchester* (1935); Simon, A., *Manchester Made Over* (1936); Stocks, M., *Ernest Simon of Manchester* (1963); Webb, R., *Early Ringway* (1978); Scholefield, R., and McDonald, S., *First and Foremost* (1979); Eyre, D., *Manchester Buses 1908-1945* (1971); Yearsley, I., *The Manchester Tram* (1962); Dougill, W., *Wythenshawe — especially Parkways* (1935); Worral, N., *Wythenshawe, A Community Unit* (1935); Manchester and Salford Better Housing — Report, 1935; (Greater) Manchester Transport — Guides, Mr. Chris Heaps of Didsbury.
5. City of Manchester Purchase of Wythenshawe Scheme, 1931; Log Books by and Information from headteachers of Wythenshawe schools; *Wythenshawe Gazetteer* and *Weekly News*; *Wythenshawe Recorder/Express*; The Royle Collection, in Wythenshawe Library; St Michael's Church Log Book; Northenden Golf Club Silver Jubilee Handbook.
6. Shaw, A., *Adult Education and the Community, Wythenshawe* (1969); Hall, M., *Community Centres in Manchester* (1946).
7. Nicholas, R., *City of Manchester Plan* (1945); Cherry, B., *Urban Change and Planning* (1960); Dudley, *Design of Dwellings — Report* (1945); Barlow Commission — Report; Wythenshawe Federal Council Letters.
8. Davidson, J., *Adult Education and the Community* (1967); Manchester City Council, *Wythenshawe, Plan and Reality* (1953, 1956); Wythenshawe Federal Council, *How Wythenshawe Lives* (1951); National Census Reports (1951, 1961); Deakin, D. J., *Looking Back at Northenden* (1983); Sutton, L., *Brooklands Estate, 1952-1973.*
9. Northenden Community Council, Festival Programme, 1951; Wythenshawe Community Councils, Civic Week Programmes; Dodd, A., *Like a Mighty Tortoise* (1978); Wythenshawe Churches and Schools Brochures.
10. Moss, M., *The Wythenshawe Project* (1978); McGlennon, C., *Sociological Study of Wythenshawe* (1971); Appleyard, A., *Correlating the Old and New in Wythenshawe* (1982); Peacock, J., and Brennan, P., Dissertations on Wythenshawe; Central Library, Manchester, *New Wythenshawe* — Factsheet, 1976.
11. Mersey Valley Guides.

Note

The Wythenshawe Committee: the body that supervised the growth of Wythenshawe, a committee of Manchester City Council, was the Wythenshawe Estates Special Committee — more usually called the Wythenshawe Committee. The minutes were typed, then pasted in 13 large, red tomes, whose total thickness is well over a metre, at present in Wythenshawe Library.

Index

A number of topics have been grouped under the headings Churches, Education, Entertainment, Health Care, Horticulture, Sport and Transport. For subjects within these areas please see the general heading.

A page number in italic type denotes an illustration.